Contributions to Economics

For further volumes:
http://www.springer.com/series/1262

Arne Beck

Competition for Public Transport Services

Institutional Framework and Empirical Evidence of Bus Services in Germany

Physica-Verlag
A Springer Company

Arne Beck
Berlin
Germany

ISSN 1431-1933
ISBN 978-3-7908-2801-6 ISBN 978-3-7908-2802-3 (eBook)
DOI 10.1007/978-3-7908-2802-3
Springer Heidelberg Dordrecht London New York

Library of Congress Control Number: 2012934369

Printed on acid-free paper

Physica-Verlag is a brand of Springer
Springer is part of Springer-Science+Business Media (www.springer.com)

Preface

My main motivation to write this dissertation has been to evaluate the successes, failures, and factors that influence the competition for public bus transport services. Using Germany as a case study, I explain the institutional framework of this public bus transport market, which several international researchers and market participants have described as incomprehensible. My objective is to provide a basic understanding of the players and their options, offer insights about the German model, and make policy recommendations for consideration by decision-makers and regulatory authorities whose goal is to increase competition for public bus transport services.

The empirical analysis presented is based on primary data that is usually not publicly available, supplemented by numerous expert interviews. I also have a personal interest in the subject, having spent more than 5 years as a consultant on issues of competition and market organization for public transport services (rail and road), now working at civity Management Consultants. To my knowledge, this is the first comprehensive economic analysis of, in the same regime: (1) market initiatives to operate commercial services under exclusivity, and (2) authority initiated tendering procedures for non-commercial services. I hope that this story of Germany's experience proves helpful for other researchers, companies, and policymakers in the struggle to fulfill societal expectations for public transport at a time of global economic uncertainties.

The dissertation is divided into five parts. Following Part I, the introduction, Part II presents a theoretical approach for the analysis of the regulatory framework and the opportunities it offers market participants, and relevant case studies. In Part III I empirically evaluate the conditions for tendering in this market and the experience with the introduction of competition for non-commercial services. The focus is on identifying the barriers to entry and other factors that influence the prices paid by public transport authorities. In Part IV I shift the focus to the competition for commercial services and try to ascertain whether or not the legal setting is successful in promoting competition in this market segment. Part V summarizes the results on Germany's experience and proposes a model for organizing the contracting and awarding of public transport services in the future.

Acknowledgments

This book, which has been written as a cumulative doctoral thesis, is the product of research conducted as an external doctoral candidate at the KIT, Karlsruhe Institute for Technology (Section for Network Economics, Institute for Economic Policy Research [IWW], Faculty for Economics). Several sections were presented previously at national and international conferences, where a number of critical remarks helped to improve this study. One earlier paper received the Michael Beesley Award (honorable mention for best workshop paper presented by a person in the early stages of their career) at the 11th Thredbo International Conference on Competition and Ownership in Land Passenger Transport (September 2009, Delft, Netherlands) due to its innovative approach.

The analysis presented here is based in large part on data provided by the responsible authorities themselves, and I especially thank these institutions for their support. Furthermore, I am very grateful to those who generously provided time for expert interviews and offered insights about the public transport market. Finally, my sincere thanks to BSL Management Consultants (Lloyds Register Group), civity Management Consultants and KCW for supporting my research.

Writing a doctoral thesis requires the support of a network of colleagues, family, and friends who both provide constructive criticism and offer encouragement throughout the process. First and foremost, I thank my wife Marianne who encouraged me to write this thesis and my family and friends who helped me through the long hours required to bring this work to fruition. For comprehensive comments that significantly improved the quality of this dissertation, special thanks to Kay Mitusch from the KIT. I am grateful to my discussion partners throughout the research phase, particularly Andreas Brenck from the IGES Institute, Mathias Walter and Katrin Augustin from the Chair of Energy Economics and Public Sector Management at Dresden University of Technology; Gernot Liedtke from the KIT; Maria Nieswand from the DIW – German Institute for Economic Research, Didier van de Velde from the Delft University of Technology, Faculty Technology, Policy and Management; Rico Merkert from the University of Sydney – Institute of Transport and Logistics Studies (ITLS) at the Faculty of Economics and Business;

Peter Kain from the Federal Bureau of Infrastructure, Transport & Regional Economics of Australia; Sascha Frohwerk from the University of Potsdam, Department of Economics; Oliver Drümmer, Caroline von Kretschmann, Mathias Lahrmann, Jörn Meier-Berberich, Mirko Schnell, Kai Sellmann, Dirk Schümann, Anna Wallbrecht, and Olaf Zeike from the former BSL Management Consultants (Lloyd's Register Group); Börge Lumma from Veolia; Rainer Peters from the Landesnahverkehrsgesellschaft Niedersachsen; Markus Ksoll from Deutsche Bahn; Melanie Oertel from KCW; Gerrit Landsberg from BBG and Partner; Chris Knowles from Lloyd's Register Group; Detlev Metzner from the Münchner Verkehrs- und Tarifverbund; Michael Winnes from the Verkehrsverbund Rhein-Neckar; and Sabine Sontopski and Sven Paasch.

I also thank all of the participants in the workshops "Beyond Competitive Tendering" and "Benchmarking the Competitive Tendering Outcome" at the 11th Thredbo Conference, and in the doctoral seminars at the Workgroup for Infrastructure Policy at the Technische Universität Berlin and at the KIT. My gratitude goes to Thorsten Beckers for publishing the preliminary working paper versions on the homepage of the Center for Network Industries & Infrastructure, Technische Universität Berlin. I acknowledge the contributions of Deborah Anne Bowen, Ann Stewart, and Linda Turner for language assistance, and Heike Albrecht for graphic assistance. Without the advice and support of all these individuals (and others who I may have omitted), this dissertation would not be possible.

Abstract

Following the worldwide trend towards liberalization of public transport services German lawmakers revised the legal framework governing their country's market in the mid-1990s. Since that time the organization of the market for public bus transport services has been characterized by a dichotomous system of licenses for commercial services, where operators are granted exclusivity, and licenses for non-commercial services, where supplementary direct subsidies are tendered out by public transport authorities. This parallel structure offers market participants a wide range of opportunities for action, but also poses challenges to operators and authorities due to an awarding system and contractual relationships that fundamentally differ among the types of services. In contrast to the apparent view of legislators, the distinction between commercial and non-commercial services is not only determined by local characteristics of the services in question, but, in fact, is largely determined by the public transport authorities themselves.

An analysis of the market for non-commercial services shows that the strength of competition is determined primarily by the tendering conditions set by public transport authorities, with some factors differing at a regional level. A crucial issue is the level of uncertainty, which has been identified as a market entry barrier and a factor in price increases – for instance, in the case of net-cost contracts. The volume to be tendered out is another important issue. Other factors that influence the price to be paid by public transport authorities include conditions that influence productivity, such as the efficiency of the operating schedule, external factors such as spatial conditions, and various risk factors. With increased experience, public transport authorities produce significantly improved results, which is why higher-level authorities may achieve more successes than smaller local ones. The analysis of the market sub-segment for commercial services shows a steadily increasing market volume. Although this sub-segment relies on market initiatives by operators, its volume is still very small. Entry barriers identified in the institutional framework clearly impede a more competitive development due to the higher level of uncertainty faced by newcomers to this market compared to the tendering market. The results presented here once again confirm the importance of a clear regulatory framework and of favorable market conditions designed by authorities to promote vigorous market development.

Contents

List of Figures

List of Tables

List of Abbreviations

A.m.	Ante meridiem
A.o.	Among others
AEG	Allgemeines Eisenbahngesetz (Common German Law for Railways also see Glossary)
AK Vergabe	Arbeitskreis Vergabe (the AK Vergabe is the workgroup for awarding within the BAG ÖPNV)
BAG ÖPNV	Bundesarbeitsgemeinschaft der ÖPNV-Aufgabenträger in der Bundesvereinigung der kommunalen Spitzenverbände Deutschlands (the BAG ÖPNV is a joint association of local acting PTAs of the Deutscher Städtetag [German association of cities], the Deutscher Landkreistag [German association of rural districts] and the Deutscher Städte- und Gemeindebund [German association for small cities and towns])
bdo	Bundesverband Deutscher Omnibusunternehmer e.V. (pressure group of the German private [small- and medium sized] bus operators)
BGBl	*Bundesgesetzblatt* (official journal for publications on new established acts, laws, regulations, etc.)
BLFA	Bund-Länder-Fachausschuss Straßenpersonenverkehr (official commission of the ministries of transport of the federal and the state government)
BMVBS	Bundesministerium für Verkehr, Bau und Stadtentwicklung (national ministry responsible for transport)
BMVBW	Bundesministerium für Verkehr, Bau und Wohnungswesen (now re-named to BMVBS)
BVerwG	Bundesverwaltungsgericht (Federal Administrative Court of Germany)
BW	Federal state Baden-Württemberg
BY	Federal state Bavaria
C.	Coefficient

CCL	Competition for commercial lines or services (also see Glossary)
CDU	Christlich Demokratische Union Deutschlands (conservative party in Germany)
DB	Deutsche Bahn AG (national railway operator, currently biggest operator for regional bus services in Germany)
DEA	Non-parametric data envelopment analysis
E.g.	Exempli gratia
EC 1370	(EC) No 1370/2007
EC	European Community
EEC	European Economic Community
EEV	Enhanced Environmentally Friendly Vehicle (ambitious emmission standard determined by the EC)
EntflechtG	Gesetz zur Entflechtung von Gemeinschaftsaufgaben und Finanzhilfen, or Entflechtungsgesetz (Demerger Act)
Etc.	Et cetera
EU	European Union
FFM	City Frankfurt am Main
FoPS	Forschungsprogramm Stadtverkehr (research program on urban transport of the federal ministry of transport)
FRG	Federal Republic of Germany
GC	Gross-cost contract (also see Glossary)
GDR	German Democratic Republic
Global player	Consolidated operators like Veolia, Arriva, Transdev, BeneX, Abellio
GVFG	Gemeindeverkehrsfinanzierungsgesetz (Local Authority Traffic Financing Act, also see Glossary)
HE	Federal state Hesse
HHA	Hamburger Hochbahn AG (municipal operator of the city Hamburg)
HMWVL	Ministerium für Wirtschaft, Verkehr und Landesentwicklung des Landes Hessen (ministry of Hesse responsible for transport)
HSB	Hanauer Straßenbahn AG (municipal operator of the city Hanau)
Hülsmann	Omnibusbetrieb Hülsmann GmbH (private medium-sized bus operator)
HVV	Hamburger Verkehrsverbund GmbH (public transport association in the Hamburg area)
I.e.	Id est
Km	Kilometer
KVK	Kraftverkehr Kinzigtal GmbH (municipal operator, former subsidiary of HSB)
LA	Licensing authority (also see Glossary for further explanations)
Ln	Logarithmus naturalis
LNVG	Landesnahverkehrsgesellschaft Niedersachsen mbH (LA for Lower Saxony)

LR	Likelihood-Ratio Test
LT	License term
M	Management contract
MBV ST	Ministerium für Bauen und Verkehr des Landes Sachsen-Anhalt (ministry of Saxony-Anhalt responsible for transport)
Municipal	Municipal- or state-owned operators
MVV	Münchner Verkehrs- und Tarifverbund GmbH (public transport association in the Munich area)
N	Number of observations per group analyzed
NC	Net-cost contract (also see Glossary)
No.	Number
NVV	Nordhessischer VerkehrsVerbund – Verkehrsverbund und Fördergesellschaft Nordhessen mbH (public transport association in the area surrounding Kassel)
NW	Federal state North Rhine-Westphalia
O	Operator
ÖPNVG	Gesetz über den öffentlichen Personennahverkehr in Hessen (Law for Public Transport in Hesse)
ÖPNVG LSA	Gesetz über den öffentlichen Personennahverkehr im Land Sachsen-Anhalt (Law for Public Transport in Saxony-Anhalt)
P.	Page
P.a.	Per annum
P.m.	Post meridiem
PBefG	Personenbeförderungsgesetz (Passenger Transport Act [also see Glossary])
Pp.	Pages
Prob	Probability
PSC	Public service contract
PT	Public transport (as services provided to the public)
PTA	Public transport authority (also see Glossary)
PTP	(Local) public transport plan (also see Glossary)
RegG	Regionalisierungsgesetz (German Law on the Regionalization of Public Transport [also see Glossary])
RMV	Rhein-Main-Verkehrsverbund GmbH (public transport association in the Frankfurt am Main area)
RP	Federal state Rhineland-Palatine
SFA	Stochastic frontier analysis
SH	Federal state Schleswig-Holstein
SME	Small- and medium-sized private enterprise
SUR	Seemingly unrelated regressions
TfL	Transport for London
traffiQ	Lokale Nahverkehrsgesellschaft Frankfurt am Main mbH traffiQ
UK	United Kingdom
US	United States of America

VDV	Verband Deutscher Verkehrsunternehmen e.V. (association of German transport undertakings)
VHH	Verkehrsbetriebe Hamburg Holstein AG (municipal operator for the suburban area of Hamburg)
vkm	Vehicle kilometer
VLG	Verkehrsgesellschaft Landkreis Gifhorn mbH (municipal operator of the suburban district Gifhorn)
VOL/A	Verdingungsordnung für Leistungen, Teil A (Official German Contracting Terms for Award of Service Performance Contracts, Part A)
VRN	Verkehrsverbund Rhein-Neckar GmbH (public transport association in the area surrounding Mannheim)
VVOWL	VerkehrsVerbundOstwestfalenLippe GmbH (public transport association in the area surrounding Bielefeld)
ZVSN	Zweckverband Verkehrsverbund Südniedersachsen (public transport association in the area surrounding Göttingen)

List of Symbols

%	Percent
$\in$	Element of
ε	Error term
~	Approximately
§	Paragraph (as used in acts of law)
§§	Paragraphs (as used in acts of law)
€	Euro
a	Fixed costs for operators
b	Variable costs for operators
bidders	Number of bidders
C	Cost function
change	Change of operator
CPI	Consumer price index of the Federal Statistical Office
DC	Fuel or diesel costs
declwage	Labor agreement standard
deposit	Security deposit in percent of *FP*
E_O	Value as expected by operator
E_{PTA}	Value as expected by PTA
expr	Level of experience of PTA for lot i, measured by specific number of the lot tendered by the PTA over time
exprsum	Sum of experience of PTA, measured by sum of all lots tendered by the PTA
extopt	Option for term extension
fedstate	Federal state in which a service is located
FP	Full price to be paid by the PTA per annum to the operator
FR	Fare revenues
Hesse	Group of observations located in the federal state Hesse
HesseX	Group of observations located in the federal state Hesse, excluding observations located in the VRN and the FFM area
I	Index to adjust p adequately
i	Subscript for the ith lot
K	Set of lots
kmpervehcl	Vehicle kilometer per annum per bus on average
LC	Labor costs (primarily bus driver costs)
lengthbus	Length per bus on average
linesno	Number of lines

Munich area	Group of observations located in the Munich area
Non-Hesse	Group of observations not located in the federal state Hesse
novechl	Number of vehicles
OC	Other costs (primarily administrative or overhead)
Other regions	Group of observations located in other regions
p	Price per vehicle kilometer paid by the PTA to the operator in the first contract year as a result of competitive tendering on a gross-cost basis
P	Price p adjusted by I
q	Quality offered/delivered by operator
q_B	Quality level maximizing profits for the operator
q_C	Quality level representing the threshold between commercial and non-commercial services
q_D	Non-commercial level of quality (as an example)
q_m	Minimum level of quality defined by the PTA in its PTP
r	Subscript for a specific region r
renewal	Renewal of vehicles during contract term
revrisk	Revenue risk measured by contract type
s	Subscript for a specific federal state s
SDS	Supplementary direct subsidies necessary to enable a non-deficit delivery of services by operators on the minimum quality level q_m
sme	Winning bidder small- or medium-sized operator
spatial	Spatial type of transport service
startoyear	Year of start of operations
submdays	Days of submission
t	Subscript for a specific year t
term	Contract term in years
VC	Capital costs (primarily depreciation of vehicle investments)
vkmpa	Vehicle kilometers per annum
x	Matrix or vector of explanatory variables
α	Constant or intercept
β	Coefficient or coefficient vector
π	Profit for operator
π_{max}	Maximum profit for operator
υ	Statistical error

Part I
Overview

Following the introduction Part I begins by distinguishing short-distance public transport services by bus from the other segments of the German market. A brief overview of related topics in the international literature is provided in Chap. 2, and both an outline of the dissertation's structure and abstracts of the sections appear in Chap. 3.

Chapter 1
Introduction and Focus of Analysis

1.1 Introduction

In the 1990s, Germany followed numerous countries in the European Union and elsewhere which were altering their regulatory frameworks in order to promote competition for public bus transport services. When assessing international attempts to introduce competition into the public transport market, one encounters a wide range of competitive and contractual arrangements, some of which are quite controversial. For example, controversy arose with the introduction of route tendering in London in 1984 as well as the deregulation of the local bus markets in Great Britain in 1986 and in New Zealand in 1989 (see Banister 1985; Beesley and Glaister 1985, and Gwilliam et al. 1985). Over the years, as more countries and regions undertook regulatory reforms, valuable experience about the functioning of competition-based regimes was gained, and many useful lessons were learned. Such lessons have served to improve upon existing models, and as a result, more countries have decided to follow the liberalization path.

In contrast to most of the market models adopted in other parts of the world, Germany's public bus transport market is characterized by a dichotomy between commercial and non-commercial services that is based on exclusivity for the licensee. To provide commercial services, operators submit an application for a license to operate on their own (market initiative). If the application is approved by the licensing authority, the licensee receives the right of exclusivity for the service sought. To provide non-commercial services, the licensee receives the right of exclusivity only after a public transport authority (PTA) has initiated a tendering procedure in which supplementary direct subsidies are also awarded to enable the licensee to provide an adequate level of service quality (authority initiative). Competition for public bus transport services may therefore occur in two ways: competing market initiatives by operators (competing applications for a license to operate commercial services under exclusivity), or a PTA's tendering procedure for non-commercial services.

A. Beck, *Competition for Public Transport Services*, Contributions to Economics,
DOI 10.1007/978-3-7908-2802-3_1,

The question arises to what extent this German market model succeeds in promoting market competition, and what lessons might be learned. The purpose of this dissertation is to identify the key factors that play a role in the successes and failures observed to date by analyzing the overall framework and the two sub-markets for commercial services and non-commercial services. Policy recommendations will be derived to improve the existing system and alternative models will be proposed to regulate tender and contract award procedures. Given the increased international discussion concerning the use of competitive instruments for commercial services (see, e.g., Lundin et al. 2009, OFT 2009, and Raad voor Verkeer en Waterstaat 2009), the results of this analysis should have important implications for improving public bus transport throughout the world.

To enable readers who are unfamiliar with the main aspects of the German framework (or, at least, the main European frameworks) to understand the institutional context, I provide case studies and examples. Lists of abbreviations, symbols, and a glossary are included as well. Moreover, this cumulative dissertation is based on self-contained essays, allowing those whose time is limited to read specific sections in isolation. As a result some overlap between sections will be inevitable.

1.2 Focus of Analysis: Competition for Short-Distance Services by Bus

The market for commercial and non-commercial passenger bus transport services is one segment of Germany's public transport market. This market (rail, light rail, and bus) has the largest market volume in the European Union and in 2008 transported 10.9 billion passengers.[1]

Most of these passengers (10.65 billion or 98.1%) regularly travel up to 50 km and/or one hour on scheduled routes (short-distance services, according to the legal definition as codified in § 2 of the Law on the Regionalization of Public Transport – Regionalisierungsgesetz, or RegG). In 2008, short-distance passengers covered a total distance of 101.2 billion passenger kilometers, and operators were able to generate fare revenues of €10.9 billion. Around 2,550 operators provided 3.4 billion vehicle kilometers by railroad track (including commuter railways and excluding long-distance services), light rail, and bus.

In 2008 as many as 51.1% of all short-distance passengers used public bus transport services. Accounting for 72.8% of all vehicle kilometers, such bus services form the backbone of Germany's public transport industry. Nevertheless, regarding passenger kilometers, the figures for rail (47.0 billion passenger kilometers) and light rail services (16.1 billion passenger kilometers) taken together are significantly higher than for bus services (38.0 billion passenger kilometers).

[1] See Reim and Reichel (2010), publishing the relevant figures of the German Statistical Office.

Given the importance of bus transport services for the country's public transport market, the following analysis concerns commercial and non-commercial short-distance passenger transport services by bus. It does not cover long-distance services either by rail or bus, nor does it address short-distance services by rail or light rail.

Chapter 2
General Literature Overview

Although not the focus of this dissertation, some remarks on related key issues discussed in articles and studies on this subject are necessary to understand the results within the broader context of research on competition for public bus transport services. However, a complete literature review is beyond the scope of this dissertation.

Much research has been undertaken on regulatory and institutional frameworks and their effects on the public bus transport market. The first to discuss the market for cab services was Chadwick (1859), who analyzed regulated competition in the market for public taxi services as compared to unregulated competition, or a free market regime. Following the wave of liberalization in the late 1980s, articles began to appear in the 1990s which assessed the outcomes and the factors influencing competition in markets where competition had been introduced at a very early stage, i.e. Britain, New Zealand, and the Scandinavian countries. White and Tough (1995), for instance, compared the results of tendering gross-cost versus net-cost contracts in Britain outside London, and showed that net-cost contracts lead both to a significantly lower number of bidders and to higher prices. Alexandersson et al. (1998) showed initial effects of tendering in Sweden, including significant cost-reducing effects. One of their main findings was that the decline in demand in Sweden during those years was not a result of the introduction of tendering or of deregulation, but was probably related to the country's deep recession.

In recent years, a number of international studies have analyzed tendering models for (non-commercial) bus services. In a study of the Swedish competitive tendering market, Alexandersson and Pyddoke (2003) identified a long period of decreasing costs and a substantial change in operators' structures. Mathisen and Solvoll (2008) focused exclusively on how the introduction of competition affected the development of the market structure in Norway, and confirmed a substantial shift towards non-local companies.

A meta-analysis of international studies on competitive tendering by Hensher and Wallis (2005) showed a significant price reduction in the first tendering round, but also some price increases thereafter. Initial findings on the introduction of

A. Beck, *Competition for Public Transport Services*, Contributions to Economics,
DOI 10.1007/978-3-7908-2802-3_2,

tendering processes in the Netherlands as part of the market reforms of 2000 presented by Hermans and Stoelinga (2005), among other authors, confirm that cost efficiency has increased but that passenger figures for bus services have remained stable despite improvements in service levels and customer satisfaction. The factors influencing the London bus tendering model examined by Amaral et al. (2006) and Cantillon and Pesendorfer (2007) again confirmed that competitive tendering results in price decreases, but that some price discrimination and strategic pricing by bidders occurs, at least in the specific London environment of multi-unit auctions. Amaral et al. (2008) analyzed collusion under both the London bus tendering model and the French model. Their paper provides evidence that transparency, the discretionary power of public bodies, and the level of competition are the key success factors in preventing collusion and corruption. They also showed that the London model improved performance indicators more than the French model.

Sharaby and Shiftan (2008) analyzed the results of introducing tendering in Israel, which again confirms increasing quality levels and decreasing prices. A notable recent paper is Wolanski (2009), who compared the efficiency levels of direct awarding and competitive tendering and analyzed the drivers of efficiency in the Polish market. He confirmed that tendering public bus transport services results in considerable improvements in efficiency.

Several papers have analyzed free, unregulated (commercial) market regimes. Romilly (2001), for instance, investigated the subsidy levels of local bus services in Britain outside London. He showed that despite the significant decrease in passenger numbers and an increase in fare levels, the government was able to reduce subsidies. Overall, his econometric model for the period 1957–1997 predicted welfare gains of around £7.7 million per annum. In a study of the ownership structures in this free market environment, Roberts (2005) showed that larger business forms have emerged that possess the size and power needed to invest and expand business in order to meet government requirements, for example, by bringing new and more environmentally friendly vehicles to the streets. In a theoretical paper, Gómez-Lobo (2007) stressed that the usual forms of competition do not work in urban bus markets, and attempted to explain why cartels arise in these markets. They are not cartels in the classic sense, but may be viewed as coordinating associations to reach the optimal equilibrium from the operator's perspective, for example, by avoiding competing buses arriving simultaneously at the same stops and hence ensuring a monopoly price for the operators. Leopairojna and Hanoaka (2007) presented a market analysis of passenger van services in Bangkok, a service type that conventional bus operators view as competitors. They recommend regulation of this free market regime to ensure the safety and quality of the services due, for example, to high overload factors, but also find there is no necessity for regulation of market quotas or exclusivity.

In general most of the studies to date on free, unregulated markets have focused on Great Britain, New Zealand, and South American and Asian countries, while studies on regulated competition have focused mainly on continental Europe, London, and Australia.

General aspects of different market models have also been discussed in the extant literature. Van de Velde (1999) presented a general classification for market organization, and discussed the different forms of market versus authority initiative for public bus transport services in Europe. A more recent overview by Macário (2005) stressed the high correlation between regulatory evolution and institutional behavior on urban mobility markets. A Sri Lankan assessment of the development of the regulatory framework for public bus transport services within the past 100 years by Kumarage and Jayaratne (2008) identified several phases that tend to repeat in a circle, starting from unregulated competition, followed by a period of consolidation under regulated private monopolies, a period of nationalization under state monopoly and now (since 1979) a period under regulated mixed competition. Gwilliam (2007), who provided evidence for a regulatory cycle, confirmed their finding. For developed countries this cycle consists of a circular flow through private competitive supply, unregulated private monopoly, regulation of private monopoly, nationalization, and then back through further regulatory reform to some type of private competitive supply.

An overview showing the wide variety of market structures and modes of market entry developed in Europe since the first efforts at liberalization in the late 1980s appears in van de Velde (2005), who described the increasing involvement of the private sector both through deregulation and competitive tendering, and the decentralization of public responsibility for the sector, and observed a trend to increased use of authority initiative. He also showed that the former market initiative has not led to competing operators within the market in most of the countries studied. Updating these observations, van de Velde et al. (2008a) described the different European forms of market organization that have arisen with the right to "the creation of passenger transport services" granted under the new European regulation (EC) No 1370/2007, and analyzed different contractual settings which reconfirm the broad variety across Europe.

In the German literature, the distinction between commercial and non-commercial services has been analyzed by several German legal scholars (e.g., Werner 1998 and 2001). Furthermore, legal aspects of tendering (Werner et al. 2004 and Klinger 2006) and competition for commercial services (Landsberg 2003; Werner 2004; Nareike and Walter 2006 as well as Recker 2007) have been discussed in many papers. However, economic papers on the institutional framework of German public bus transport services and competition for this market are rare. A brief overview of main aspects was presented by van de Velde (2005). In recent years, Sterzenbach (2008) has looked at public funding, while Knieps (2004) as well as Beck and Wille (2011) examined the structure of the German "Verkehrsverbünde" (public transport associations). A basic overview of this kind of market organization is presented by Pucher and Kurth (1996).

Research on the economic effects of tendering includes Achenbach 2006; Augustin and Walter 2009; Beck and Wanner 2007; Beck and Wanner 2008; Berschin 2003, and von Berlepsch 2005. A few papers consider competition for commercial services (e.g., Beck 2007; Beck and Wille 2009, and Walter et al. 2009).

Nevertheless, to my best knowledge, there are no economic papers which analyze the effects of commercial and non-commercial services within one (regulated) market. Thus, this dissertation is the first comprehensive economic analysis of the German bus industry that considers the distinction between commercial and non-commercial services.

Chapter 3
Structure of the Book

As mentioned, this dissertation is divided into five parts. Following this introductory Part I, Part II presents an overview of the regulatory framework for the German bus industry. The implications of the legal framework for the economic setting are analyzed and the prospects and challenges discussed, followed by a case study of different institutional models within this framework and an overview of international alternatives to competitive tendering. Part III evaluates competition for non-commercial services, first analyzing important aspects of the regulatory framework for this market segment, followed by investigating the effects of competition and the key factors affecting the development of this market from the public transport authority perspective. Part IV focuses on the competition for commercial services. Here, the regulatory framework and the market development of this segment are analyzed in detail to evaluate whether or not the current legal setting succeeds in promoting competitive development. Part V concludes and makes policy recommendations for adjusting the existing German framework. The abstracts of the essays of Part II to Part V are presented below.

3.1 Abstract of Part II: Framework

This part begins with an essay in Chap. 4 that looks at the key feature that distinguishes Germany's public bus transport from other countries – the distinction between commercial and non-commercial bus services. The analysis shows that – contrary to the apparent views of legislators – costs and revenues are not the only parameters determining whether or not operators can provide services in a commercially viable manner. Apart from the local characteristics of the specific service, the analysis stresses that the classification of services as commercial versus non-commercial is determined in large part by the public transport authorities that set the minimum quality standards to be provided by operators. It can be seen that the authorities awarding the contracts can sometimes significantly affect market organization depending on how they use their regulatory clout. Further, market

A. Beck, *Competition for Public Transport Services*, Contributions to Economics,
DOI 10.1007/978-3-7908-2802-3_3, © Springer-Verlag Berlin Heidelberg 2012

organization differs substantially with respect to the award structure and the contractual relationships, hence creating challenges for operators and authorities in this embryonic market.

The next essay, presented in Chap. 5, discusses the past decade's debate over introducing competition in Germany's bus sector and the forms of competition that have the potential to enhance quality and efficiency. The main characteristics of this market are analyzed as well as the opportunities for introducing or promoting competition. The analysis is based on cases that are central to the debate, and evaluates their successes and failures. To provide a more complete context for the analysis of market participants' behavior, the institutional changes affecting these cases are also discussed. The analysis shows that there are several ways to introduce competition, through tendering of non-commercial services or through competition for commercial services, either authority initiated or market initiated. The array of possibilities for the German market allows both PTAs and operators numerous opportunities to take action. While most other EU Member States have decided in favor of a specific market model (authority initiated competition in Sweden and Denmark; market initiated competition in GB outside of London), Germany has introduced a parallel structure comprising authority initiated *and* market initiated competition, both of which are remarkably successful in enhancing the level of quality and efficiency, although with failures in some areas.

Most countries contemplating the introduction of competition-based organizational frameworks failed to perceive the UK's deregulated bus regime as the best way forward. Absent in-depth analyses of the British model, deregulated regimes were either dismissed, or became the subject of contentious debate. The rush to competitive tendering was fueled by the European Commission's endeavor to enact legislation promoting competitive tendering of exclusive contracts as the preferred means of organizing local public transport markets. Yet, deregulation in various guises may well play a growing role in local and regional transport, i.e. in long-distance coach transport and in (international) European railway markets since early 2010. The final essay in this Part II, presented in Chap. 6, discusses whether such competition-based institutional alternatives to competitive tendering can provide efficiency and service improvements, how they might be regulated, and how non-competitive direct awards might still guarantee good performance. Several market models to increase operator participation are proposed.

3.2 Abstract of Part III: Competition for Non-Commercial Services

The fourth essay of this dissertation, presented in Chap. 7, begins with a detailed examination of the regulatory framework for public bus transport services, the basic structures, and the typical award schedule for tendering. Next follows a description of the barriers to entry and the impact of uncertainty on public bus transport services.

A study of 34 public service contracts in Europe shows that when concluding a public service contract, operators must cope with a variety of risks that have different impacts and that can be controlled only to varying degrees. With respect to Germany the study shows that revenue risk for public bus transport services is of particular importance. This essay then concludes by discussing a structure for identifying and distinguishing different types of risks, and explains the major economic effects of risk in tendering.

The fifth essay, presented in Chap. 8, evaluates general developments in this market segment and the impacts on market participants. Following a prolonged transition period with only a few isolated cases of competitive tendering for public bus transport services, the number of tenders has actually grown in recent years, but with complex results. From the public transport authority view, the main effects are decreased subsidy payments with relatively low expenses relating to the tendering process (allocation, contract management). The overall level of competition is high, with 5–7 bidders per tender on average. It has somewhat declined in recent years. Barriers to entry are identified at significant levels for several parameters, especially for the volume tendered and the revenue risk to be borne by the operator out of net-cost contracts. Small- and medium-sized transport operators have been able to increase market share in the starting phase of tendering, although with diminishing success later. Due to new requirements for competitive tendering, the quality of public transport available has improved considerably, and environmental standards are better implemented and sustained. From an employee point of view, there is no evidence that wages will be less than for private operators, although they are currently far below the wages for public incumbent operators.

The final essay of Part III, presented in Chap. 9, analyzes tender results for non-commercial public bus transport services in Germany measured by prices per vehicle kilometer and focuses on the factors affecting these prices. By using alternative regression techniques, we show that prices have regionally varying determinants. For example, where prices have increased over time in most of Hesse (the state with the largest number of contracts tendered to date), prices in the Munich area appear to have decreased. Optimization of bus services generally has a cost-decreasing impact, which confirms that setting appropriate conditions allows PTAs to reduce prices. Stochastic frontier analysis reveals that tender prices in Hesse are slightly less efficient, and that the PTA's experience has an efficiency-increasing impact. These findings suggest that establishing a higher (overarching) tendering authority would likely enable further price reductions.

3.3 Abstract of Part IV: Competition for Commercial Services

Identifying the prospects and constraints of the market segment for commercial services again requires a more detailed analysis of market development and the regulatory framework. This essay shows that after decades of relative stagnation, the competitive market for commercial public bus transport services is finally taking off.

Nevertheless, compared to its total market volume, there are relatively few cases of observable competition. An empirical analysis of the level of competition within this market segment compared to the market segment for tendering of non-commercial services confirms the existence of barriers to entry. Clearly, the barriers impede competitive developments in an embryonic market based upon market initiative by operators. An important barrier is the overall level of uncertainty regarding competitive procedures for commercial services, which is significantly higher than usual in tendering procedures for non-commercial services. The high uncertainty poses more disadvantages for newcomers compared to incumbents. The analysis provides evidence that the regulatory framework has a major influence on the market development.

3.4 Abstract of Part V: Conclusion and Outlook

Part V summarizes and discusses the findings of the seven essays presented. It concludes that the policy implications derived in Parts II to IV show that competition for commercial services is an interesting alternative to competitive tendering, but several problems still exist within the framework.

Therefore, the closing eighth essay in Part V presents and discusses one proposal to clarify and improve the existing German framework by making a slight adjustment. Avoiding a more radical change and added costs, it preserves the dichotomy between commercial and non-commercial services and offers a variety of options to authorities and operators. Local market participants are free to select the model that fits their objectives, including the PTA's opportunity to award the services directly. The proposal would enable competition of different awarding modes within the market without any clear preference on the part of the legislative body.

Part II
The German Institutional Framework

This part consists of three chapters. The first analyzes the institutional framework for contracting and awarding public transport bus services in Germany. Here, I focus on the distinction between commercial and non-commercial services. The second examines some of the models used to introduce competition in the different federal states. I present and evaluate the main successes and failures of different approaches where stakeholders tried to improve the national institutional frameworks in their own sphere of responsibility. My aim is to provide insights about the use of regulatory tools by market participants and to identify the pros and cons of each approach. The third presents an overview of international frameworks and discusses some new issues to implement a more market-oriented approach.

Chapter 4
The Distinction Between Commercial and Non-Commercial Bus Services

4.1 Introduction

The institutional framework of the German public bus transport system is structured around a fundamental distinction between commercial and non-commercial services. Most legislators seem to view this distinction as unambiguous, since – in their thinking – local conditions (population density, land use patterns, etc.) mainly determine the costs and revenues of public transport bus services. For example, the revenue potential of an urban bus line will usually be higher than that of a rural one. Conversely, costs per vehicle kilometer will usually be lower in rural districts than in cities due to the higher average speed.

If this distinction were truly unambiguous, classifying services as commercial or non-commercial would largely depend on the local characteristics of the specific service, and thus would be exogenously determined. The issue becomes whether local conditions are really the only distinguishing feature for operators, or whether market participants might also have a significant impact on this distinction. Considering the usual influence of authorities on this industry, it is fair to assume that their activities do have a major impact on the distinction between commercial and non-commercial services. To enable further analysis, the regulatory framework must be examined to consider the possible courses of action available to market participants.

The various regulatory and institutional frameworks and their effects on the public bus transport market have been the subject of numerous papers. As observed in the general literature review in Chap. 2 above, tendering models for (non-commercial) bus services have been analyzed in several international articles in recent years. Furthermore, some papers have analyzed free, unregulated (commercial) market regimes, primarily with a focus on Great Britain, New Zealand, and several South American and Asian countries.

The different market models and their main distinctive aspects have been discussed in only a small number of papers. Van de Velde et al. (2008a, pp. 113–115, pp. 24–25) described the different European forms of market organization with a note on the

A. Beck, *Competition for Public Transport Services*, Contributions to Economics,
DOI 10.1007/978-3-7908-2802-3_4, © Springer-Verlag Berlin Heidelberg 2012

developments expected under the new regulation (EC) No 1370/2007. Within the German literature, the distinction between commercial and non-commercial services has so far been primarily a legal debate. Economic papers are rare, with only a few articles examining tendering from an economic perspective, or investigating competition for commercial services.

However, to the best of my knowledge, economic papers analyzing the effects of commercial and non-commercial services within one (regulated) market have not yet been published. Perhaps this is why researchers as well as global players entering the German public transport market usually describe the regulatory framework as basically incomprehensible to outsiders.[1] Thus, my aim is to present an economic analysis of the institutional framework and the distinction between commercial and non-commercial services in order to help all players understand the major options for action.

The analysis outlined in this essay is structured as follows. The main aspects of the far-reaching market reforms of the mid-nineties are described in Sect. 4.2. The current legal framework which forms the basis for the subsequent discussion is described in Sect. 4.3. Based on a European perspective, Sect. 4.4 then explains the current institutional framework. The German institutional framework is discussed in the context of the theoretical approach presented in Sect. 4.5. This constitutes the starting point for the analysis of market participants' possible courses of action and discussion of the results from the viewpoints of authorities and operators presented in Sect. 4.6. Here, I also analyze whether market participants are able to significantly influence the categorization of their services. Section 4.7 summarizes the results of the section.[2]

A List of Abbreviations and a List of Symbols are included in the first few pages of the book; a Glossary and a List of the Acts of Law follow the Appendix. These lists are intended to facilitate understanding of specific terms for readers unfamiliar with the regulatory framework of German public bus transport. Where appropriate, case studies are included to ease understanding of the specific aspects.

4.2 Market Reform in the Mid-1990s and Major Innovations

The market reform in the mid-1990s occurred in reaction to the changing regulatory environment in the European Union (EU) and as a result of a long period of increased loss-making by the national railway operator, Deutsche Bundesbahn. This process also initiated debate about comprehensive reform of the entire public transport sector. In addition, Regulation (EEC) No 1191/69 and its revised version, (EEC) No 1893/91, encouraged more competition for subsidies within the EU.

[1] This is my conclusion after more than 5 years of consultancy work in the German public transport system on behalf of KCW, BSL Management Consultants and civity Management Consultants, and from numerous discussions with foreign researchers and practitioners.

[2] This Chap. 4 is based largely on Beck (2009b and Beck 2012).

Their transposition into the German legal framework pushed the national debate further. As part of this discussion, the federal states (Länder) demanded new regulation of public transport organization for all sectors, arguing that the positions of the existing operators were highly protected by and within the current regulatory framework (see Werner 1998, pp. 2–3).

The market reform in Germany went into effect on January 1, 1996. At the national level, the federal constitution (Grundgesetz), the Common German Law for Railways (Allgemeines Eisenbahngesetz, or AEG) and the Passenger Transport Act (Personenbeförderungsgesetz, or PBefG) were amended, and the Law on the Regionalization of Public Transport (Regionalisierungsgesetz, or RegG) was introduced. By shifting responsibilities to the Länder and asserting the principle of subsidiarity, the new laws made them responsible for regulating public transport in detail. The federal government retained very few regulatory responsibilities especially for the railway sector.

Regarding competition and market organization, the main innovation from a regulatory point of view was the introduction of a definition for so-called "non-commercial" services. For these services direct subsidies were to be paid by the PTA to render them profitable for operators. The new regulations required the subsidies to be subject to tendering, unlike services are classified as commercial. For commercial services a license that provided exclusivity to the licensee and some compensatory payments, e.g., for reduced fares for pupils and the disabled, were expected to be sufficient to enable commercial operations. The major innovations are summarized below.

Major innovations of market reform in the mid-1990s

1. Establishment of the supply–demand (principal-agent) principle, where PTAs plan, organize, and finance public transport services at what they consider an appropriate level of quality (see §§ 1, 3 and 4 RegG), when they consider the results of market initiatives to be insufficient. In conjunction with the amendment of the federal law, the states changed their public transport laws to accommodate the legal framework established at the federal level. Almost all states assigned the PTA responsibilities for public transport by bus and light rail to the rural districts or larger district free cities (municipalities) (see Barth 2001, pp. 127–128).
2. Introduction of the obligation for PTAs to define minimum standards for public transport services, via (local) public transport plans (PTPs) (see § 8 [3] PBefG).
3. Introduction of the definition of non-commercial services ("gemeinwirtschaftliche Verkehre"). If direct subsidies are paid by the PTAs, the regulations require these subsidies to be tendered (see §§ 8 [4] and 13a PBefG and [EEC] No 1191/69).

Despite this fundamental legal distinction, it is well known to market insiders[3] that most PTAs and operators continued to classify subsidies as non-operational revenues, which enabled them to classify services as commercial according to § 13 PBefG. In practice, the incumbent operators have experienced "an almost automatic renewal" of their licenses (see van de Velde 1999, p. 151) and subsidies. In a few cases the PTAs have classified services as non-commercial and tendered financial support. This scenario explains why innovation in the regulatory framework has still failed to induce the authorities to introduce competitive instruments to any appreciable degree.

However, analyzing the intentions of authorities (and operators) to carry on with the renewal of licenses and subsidies is not the focus of this analysis. Rather, this dissertation focuses on the increasing number of competitive cases and the surrounding conditions.

4.3 Current Legal Framework in Germany

The distinction between commercial and non-commercial services is one of the key elements of the German legal framework for public transport bus services in 2009.[4] The characteristics of commercial and non-commercial services in terms of financing and/or exclusive rights and awarding procedures are explained in the following section.

4.3.1 Financing Structure for Commercial and Non-Commercial Services

The funding structure of local and regional public bus transport services in Germany is characterized by a system of subsidies provided by a multitude of agencies at all three tiers of government.[5] Payments are made using a broad variety of instruments. Based on Fig. 4.1 below, the basic funding structure divided according to federal, state, and local tiers is described next.

[3] Thanks to numerous experts interviewed for market insiders'.

[4] As the legislative body has not yet agreed upon an adjustment of the legal framework, this framework is still in place, although the new (EC) No 1370/2007 is valid from December 3, 2009. So far, in practice no significant alteration has been observed with respect to the distinction between commercial and non-commercial services and other major regulations described here.

[5] See Hickmann (2004, p. 34), Sterzenbach (2008, pp. 75–104) and Wissenschaftlicher Beirat beim BMVBS (scientific council at the federal ministry of transport) (2008, pp. 82–86) for a detailed explanation of the financing structure in Germany.

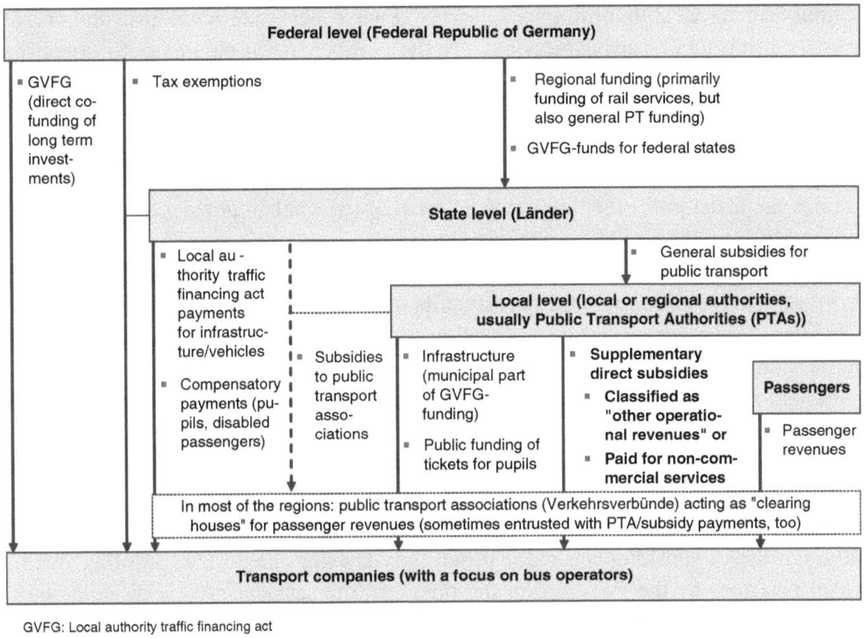

Fig. 4.1 Funding structure for public transport services by bus (Source: Own figure based on Hickmann (2004, p. 34) and Sterzenbach (2008, p. 80))

The federal level (the top tier: the Federal Republic of Germany) provides direct co-funding for selected long-term investments in major infrastructure projects. These are based on the Local Authority Traffic Financing Act (Gemeindeverkehrsfinanzierungsgesetz – GVFG). Furthermore, the federal government waives taxes through reduced tax scales and tax exemptions for public transport (for value added tax, for motor vehicle tax, for petroleum tax in case of vehicles powered by natural gas or [temporary] biodiesel, for real property tax, and for local business tax).

The states (the second tier: the Länder) also waive some tax revenues to assist the industry. To subsidize public transport services within their territory, the states receive so-called “Regionalisierungsmittel” (regional funds, paid according to § 5 RegG). These funds, which totaled €6.675 billion in 2008, are used primarily for funding rail services. Nevertheless, the states use a portion of these funds for general public transport purposes.[6]

The Länder also receive funds from the federal government to support infra-structure investments (e.g., for depots) and/or vehicle investments at the local level

[6] See SCI (2006) and Wissenschaftlicher Beirat beim BMVBS (2008, p. 84).

(amounting to €1.336 billion per year).[7] Two other state-level instruments of primary importance for bus services are the compensation payments to operators for reduced fares for pupils (including trainees and students up to a specific age) and the disabled.[8] According to Hickmann (2004, p. 34) and Sterzenbach (2008, p. 93), compensation for reduced pupil fares is one of the main sources of public funding for operators of short-distance services in the German public transport system. The Länder can also make other payments to local or regional authorities to enable them to directly fund their public transport services.

The local or regional authorities (the third tier) which usually act as PTAs for bus services provide infrastructure investments under the GVFG through co-financing subsidies. Some local school authorities cover the remaining costs of students' public transport tickets.

Where necessary to ensure adequate service, the PTAs pay direct supplementary subsidies to operators. Whether or not such payments are considered "other operational revenues" is the fundamental basis that distinguishes between commercial and non-commercial services. If these subsidies are classified as other operational revenues, the services are classified as commercial according to § 8 (4) PBefG, although direct subsidies are paid. When they are not categorized as other operational revenues by the PTA and/or the operator, the services are classified as non-commercial.

To enable municipal operators to deliver adequate levels of service, PTAs also use deficit compensations and cross-subsidies for supplementary funding. In the case of deficit compensation the PTA assumes the loss for the financial year. In the case of cross-subsidies, a profitable municipal company (such as municipal energy suppliers) will assume the loss. The municipal owner is then able to accrue financial benefits resulting from reduced corporate tax payments due to the owner's relationship with the profitable municipal company.

Direct awarding to municipal operators (in-house awarding) and private operators is the major type of awarding in Germany. Nevertheless, as described above, it is not the intended focus of this dissertation since the major market trend is the introduction of competition. Therefore, the funding scheme for direct awarding mechanisms will not be considered in detail.

In addition to the importance of public co-funding for public transport services it should be kept in mind that a significant share of revenues for operators also consists of fare revenues. To distribute fare revenues between operators (and to promote the use of the public transport system) public transport associations

---

[7] See §§ 1 and 2 GVFG and the Demerger Act (Gesetz zur Entflechtung von Gemeinschaftsaufgaben und Finanzhilfen, also known as Entflechtungsgesetz – EntflechtG). Note that data on the quantitative volume of further instruments of public co-funding is usually not published and even making estimates is difficult.

[8] Under § 45a of the Passenger Transport Act and §§ 145 ff. of the Ninth Code of Social Law.

(Verkehrsverbünde) have been founded in many regions.[9] Using a database of 150 German PTAs, Graetz et al. (2007, p. 11) showed that a public transport association existed for more than 80% of the PTAs in their study. Usually these associations act as clearing houses to distribute fare revenues among operators. Several associations have also been entrusted with the duties of PTAs at the regional and/or at the local level, including the administration of the provision of (supplementary) subsidy payments to operators. Some states – usually in coordination with PTAs – subsidize the public transport associations in their territory.

In summary, the financing structure in Germany is not only rather complex, differing between the states, but often also differing at the regional and/or local level without any clear obligation for authorities to publish complete information on public funding.[10] Furthermore, my examination shows that German legislation provides authorities with a certain level of freedom to structure their financing schemes according to their local needs. In contrast to the incumbent operators, the multitude of financing instruments available makes it difficult for newcomers to assess the subsidies to be expected. Sterzenbach (2008, p. 105) therefore classifies the German financing structure for public transport with its numerous financing sources and streams as "intransparent". A similar statement was made by the scientific council at the federal ministry of transport (see Wissenschaftsrat of the BMVBS 2008, p. 82), which describes the German financing structure as "historically developed, complicated and widely intransparent". For the purpose of our analysis bear in mind that the market participants themselves have a major influence on whether or not services are classified as non-commercial or commercial. This may be done by classifying public co-funding as being or not being direct subsidies.

4.3.2 Awarding of Exclusive Rights for Commercial Services

There are three main participants in the market for commercial public transport services by bus: PTAs, the licensing authorities (LAs), and operators. Figure 4.2 below provides a brief overview of the obligatory collaboration under the PBefG.

If operators decide to initiate new, or continue existing commercial services, they must apply for a license which is granted by the LA (see § 2 [1] and § 11 [1] PBefG). The application must contain the major characteristics of the service planned, e.g., line length and route, timetable, tariff system, and number and type of vehicles (see § 12 [3] PBefG). The license can be granted for only one line, or for

[9] See van de Velde et al. (2008a, p. 53) for a short explanation of the German Verkehrsverbund. For a more detailed explanation on the Verkehrsverbund as a typical German association that coordinates fare levels and systems, sales and distribution, timetables and passenger information in one geographic area and splits fare revenues among its participants see Pucher and Kurth (1996).

[10] See Sterzenbach (2008, pp. 97–101).

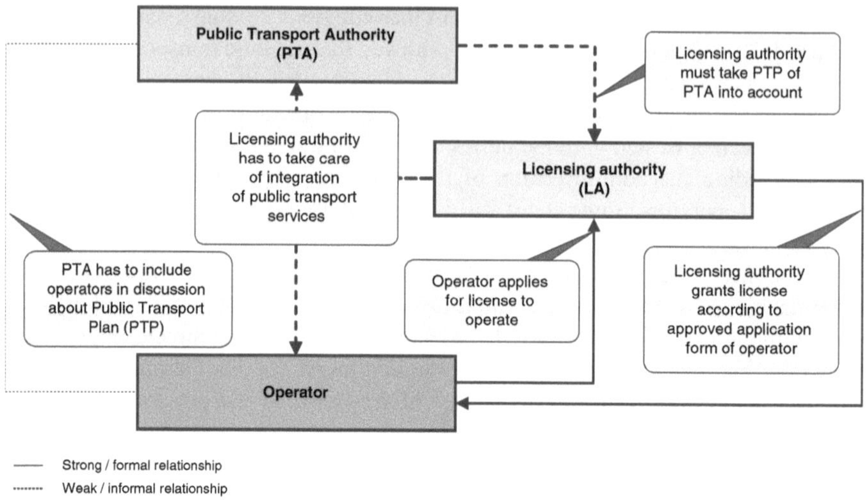

Fig. 4.2 Major participants in the market for commercial services

a network (see § 9 [2] PBefG), e.g., a city. Following approval by the LA, operators are obliged to deliver the approved service for the full license term, usually 8 years.

The responsibilities of LAs within the national market are to safeguard the security of operations for passengers and to secure the continuous delivery of services to passengers during both the validation of applications and the license term. The main tasks are to provide access to the profession of being a bus operator via a verification of the company. This permits the operator to provide public bus transport services in general. In case of commercial services, LAs also provide access to the market. Both of these obligations are conducted through the process of granting of licenses. LAs can reject applications if they expect problems with security or continuous delivery of public transport services (for minimum requirements for market entry, see § 13 PBefG and Werner 2001, pp. 61–63).[11]

LAs are also obligated to ensure commercial stability for existing services, e.g., they can reject new applications to establish commercial services if the demand for public transport can be met by existing providers. An incumbent provider may also agree to adopt parts or all of the proposals of competitors if profitable (see Werner 2001, p. 97).[12,13] To date, the competing applications of newcomers against

[11] According to Gerrit Landsberg, lawyer at BBG und Partner, the main focus is on awarding concessions and includes very weak instruments to withdraw these authorizations (licenses) or impose fines if operators do not deliver services as promised (see also §§ 25 and 61 PBefG).

[12] Lawyers continue to discuss the extent of this form of exclusive right; see Werner (2004, pp. 91–96).

[13] These rules effectively establish an exclusive right granted via a license (see § 13 [2] PBefG and BLFA 2006, p. 2).

existing lines have seldom been observed during the license term. Nevertheless, they are allowed in principle (see Beck 2007, p. 426).

In fulfilling their responsibilities, LAs must take into account the (local) Public Transport Plan (PTP), but lack any clear guidelines on this subject (§ 8 [3] PBefG). They can merely deny applications which do not comply (§ 13 [2a] PBefG), but there is no clear obligation to do so. According to Werner (2001, p. 90) and Gerrit Landsberg, PTPs nevertheless are usually a minimum standard for LAs.

LAs are also mandated to look after the integration of public transport services (according to § 8 [3] PBefG), especially with respect to cooperation schemes such as tariff or public transport associations (Verkehrsverbünde). Again, the law merely requires taking this issue into consideration when making administrative decisions without a clear obligation to initiate particular actions.

When different operators compete to operate specific commercial services after the expiration date of an existing license or compete for a new license, the situation is classified as Competition for Commercial Lines or services (CCL). If a CCL occurs, the LAs still must validate all offers. The first step of the validation procedure is to examine compliance with the above-mentioned minimum criteria (security aspects, economic capability, reputation, delivery of appropriate service according to PTP, etc.; see §§ 12, 13, and 14 PBefG and Werner 2001, pp. 90–102). In the second step the LA selects the best of the remaining offers with respect to fulfilling public interests (mainly quality aspects from a passenger point of view, e.g., frequency, tariff system, etc.; see Werner 2001, pp. 102–104).

The rights and obligations of the PTAs concerning commercial services are limited. According to § 1 RegG, their main task is to determine and secure an adequate minimum level of public transport service in their territory. Thus, it is the PTAs' responsibility to provide services of general interest.[14] Usually, a direct contractual relationship between a PTA and a licensee does not exist within the market for commercial services. In this case, the PTP is the chief instrument used by the PTA to fulfill its obligation to provide an adequate level of services (see Barth 2001, pp. 56–63 as well as pp. 94–97, for the importance of the PTP in this matter). PTAs must include operators when discussing the establishment or adjustment of the PTP.

4.3.3 Granting Supplementary Subsidies for Non-Commercial Services

If the provision of services is not commercial, i.e. it uses exclusive rights only, supplementary direct subsidies are necessary. If these funds are not categorized as other operational revenues, the subsidized services must be classified as non-commercial. According to § 8 (4) PBefG, PTAs are then obliged to tender these

[14] See Forsthoff (1938, pp. 36–37), and European Commission (2001) for the classification of public transport (PT) services as services of general interest.

supplementary direct subsidies. In contrast to commercial services, the PTA itself initiates the services in question, usually through tendering procedures under the legal rules of the Official Contracting Terms for Awarding Service Performance Contracts, Part A (Verdingungsordnung für Leistungen, or VOL/A).

Following the award of the contract, the winning bidder applies to the LA for a license to operate (see Werner 2001, p. 36). However, in the case of a competing application for commercial services, the LA must decide in favor of the commercial market initiative (priority of commercial services; see § 8 [4] PBefG and Werner 2001, pp. 82–83), as long as the minimum criteria are met. This is also the case during or after a tendering procedure, as long as the LA has not approved the service.

It is important to note that PTAs usually do not have any direct influence on the procedure for controlling the quality provided by the operator of commercial services authorized by the LA. PTAs may only notify the LAs when quality is not delivered by the operator as defined in its application, in contrast to the use of a public service contract with clear obligations.

4.3.4 *Comparing of Competition for Commercial and Non-Commercial Services and Direct Awarding*

In summary, the analysis of the current framework shows that competition for public transport services by bus is possible either (1) for non-commercial services via tendering, or (2) for commercial services via CCL. A third aspect occurs where (3) no competition takes place and licenses are re-granted to the incumbent operator.

The Public Transport Act revised in the mid-1990s deemed supplementary direct subsidies by the responsible PTA necessary to ensure that *non-commercial services* ("gemeinwirtschaftliche Verkehre") are provided at a quality level defined as adequate by the PTA. The PTA must award such funds at the lowest cost possible (usually through tendering). Therefore, the non-commercial services have been classified as authority initiated. Although subsidies are awarded by the PTA, the winning bidder of the *tendering* procedure must apply to the LA for a license to operate the non-commercial lines. The LA grants the license on the condition that a set of minimum criteria is met (e.g., services with a minimum quality level as described by the local PTP developed by the PTA). Effectively, such a license to operate always includes the right of exclusivity for the licensee during the license term. To ensure the commercial stability of existing services, the framework requires LAs to reject new applications to establish commercial services if the demand for public transport can be met by existing providers.[15]

[15] If a new application to operate a bus line competes with existing public transport services, and the operators of the existing lines claim convincingly that the profitability of these services is jeopardized, the licensing authority must reject the new application. In reality this has resulted in a status of exclusivity for holders of existing licenses (incumbent operators).

For *commercial services* ("eigenwirtschaftliche Verkehre"), supplementary direct subsidies by the PTA pursuant to § 13a PBefG are not deemed necessary. Instead, the sum of fares, compensatory payments for fare reductions (e.g., for students), and other operational revenues cover or exceed the operating costs. To launch such services, operators only have to submit an application to the LA; these services are classified in this dissertation as operator initiated (or market initiated). There is no direct relationship between the PTA and the operator for such services. The LA grants the applicant exclusive rights for the license term, usually eight years. Upon request, LAs are obliged to inform operators about the termination date of existing licenses. When there are competing applications for commercial services/lines (this dissertation classifies them as *competition for commercial lines or services [CCL]*), the LA must select the best bid with respect to the quality offered.

In the licensing process, the institutional framework gives priority to commercial services. If there are competing applications for non-commercial services and commercial services of comparable quality, LAs always have to decide in favor of the commercial operator initiative. This general rule even applies during or after a tendering procedure, e.g., if a bidder becomes aware of the commercial feasibility of the services in question while deciding its own tender or if a losing bidder tries to secure the volume of the service in question for its own operations after the tendering procedure ends.

A third type of services, legally defined as commercial, but in reality co-funded by local authorities, needs to be mentioned due to its predominance in Germany. Here, supplementary direct subsidies are defined as other operational revenues by both the authority and the operator. According to the legal definition in § 13 PBefG, these services are classified as commercial and the licenses are granted by LAs. In fact, most public bus transport services in Germany are still awarded directly in this manner (see e.g., Schnell 2009, p. 24), combined with the *renewal of the incumbent's license*. According to the legal framework of 2009, PTAs are not mandated by law to award these public funds in a competitive procedure. However, operators applying for licenses for real commercial services without any need for supplementary direct funding can always compete with the incumbent operator. The service categories by award type and characteristics are summarized in Fig. 4.3.

While in 2009 direct awarding through renewal of the incumbent's license was still the norm (~ 91.5% market share), tendering was observed for ~ 6% and CCL procedures for a mere ~ 2.5% of the market.[16] Clearly, the central aim of the 1990s reform, to encourage competition, has not been realized.

Nevertheless, the main aspect of the analysis in this dissertation is competition for public transport services by bus in Germany as this has been a major subject of discussion among market participants in recent years. We will therefore not discuss direct awarding of licenses in more detail here.

[16] Estimation based on BSL Management Consultants database.

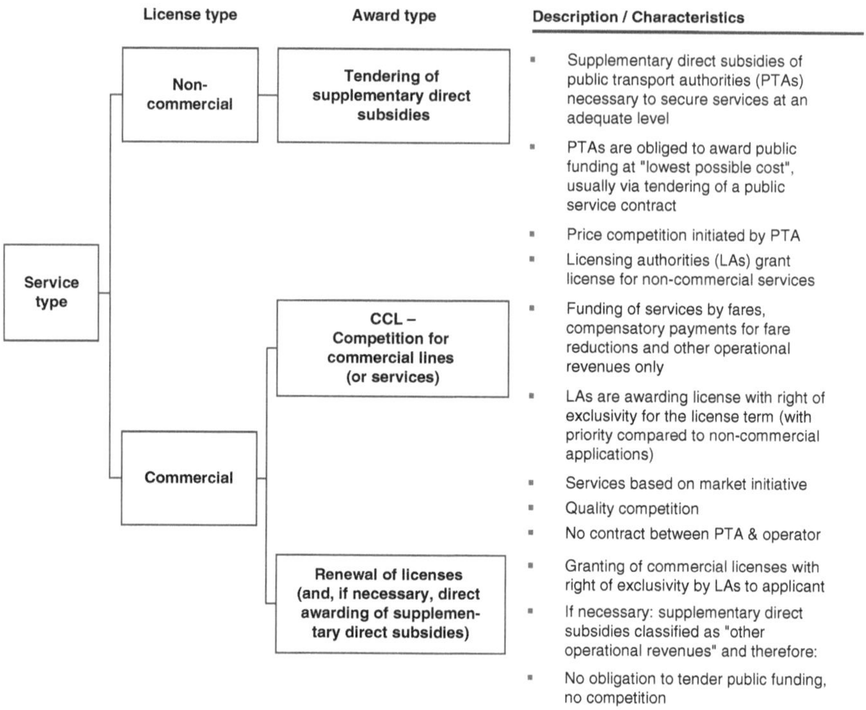

Fig. 4.3 Categorization of services according to type of award

4.4 A European Perspective on Institutional Frameworks and on the German Case

The institutional framework for contracting and awarding exhibits wide variations across the EU Member States. The specific feature of Germany's institutional framework is that distinctive aspects from institutional frameworks, such as competition *for* the market (Scandinavia) or competition *within* the market (Great Britain outside London), which usually are found only within one specific area, exist side by side within one market. In order to provide a different viewpoint in addition to the legal analysis presented in Sect. 4.3 I therefore explain the major aspects of contracting and awarding as applied in numerous EU Member States, followed by a more detailed description of the applications used in Germany.[17] The following aspects are discussed: (1) contractual relationship, (2) level of freedom given to operators to design the service, and (3) difference between market and authority initiatives. Where appropriate, case studies are included to ease understanding of the specific aspects.

[17] The database for this analysis of the German market is presented and discussed in detail in Chap. 5 as well as in Part III and Part IV.

4.4.1 Contractual Relationship for Commercial and Non-Commercial Services

4.4.1.1 The European Perspective

A contract defines rights and duties of the contracting parties. For matters of public transport services the International Association of Public Transport (2005, p. 22) defines the specific aspects of public service contracts (PSCs) as "Contracts are the mechanisms to formalize the relationship between the authority and an operator. The organizing authority is responsible for its transport policy.... The operator contributes to the realization of this policy in the framework of a contractual relationship." As seen in Fig. 4.4 the authority defines the operator's obligations and the operator must fulfill the contract, in return receiving the right to a public compensation (e.g., via exclusivity and/or supplementary direct subsidies).

Article 2 of the new (EC) No 1370/2007 states that the compensation encompasses any benefit, particularly financial, granted directly or indirectly by an authority during the period of implementation of the public service obligation, or in connection with that period. The authority must grant the compensation after ensuring that the operator has fulfilled the obligations according to the contract. Consequently, the contract documents the obligations of the operator within public transport services as well as its rights (e.g., exclusivity, compensation, subsidies, etc.).

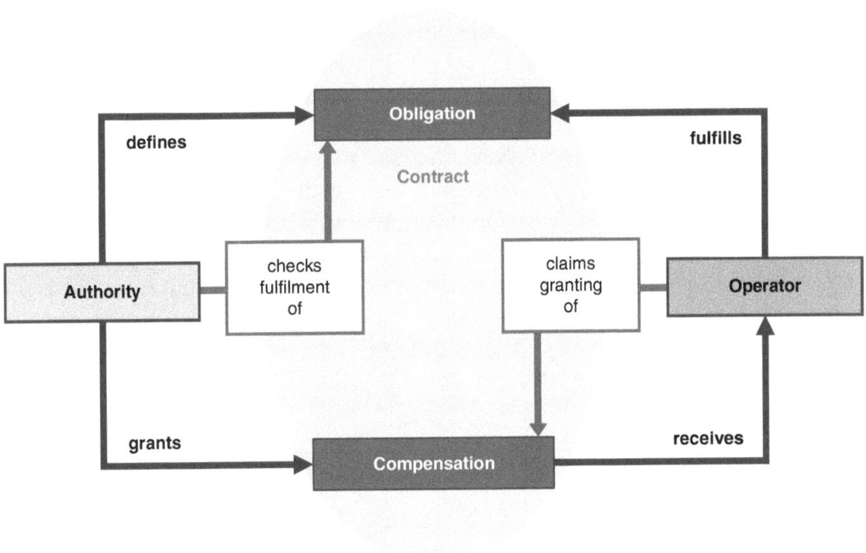

Fig. 4.4 Rights and obligations of the parties in a public service contract (This figure as well as this sub-section on contracts in Europe is based on my own research conducted as a member of the research group that developed a guidebook for the European Commission on how to award services properly (see van de Velde et al. 2008a, a study based on 34 contract cases in Europe))

The contract then serves as a means of checking whether or not the obligations of the two parties have been fulfilled as agreed. According to this EU definition, the contract fixes the fulfillment obligations of the operator, and (usually) the payment obligations of the authority. According to Article 3.1 of (EC) No 1370/2007, any grant of an exclusive right and/or other compensation given to the operator by the authority must be awarded within the framework of a public service contract.

For the purpose of this analysis, the definition of a contract extends beyond the classical sense (i.e. a written document confirmed by both contractual parties by signature) to include one or more legally binding acts that confirm some form of agreement between the two acting parties – the authority and the operator. This broader definition corresponds to the definition used by the EU Regulation on public service obligations ([EC] No 1370/2007 article 2 [i] together with article 2 [e]).[18]

4.4.1.2 The German Case

As explained in Sect. 4.3.2, operators in German public transport must apply for a license to operate commercial services before tendering. The license is granted by the LA for specific public transport services for the license term (see Fig. 4.5). For commercial services, it is the LA's responsibility to select and monitor the operator, thus forming a very weak form of contract between authority and operator. The LA only has to account for the PTP and any other comments of the PTA. Analyzing this contractual setting for commercial services shows that a public service contract between operator and PTA is not foreseen (and unusual).

In fact within the market for commercial services, the only direct relationship is between the LA and the licensee. Nevertheless, from an economic point of view, it can be classified as a contract between a state authority and the operator in a principal-agent relationship. This contract (the license and the legal obligations of the LA) sets out the rights and obligations of both parties. It regulates the obligation of the operator to deliver the service as approved (see § 21 [1] PBefG) and the right to receive a specified level of exclusivity in return. During the license term, the LA acts as an inspection authority to secure the delivery of public transport services (see § 54 PBefG and Werner 2001, pp. 131–145). Nevertheless, the assertiveness of this type of contract is low.

On the contrary, non-commercial services are characterized by a supplementary public service contract. This document signed by both parties fixes the obligations to be fulfilled by the operator and the necessary direct subsidies, thus establishing a

[18] Note that (EC) No 1370/2007 became effective on December 3, 2009 after I finished the analysis. Nevertheless, the regulation provides a clear, unambiguous definition of the extent of a public service contract on a general level that is accepted by all EU Member States, making it appropriate to include its main definitions for contracts here.

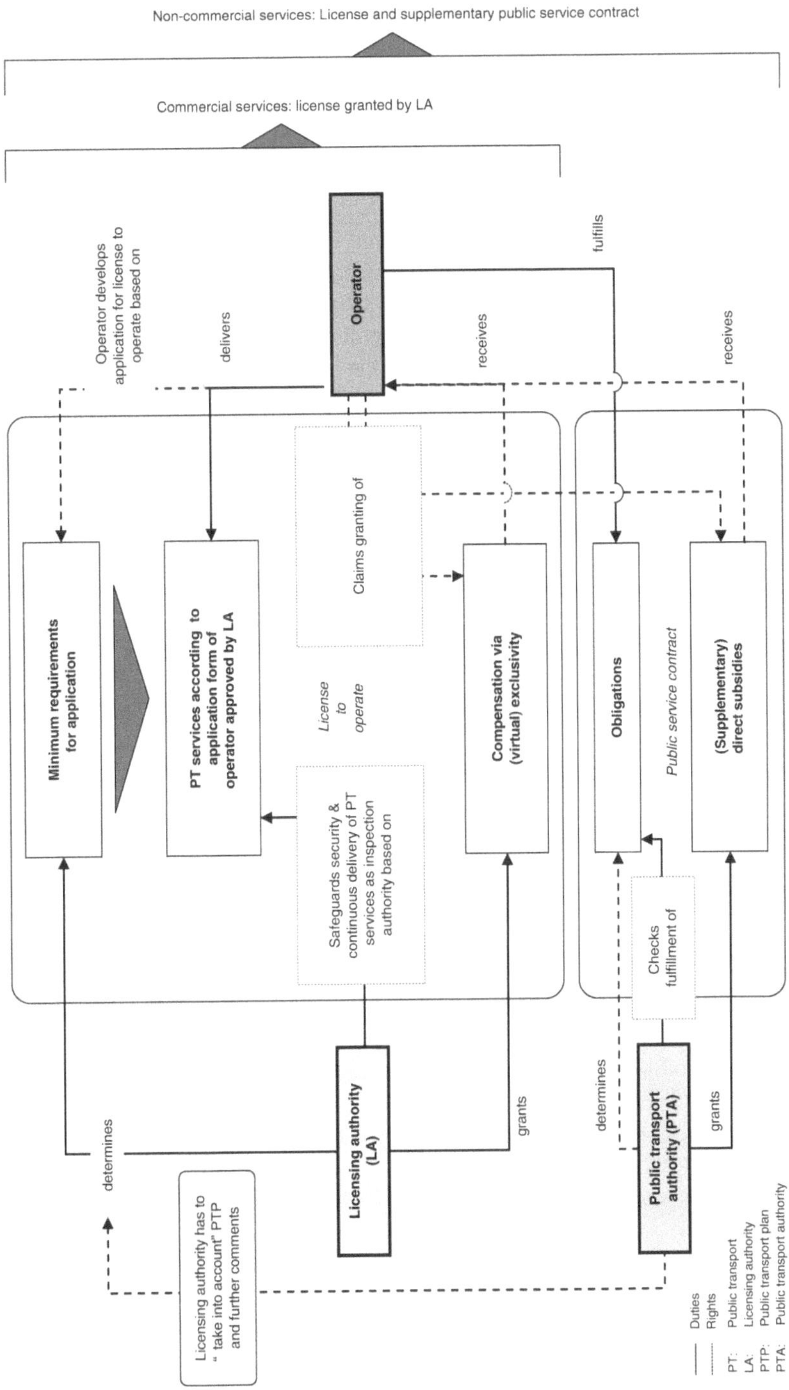

Fig. 4.5 Contractual relationship for commercial and non-commercial services

direct contractual relationship between the PTA and the operator. For example, gross-cost contracts determine that the revenue risk is borne by the PTA and thus the PTA must pay the full costs of the operations (plus a profit margin), while net-cost contracts determine that the revenue risk (and chance) is borne by the operator and thus only supplementary public co-funding is necessary. Furthermore, when using tendering, PTAs are able to select and monitor the operator independently. After the awarding procedure, the LA grants the non-commercial license.

Drafting a suitable contract is an important task. As van de Velde et al. (2008a) found, there is a great variety of contractual practice across Europe, which is also true for Germany (see e.g., Sect. 4.4.2, Chaps. 5 and 7). The specific local circumstances and the different transport policy aims of the different authorities obviously result in requirements tailored to the locale. Consequently, public service contracts have to be designed properly to fulfill these requirements. Agreements must be reached between authorities and operators regarding risk allocation, planning, design of services and control of performances. The next section describes the design of services and the freedom of operators. Other aspects, especially the allocation of risk, and their effects on the results of tendering, are described in Part III.

4.4.2 Operators' Level of Freedom to Design the Service

4.4.2.1 The European Perspective

When developing the contractual relationship between the PTA and the operator, an important factor is the minimum quality level derived from the transport policy aims of the political decision-makers. This requires determining the extent to which the PTA will prescribe the design of public transport services. A non-ambiguous division of tasks, responsibilities, and competences between the authority and the operator is needed.[19] The allocation of decision-making regarding the design of services will then limit the freedom of the operator to contribute to (e.g., by making suggestions) and to design the services (see Fig. 4.6).

When the PTA grants the operator a high degree of freedom, there may be less need to describe several aspects in detail when determining the minimum quality level. In this case, the authority guides the design of public transport services via functionally described aims. This case will be referred to as functional planning (see Fig. 4.7).

An example of a functional design of services is a minimum quality determining that 80% of a city's inhabitants must live in a radius of 400 m maximum walking distance to the next bus stop (influencing the location of bus stops set by the

[19] See also International Association of Public Transport (2005, p. 10).

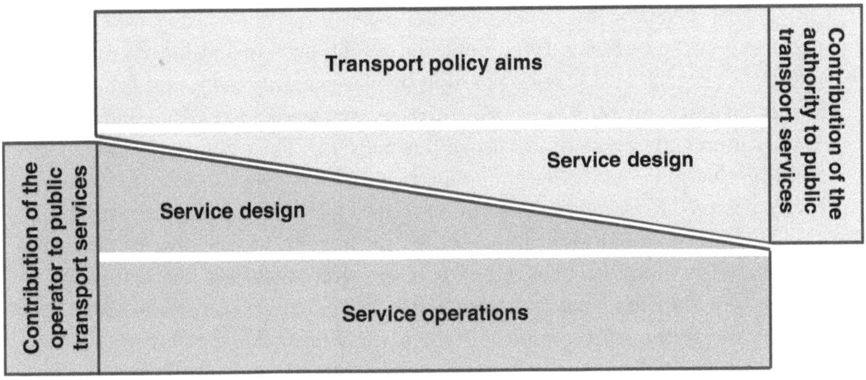

Fig. 4.6 Contributions of contracting parties to public transport services (This figure as well as this section on contracts in Europe is based on my own research conducted as a member of the research group that developed a guidebook for the European Commission on how to award services properly (see van de Velde et al. 2008a and 2008b, a study based on 34 contract cases in Europe))

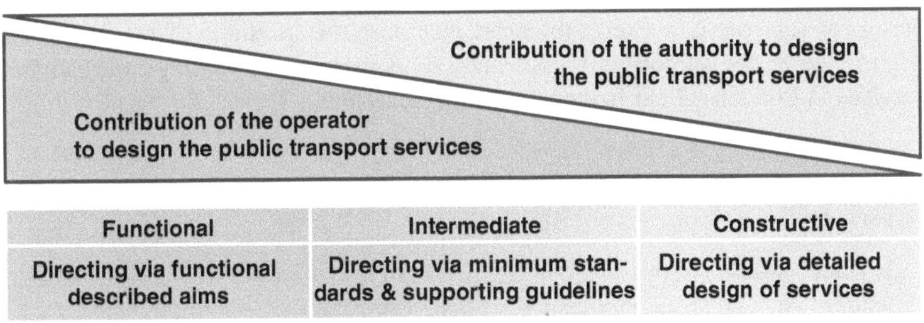

Fig. 4.7 Classification of contractual relationships

operator). A case study on functional awarding of regional and urban bus services in Grenland (Norway) is presented below.

Case study Grenland (Norway): Functional awarding of regional and urban bus services[20]

According to the public transport plan the main objective for the public transport in the region Telemark 2003–2009 was to increase the number of public transport trips per inhabitant from 39 to 50 in the short run and up to 70 in the long run. These policy aims were translated into requirements for

(continued)

[20] This case study was presented in detail by van de Velde et al. (2008a, p. 53) and (2008b, pp. 34–35).

operators via the public service contract, which established the contractual goal to develop the best service possible by using quality tendering for a fixed subsidy level (quality competition). Grenland tendered a network contract for the operation and design of the urban bus network. The operator is subjected to full production cost risk and revenue risk and has considerable freedom in service design during the lifetime of the contract. Due to the high contribution of the operator to the design of the public transport services, this contract can be classified as functional, since the operator is free to: decide the bus size and frequency within the financial framework of the contract and the capacity constraints for the buses; adjust the service within the framework of the opening hour and the capacity constraint for the buses; and adjust fares within the regional fare scale.

When the PTA desires to contribute to the service design to a large extent, the operator then has less or no direct involvement with service design. This case will be referred to as constructive planning (see Fig. 4.7). An example of a constructive design of services is a fixed timetable, including the locations of bus stops, all determined by the authority. A case study on constructive awarding of urban bus services in London (Great Britain) is presented below.

Case study London (Great Britain): Constructive awarding of urban bus services[21]

London awarded about 700 contracts for single bus routes in a competitive tender. The operators only bear the production cost risk, while the authority bears the revenue risk. All service planning is done by Transport for London (TfL). The London example is unique in the UK, since the rest of Great Britain has a deregulated system. The main public transport policy goals of the city of London are set in the Mayor's Transport Strategy. With respect to a complex route network London decided in favor of a high contribution of the TfL to the service design (constructive contract). TfL London Buses defines the network and specifies minimum service levels in detail, including times of first and last buses. TfL defines the ticket products, and sets the fares. TfL is also responsible for all marketing and information, sets and monitors performance standards, and maintains stops, shelters, and stations. During the contracting period routes and timetables can be changed at TfL's discretion if circumstances have changed.

[21] This case study was presented in detail by van de Velde et al. (2008a, p. 54) and (2008b, pp. 49–52).

In reality, of course, most contractual relationships must be classified as intermediate, since the PTA guides public transport services in its area of responsibility via a mix of functionally described aims and constructively described minimum standards. This dissertation uses the terms functional and constructive planning to describe the operators' level of freedom to design the services. Other studies, i.e. Atkins (2005, p. 5) differentiate between an "outline specification" (similar to functional) and a "detailed specification" (similar to constructive).

4.4.2.2 The German Case

When classifying the structure of contractual relationships as presented in Sect. 4.4.1, clarification about the contribution of operators and authorities is necessary. The analysis of competitive awarding procedures shows that commercial services are usually characterized by a high level of operator freedom (see Fig. 4.8). The PTA determines the minimum quality level only within its PTP, usually by setting functional aims and some minimum quality standards (see e.g., Kreis Dithmarschen 2003). A few German PTAs determine the minimum quality level in their PTP in a more detailed (intermediate) fashion (see e.g., Region Hannover 2008). Thus the contractual relationship for commercial services is usually characterized by a high level of freedom for the operators.

A case study on CCL within the rural district of Wittenberg that also shows a high level of freedom for the operator to design the services is presented below.

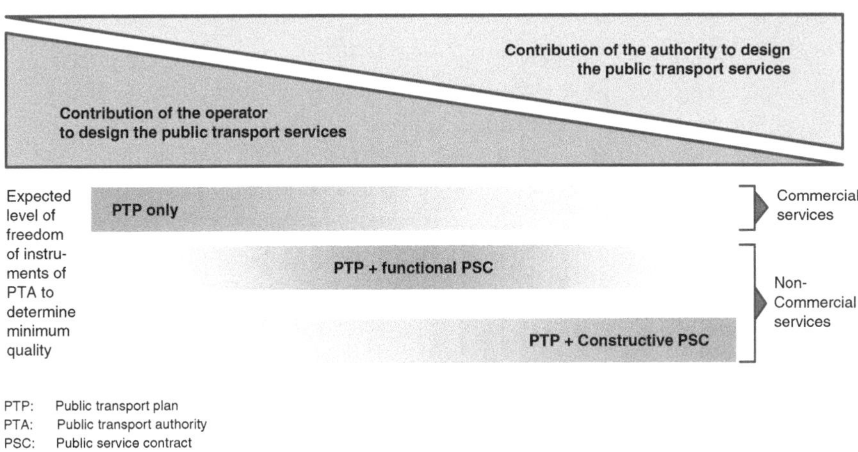

Fig. 4.8 Classification of contractual relationships in the German case

Case study Wittenberg (Germany): Competition for commercial lines[22]

The rural district Wittenberg promoted a CCL procedure in its area of responsibility. The minimum quality standards are fixed in the PTP. Wittenberg offered a fixed compensation to operators (lump sum payments and payments per passenger), published by the rural district in advance. The operator's bid largely defines the service design. It must develop a plan for the location of bus stops, a timetable, a vehicle schedule and a fare structure (based on existing fares). Nevertheless, operators must negotiate every change in service design with the rural district. Even fare increases must be authorized.

In contrast, non-commercial services are usually characterized by an intermediate (PTP and functional PSC), or a constructive contractual relationship (PTP and constructive PSC). The contractual terms precisely define the role and prerogatives of the authority and the operator during the contract period in addition to the existing PTP, and form the basis for calculations by the operators. The service level required by the authority can be described functionally, e.g., for the city of Elmshorn as shown in the box below.

Within the framework of functionally described minimum standards for Elmshorn, the operator was free to design its own routes, move existing bus stops and design the timetable. This case can be classified as an intermediate case with a high level of freedom to design the service. A case study on a constructive contractual relationship with tendering of gross-cost route bundle contracts of non-commercial services within the city Frankfurt on the Main is described below.

Case study Elmshorn (Germany): Functional tendering of non-commercial services[23]

The suburban district Pinneberg (located in the Hamburg area) tendered a gross-cost contract for a 5-year period starting in 2005 for the city of Elmshorn. The contract includes a comparatively high bonus payment for passenger increases, introducing an incentive for this political aim. The operator receives €0.35 for each newly gained passenger (calculation basis set within the first year of operation to avoid incalculable risk). The service offered by the operator was described functionally as: bus service must cover a certain area. Minimum requirements for service are: stops located in

(continued)

[22] A detailed description of the other aspects of this case appears in Sect. 5.4.2.

[23] This case study was presented in detail by van de Velde et al. (2008a, pp. 67–68) and (2008b, pp. 22–24).

densely populated areas with 2 departures per hour, stops located in industrial areas with 1 or 2 departures per hour, stops in rural areas with 1 departure per hour, and stops during rush hour in some remote areas with 1 departure per hour. Further requirements include: (1) departures with fixed scheduled frequency set by the operator; (2) direct link to the city center from every stop and maximum travel time of 15 min from a bus stop within densely populated areas to the city center; (3) two specific bus routes, mainly intended for student transport, supplied according to fixed routes and timetables; (4) low-floor buses; and (5) fare structure and passenger information in accordance with the standard set by the PTA.

Case study Frankfurt on the Main (Germany): Constructive tendering of bus services[24]

The Lokale Nahverkehrsgesellschaft Frankfurt am Main mbH traffiQ (traffiQ), the tendering authority of the city Frankfurt on the Main, determines the service design before the contracting/tendering process in a detailed manner (routes, timetables, fares, detailed quality standards for buses and operators staff). The candidate/operator does not define any item of the service design during the tendering process. The bidder must submit an offer fulfilling all of these demands; otherwise, the bid is excluded. The operator cannot change service design (routes, timetables, and fares) during the contracting period. It can suggest changes, but they must be ordered by traffiQ. Changes are only possible within a specific range, such as +/– 5% of the scheduled hours. The operator must fulfill the precisely described contract demands. traffiQ has some operational competences as it determines the timetable and the type of buses for the different lines. In a few cases, the operator can choose between bus types, but within the available costs for the bus type.

In summary, these classifications and examples show the variety of contractual relationships with respect to the operator's freedom to design the service in Germany. For the following explanations please keep in mind that there are three major types of contractual relationship. These are (1) commercial services with a PTP,

[24] This case study was presented in detail by van de Velde et al. (2008a, p. 48) and (2008b, pp. 27–27). Other examples of the high number of constructive contractual relationships for non-commercial services within Germany are the tendering documents for the suburban area of Munich (see MVV 2009) and for regional bus services in the greater Frankfurt on the Main area (see RMV 2005).

(2) non-commercial services with a PTP *and* an additional *functional* PSC and
(3) non-commercial services with a PTP *and* an additional *constructive* PSC.

4.4.3 Market Versus Authority Initiative

4.4.3.1 The European Perspective

From a legal perspective, Europe's public transport service regimes can be divided in two categories: authority initiative and market initiative. The chief distinction is whether the right to initiate the creation of a service is the responsibility of an authority (which could, however, delegate it to an independent operator), or is determined by in the market, for anyone to use.[25]

It is important to note that the (EC) No 1370/2007 as the new European-wide regime allows for both organizational forms. Article 2 (e) clearly states that a public service obligation can be defined (authority initiative) or determined (market initiative) by a competent authority. The use of the word, determined, implies that something is fixed at the end of a process set in motion by someone else, in this case the market (the operator). In other words, it does not matter who initiates the process as long as it leads to a signed public service contract, and the choice is left to the EU Member States. The balance of power and responsibilities between the authority and the operator will vary, depending on which of the regimes is applied at the national level.

In authority initiated regimes, authorities which have received the responsibility for transport (i.e. the transport authorities) have the legal monopoly of initiative. This means that autonomous market entry is in principle legally impossible and all production or market entry is the result of a conscious action by the authorities to produce services or to request their production. An example is the French public transport legislation (outside the Paris region), whereby this framework identifies local and regional authorities in charge of the organization of passenger transport services. According to French law, the authorities are entitled to produce the transport services themselves unless they make a conscious decision to delegate this prerogative to other transport operators. In such a case, the law requires the authorities to use a specific competitive awarding procedure to select the operator responsible for the services. This legal regime does not foresee the possibility of non-contracted transport operators to initiate transport services independently. All activities of the public transport operators must be based on a request from a designated organizing transport authority.

In market initiated regimes, the supply of transport services is based upon the principle of autonomous entry resulting from a market process with more or less

[25] This section on frameworks in Europe is based on van de Velde et al. (2008a); for details on this issue in other parts of Europe, see van de Velde (1999) and (2005).

regulatory checks at the entrance. It varies from pure open entry systems to strongly regulated authorization or license regimes, and various intermediate systems. The purest example of a market initiative regime in local public transport in Europe is Great Britain (outside the London area). Operators have the right to provide services upon their own initiative, according to routes, timetables and fares determined by their own commercial insights. There are no exclusive rights, meaning that direct competition between bus operators on the streets is allowed, even though this is usually not the case.

Note that a regime based upon the legal principle of market initiative does not necessarily mean that the (transport) authority's role is insignificant or even non-existent. An authority can arrange for the provision of additional services when the market fails to provide them and when such services are desirable and apt to prompt the realization of transport policy goals. However, this does not transform the legal regime into an authority initiated one; rather, it only indicates that in such market initiated regimes the authority itself may provide additional services in order to correct a market which fails to provide adequate services from an authority point of view.

Again using Britain (outside London) as the example, regional transport authorities arrange for the provision of additional passenger transport services where such services are not provided by the commercial, deregulated bus market, based upon their transport policy objectives (e.g., accessibility standards for various urban areas, mobility standards for various groups, and the like). They also identify areas with insufficient passenger transport service supply and define the needed additional services. Typically, services requested by authorities and not provided by the free market are evening services and Sunday service, but this varies according to the specific market conditions. These regional authorities in charge of public transport then organize competitive tendering procedures to select operators in addition to the existing commercially supplied services. Note that the additional services ordered by authorities do not benefit from any exclusive right. Nevertheless, this important intermediate case shows that pure regimes of market initiated services are rare since they require public transport authorities to waive any form of market intervention.

4.4.3.2 The German Case

Like Great Britain the German legal regime for local public transport services by bus described in Sects. 4.3.2 and 4.3.3 is also based upon market initiative. Unlike the British regime, however, the provision of passenger transport services is subject to the award of a license which effectively gives the operator an exclusive right for a specified period. Thus, the public impact on the market in Germany shows a higher level than in Great Britain.

Furthermore, in Germany licenses are awarded by designated regulatory authorities which must consider the public transport plan of PTAs in their award decision. Nevertheless, similar to Britain outside London, the authorities are free to tender financial subsidies for non-commercial services. Another distinctive aspect of the German market is the existence of a dichotomic system of market and authority initiatives within one area. In contrast, Great Britain has assigned the two aspects to different areas (market initiative outside London; authority initiative in the London area). The Netherlands changed from a market initiated system to an authority initiated system during its market reform in 2000. For the latter, "the new law implies the market initiative with PTAs" (Hermans and Stoelinga 2005, pp. 293–295).

4.5 A Theoretical Model That Captures the Current Institutional Features in Germany

As discussed in Sects. 4.3 and 4.4, permits for commercial and non-commercial public transport bus services in Germany are awarded through a system of controlled competition *for* the market (exclusivity and, if necessary, supplementary direct subsidies). Moreover, the role of the PTAs is weak within the market for commercial services compared to their strong position in the market for non-commercial services. Nevertheless, even in the market for commercial services, their position is stronger than in open market regimes like Great Britain (outside London) where competition *within* the market exists and the PTAs merely arrange to provide additional services. In the market for commercial services in Germany, PTAs are at least obliged to set minimum standards in the PTP applying to all operators.

To enable an analysis of the interactions between commercial and non-commercial services in Germany in case of competition, I introduce a theoretical setting for the current institutional framework. The following assumptions and definitions are based on the descriptions in Sects. 4.3 and 4.4 and on procedures observed in various cases[26] focusing on the competitive bus market. As already emphasized, this dissertation does not analyze the direct awarding of licenses.

4.5.1 Awarding via Auctioning

First, I assume that the award of a license provides real exclusivity and obliges the operator to deliver the service, or services, of general interest as promised for the entire license term. Awarding of licenses to operate specific public transport bus services occurs either through quality competition in the case of competition for commercial lines or services (CCL), or through price competition in the case of tendering for supplementary direct subsidies for non-commercial services (tendering).

---

[26] The database for this analysis of the German market is presented and discussed in detail in Chap. 5 as well as Part III and Part IV.

Second, I assume that the LA and the PTA, especially in the case of non-commercial services, act as *one authority* from an operator's point of view.[27]

Both the LA and the PTA are required to design the detailed conditions of the validation procedure largely on their own. Thereafter they assign an exclusive right and, in the case of non-commercial services, provide supplementary direct subsidies to the winner of the validation procedure. I conclude that this awarding mechanism is quite similar to the design of auctions where the authority can thus be classified as an auctioneer.

According to economic theory auctions are characterized by an auctioneer that sells a specified commodity at the highest bid price offered by potential buyers. Wolfstetter (1999, p. 184) defines an auction as "a bidding mechanism, described by a set of auction rules that specify how the winner is determined and how much he has to pay."

In contrast to a usual auction procedure, as a form of public sale Germany's awarding procedure for licenses to operate commercial or non-commercial services can be characterized as a reverse auction. The bidding mechanism takes place to specify (1) the amount of quality the winning bidder will provide to passengers for the license in case of a CCL, or (2) the amount of supplementary direct subsidies the winning bidder will receive for providing the non-commercial minimum level of quality set by the PTA in addition to exclusivity. From the authority perspective this is a demand auction, or procurement by tender, in which the authority provides the winning bidder with exclusivity and, if necessary, direct subsidies in return for the provision of public transport services (competition *for* the market).[28]

The procedural conditions of the authority are, in effect, a take-it-or-leave-it offer for applicants (or bidders) in accordance with normative principal-agent theory.[29] Submission of an application (or submission of a bid in the case of non-commercial services) obliges the applicants (or bidders) to provide the services upon acceptance of the application (the bid) by the authority. Although final details are sometimes clarified in subsequent negotiations, the major parameters of the application (the bid) usually do not change. The four forms of auction design are briefly described below.

Four Main Forms of Auction Design

Economic theory distinguishes four main forms of auction design: (1) the English auction method, (2) the Dutch auction method, (3) the first-price sealed-bid auction method, and (4) the second-price sealed-bid, or Vickrey auction method (see Wolfstetter 1999, pp. 182–186 as well as Krishna 2002, pp. 2–3).

(continued)

[27] Although some disputes between the LA and the PTA have been published, both authorities usually closely coordinate their decision-making process in reality.

[28] As explained above, this market mechanism differs from open market regimes such as in Britain outside London, which are characterized by competition *within* the market.

[29] See Richter and Furobotn (1999, pp. 172–176) and Fees (1997, p. 585 and p. 588) for the normative principal-agent theory.

In an English auction, also known as an open ascending auction, the auctioneer starts with a minimum price and increases it by steps until only one bidder remains. In a Dutch auction, also known as an open descending auction, the auctioneer starts with a very high price in a sales event and reduces it by steps until the first bidder signals acceptance. Both mechanisms termed as open auctions since the sale event is usually public.

In a sealed-bid auction, all bidders simultaneously submit sealed bids such that no bidder knows the bid of any other participant and each bidder has just one round. In a first-price sealed-bid auction, the highest bidder wins and pays the price submitted. In a second-price sealed-bid auction, first described by Vickrey (1961, pp. 20–23), the highest bidder wins and pays the second-highest bid rather than its own bid.

An examination of Germany's awarding procedures shows that the license to operate the service in question is awarded to the best bid without any deduction; therefore, a second-price auction is not suitable. Nor is there evidence for an open descending auction. Instead, the design of tendering procedures as is typically recommended and usual for bus tendering procedures (see VDV 2007) resembles the first-price sealed-bid auction. However, the existing regulatory framework for CCL procedures enables competitors to outbid each other if the LA does not limit the maximum number of adjustments to the application made by the applicants. Such CCL procedures resemble the English auction (see Recker 2007, p. 71, and Beck 2007, pp. 426–429). Recently, LAs have begun to limit the number of adjustments (usually only one trial) and thus I assume an auction design based on the first-price sealed-bid auction with only one round for CCL procedures.

Note that when developing the auction design, the principal (the authority) usually strives to minimize the supplementary direct subsidies to be paid, or, in the case of a CCL procedure, strives to maximize the quality offered by the winning bidder. This course of action is optimal for the auctioneer. From a welfare perspective an auction design is efficient if the bidder with the (ex post) highest willingness to pay wins. In the model presented here this is theoretically equivalent to the most efficient operator winning, i.e. the bidder able to raise the highest fare revenues and/or realize the most efficient cost structure.[30]

[30] See Krishna (2002, p. 5 f.) and Laffont and Tirole (1993, p. 318).

4.5.2 A Model for the German Institutional Setting

As already explained above, CCL procedures are executed by LAs, whereas PTAs are responsible for tendering procedures, but I assume that both act as *one authority* from an operator point of view. The quality provided to passengers is measured by a one-dimensional index number $q > 0$ (e.g., the quality measured by the schedule frequency of the services). The minimum quality level q_m to be delivered by operators according to the PTP is the fixed level set by the PTA.

The fare revenue risk is borne by the operator in the case for CCL procedures. Public service contracts which will be used in the case of tendering also oblige the operator to bear the fare revenue risk and are classified as net-cost contracts.[31] I assume that the level of fares (the price) is set by all members of a Verkehrsverbund, since it is one of their main tasks (see Knieps 2004, p. 80). For simplicity, prices (or fare levels) are therefore determined exogenously.

Subsidies for fare reduction, e.g., compensation for pupils and the disabled, and supplementary direct subsidies classified as other operational revenues are equal and fixed for all operators so they can be normalized to zero. All other supplementary direct subsidies (*SDS*) necessary to sustain the level of service with the minimum quality level q_m, are net subsidies from an operator point of view.

There are five steps in the model's time sequence (see Fig. 4.9). In the first step, the PTA determines q_m. Thereafter the LA manages the CCL procedure as an auctioneer if operators apply for commercial services. CCL bids satisfying $q \geq q_m$ can be submitted by operators. If more than one operator submits such a bid, the operator offering the highest quality q will win the exclusive right. If no bids in terms of quality $q \geq q_m$ are submitted to the LA, the PTA acts as an auctioneer for the tendering procedure to award the supplementary direct subsidies necessary to operate the services.

The box below explains each step in detail.

Time sequence of the model

1. The PTA sets q_m
2. Operators test if operations are commercially feasible and, if so, may submit their bids in terms of quality $q \geq q_m$
3. The LA verifies if operations are commercially feasible for operators:
   (a) If bids are submitted, the LA (the auctioneer for commercial services) prepares a CCL and the model continues with step 4a
   (b) If no bids are submitted, the services in question are non-commercial; the LA informs the PTA and the model continues with step 4b

(continued)

[31] Since revenue risk is not explicitly addressed in this model, gross-cost contracts are basically equivalent to net-cost contracts if subsidies are redefined accordingly.

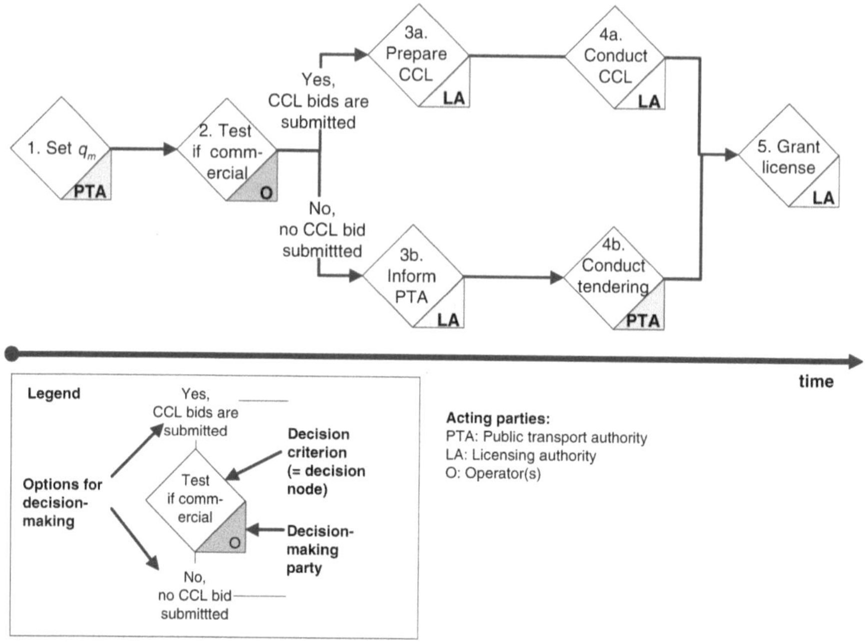

Fig. 4.9 Time flow of the model

4. The auctioneer conducts a procedure to award the services:
   (a) In the case of commercial services, the LA conducts a CCL procedure and selects the best bid in terms of quality
   (b) In the case of non-commercial services, the PTA conducts a tendering procedure to award supplementary direct subsidies
5. Finally, the LA grants the license to operate commercial services to the best operator with the highest q or, in the case of non-commercial services, to the winner of the tendering procedure.

In the model the cost function (C) is the same for all operators. Costs depend on the quality q offered and $C(q)$ shows a convex shape. Fixed costs (e.g., for building a bus depot, vehicle purchases, etc.) are on the level $a > 0$. The cost function is thus

$$C(q) = a + b(q) \tag{4.1}$$

where $\partial C(q)/\partial q > 0, \partial^2 C(q)/\partial q > 0$ and $C(0) = a$.

The real sum of all fare revenues to be generated by the operator from the license depends on the quality delivered to passengers ($FR(q)$).

Profits (π) for operators are

$$\pi(q) = FR(q) - C(q). \tag{4.2}$$

Operators enter the market and submit an offer for the specific services as long as they expect $\pi \geq 0$ (participation constraint) for $q \geq q_m$. Due to perfect competition, in equilibrium operator profits are $\pi = 0$.

4.6 Market Participants' Opportunities

4.6.1 *The Distinction Between Commercial and Non-Commercial Services*

Figure 4.10 shows the cost function *C(q)*, as described previously, and the fare revenue function *FR(q)*, the latter assumed to be linear. Note that the profit maximizing level of quality is q_B. Thus, for any minimum quality level q_m, such that $q_m \leq q_B$, a firm will try to enter the market and choose $q = q_B \geq q_m$.

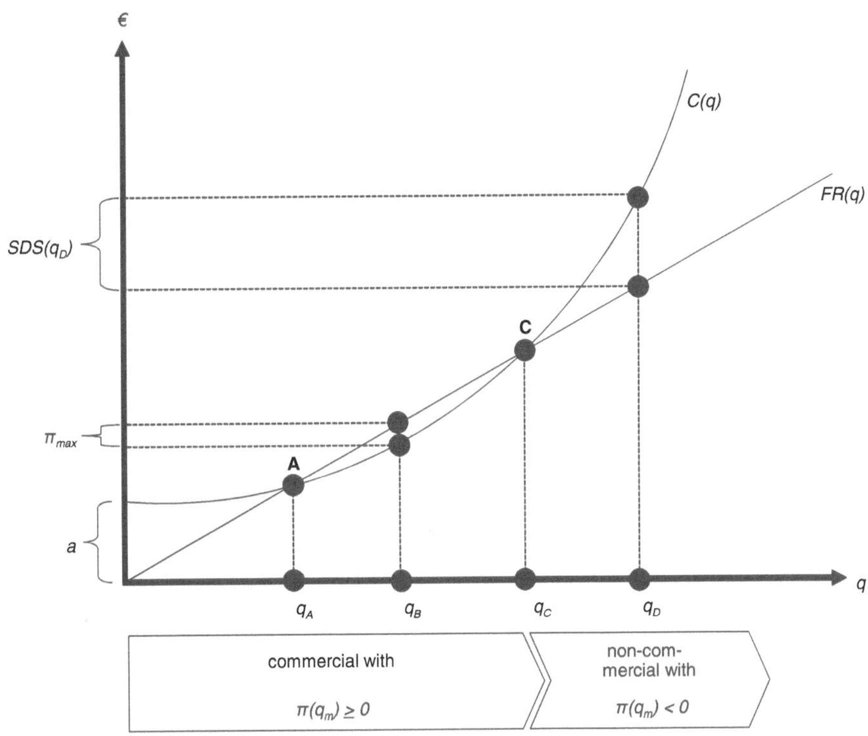

Fig. 4.10 Commercial and non-commercial services from operator's perspective

However, since profit is strictly positive at q_B, other firms will try to win the exclusive license by offering an even higher quality $q > q_B$. Anticipating a competitive CCL process will lead operators to a bid up of quality until $q = q_C$, where profits are reduced to zero. If $q_B < q_m \leq q_C$, the same competitive CCL process will start at q_m and lead to $q = q_C$.

To summarize, any $q_m \leq q_C$ will lead to a CCL process with the result $q = q_C$. Supplementary direct subsidies are unnecessary here and these services must be classified as commercial. Note that if there was a monopolist (contrary to our assumption), it would set $q = max\{q_B, q_m\}$ for any $q_m \leq q_C$, with its maximum profits being π_{max}, as indicated in Fig. 4.10.

Again, in reality most commercial services do not experience any CCL and the explanations about a monopolistic market depict the usual experiences for German incumbent operators. In contrast, CCL, assumed for our model, leads to $q = q_C$ if $q_m \leq q_C$, which will provide passengers a higher level of quality than a monopolistic market. According to Germany's specific institutional framework, here the operators must participate in a competitive procedure for the right of exclusivity managed by the LA (the auctioneer).

Now suppose $q_m > q_C$. Since $\pi(q) < 0$ for any $q \geq q_m$, the level of q_m is too high to be commercially feasible for operators. Thus, these services are classified as non-commercial services. If, for example, the PTA sets $q_m = q_D$ as shown in Fig. 4.10, supplementary direct subsidies $SDS(q_D)$ are necessary to enable operators to deliver the services without incurring a loss.

Thus, for $q_m > q_C$, services are non-commercial and operators' profits are

$$\pi(q_m) = FR(q_m) + SDS(q_m) - C(q_m) > 0. \tag{4.3}$$

Again assuming perfect competition in the tendering procedure, operators will receive supplementary direct subsidies of the level

$$SDS(q_m) = C(q_m) - FR(q_m) > 0 \tag{4.4}$$

and make zero profit.

From the PTA's perspective, the required amount of subsidies $SDS(q_m)$ is necessary to compensate operators for the deficits that result from the obligation to deliver a quality level which is higher than commercially feasible.

In summary, the main characteristic of non-commercial services is that operators' bids must be based upon a minimization of $SDS(q_m)$ instead of a maximization of q in order to win the auction. At the threshold q_C, the auction thus changes its character from a quality-auction (for $q_m \leq q_C$) to a reverse subsidy auction (for $q_m > q_C$). All of these levels of q_m are empirically relevant since several PTAs foresee a high, non-commercial level of q_m in their PTPs (e.g., traffiQ), whereas numerous other PTAs foresee a high commercial level of q_m in their PTPs (e.g., rural district Wittenberg), several PTAs foresee a low commercial level of q_m in their PTPs (e.g., rural district Dithmarschen), and even some PTAs exist without updated (and thus legally invalid) PTPs, implying $q_m = 0$.

4.6.2 The Threshold as a PTA's Break-Even Point

Figure 4.10 depicts the threshold at q_C, with $SDS(q_C) = 0$ where all revenues are expected to balance operational costs for the minimum level of quality ($FR(q_C) = C(q_C)$). This is the PTA's break-even point. Starting with q_C, the decision regarding the level of q_m determines whether subsidies are necessary (non-commercial lines with $q_m > q_C$) or not (commercial lines with $q_m \leq q_C$). Generally speaking, if the PTA decreases or increases q_m for a specific service, ceteris paribus, the services are more likely to become commercial or non-commercial, respectively. Setting q_m then determines the difference between the level of services of general interest in a controlled competition regime (tendering) and what might be commercially viable in a market regime allowing operators to develop/initiate services on their own in order to compete for exclusive rights.

PTAs are able to influence the commercial or non-commercial market organization to be selected for their services within this institutional framework. Political considerations about the level of services of general interest to be provided (level of q_m), the level of direct influence on services desired (with or without a direct contractual relationship between PTA and operator), and budgetary constraints[32] all affect a PTA's decision. Thus, the hypothesis that in a competitive market for public transport bus services local parameters for costs and revenues are the only criteria that allow an operator to deliver such services commercially is rebutted.

Operators might welcome the possibility of both commercial and non-commercial services within a single market. In contrast to other European states, such a dichotomic market provides business opportunities for market initiatives *and* authority initiatives. However, a conscious decision regarding q_m is necessary to provide clarity for operators about the market model to be expected before they invest time and funds to develop a bid. Moreover, questions arise whether sufficient analytical capabilities are in place within PTAs. This is even more important as they usually lack sufficient competencies in this respect.

4.6.3 The Challenge of Different Expectations

The critical factor when determining whether services are commercial or non-commercial is market participants' expectations of the revenues to be generated from a license at or around the exact position of q_C with a given $q = q_m$. The results may differ between operators (O) and PTAs. Letting E_O and E_{PTA} denote the expectations of operators and the PTA, respectively, one could imagine a case

[32] Treasurers, for example, are able to "optimize" q_m with the aim of minimizing $SDS(q_m)$ before any tendering procedure for non-commercial services has to be initiated.

where $E_O[FR(q_m)] \neq E_{PTA}[FR(q_m)]$ and therefore $E_O[SDS(q_m)] \neq E_{PTA}[SDS(q_m)]$ with $SDS(q_m) = C(q_m) - FR(q_m)$.

Different prospects for passenger reactions to q can be classified as usual market developments, yet there are some problems. The major issue is that operators may anticipate a different model of market organization (commercial or non-commercial) than PTAs. Even market participants' expectations about the awarding procedure (quality versus price competition; market versus authority initiative) and of the contractual relationship (license between operator and LA, or additionally, a direct public service contract between operator and PTA) may differ and they will thus prepare themselves in different ways depending on the expected awarding type.

If operators' expectations are $E_O[FR(q_m) - C(q_m)] \geq 0 > E_{PTA}[FR(q_m) - C(q_m)]$, the case will benefit the PTAs' budget, but PTAs may have preferred to conclude a public service contract directly with the operator. An analysis of 117 CCL cases with start of operations within 2003–2008 shows that 31% of the 70 market initiatives experienced different forecasts: here, the PTAs originally initiated tendering, but operators decided to apply for a license to operate these services commercially. Most of these cases occurred in the state of Hesse, which decided to declare all public transport services as non-commercial and now has the highest number of tendering procedures in Germany (see Chaps. 8 and 10). Where there were large differences between E_O and E_{PTA}, the PTAs could have shown interest in increasing q_m, yet they may have supported a quality increase for specific criteria that proved both uneconomic for operators (e.g., services during evening hours or for disabled persons), and for the PTAs (due to budgetary constraints).

Another issue arises when PTAs do not begin tendering early enough, e.g., in the case of $E_O[FR(q_m) - C(q_m)] < 0 \leq E_{PTA}[FR(q_m) - C(q_m)]$. Problems then arise in carrying out a formal tendering procedure, allowing bidders to develop well-calculated bids and enabling the winner to adequately prepare for start of operations. VDV (2007) recommends a preparation phase of almost two years for a tender. In contrast, operators usually submit applications to operate commercial services only a few months before the start of operations.

4.6.4 Effects of Commercial Services for Market Participants

For $q_m \leq q_C$, services are commercial with $SDS(q_m) = 0$ and the quality offered by the operator will be $q = q_C$. Although unknown in Germany so far, it might be interesting to investigate the amount of franchise fee $SDS(q_m) < 0$ operators would need to pay for an exclusive license to operate a specific (commercial) service on a quality level $q = q_m < q_C$.[33] Since the fare revenues should be $FR(q_m) > C(q_m)$ here, operators would pay a franchise fee for the right of exclusivity to operate the

[33] E.g., for a specific concession area instead of organizing a quality competition in a CCL.

specific services for the license term. With respect to Fig. 4.10, this franchise fee would be $SDS(q_B) = \pi_{max}$ for any $q_m \leq q_B$ or $SDS(q_m) = \pi(q_m)$ for any $q_B < q_m \leq q_C$. Note that the quality delivered would never fall below q_B. The PTA could use the fee for cross-subsidies for non-commercial services and/or for general budget purposes. Given q_m, this would lead to a maximization of the easy to validate single-dimension monetary criterion $SDS(q_m)$ by operators.[34]

However, the existing institutional framework leads to a maximization of a difficult to validate and (in reality) multi-dimension criterion q, where operators have to raise the quality level q which they offer to win the CCL procedure, until $q = q_C > q_m$. This framework protects a specific level of quality $q_C > q_m$ for passengers instead of reducing the PTA's debt. Despite the potential to solve budgetary problems, the German market organization for commercial services produces the effect that quality competition leads to a maximization of the quality offered to passengers.

On the other hand, the current regulatory framework enables operators themselves to determine their q according to market needs. The quality choice of q is based on marginal revenues and marginal costs with respect to q as expected by operators. Therefore, the level of freedom for operators to design the service is higher in the market for commercial services than in tendering procedures which typically use gross-cost contracts with a detailed service specification.[35] Operators are to some extent able to bridge the gap if the PTA does not put much effort into determining a high level of q_m in its local public transport network.

PTAs that do not wish to become involved in public transport via a public service contract may prefer commercial services, thus avoiding the need to conduct tendering, control the quality delivered, and settle accounts. PTAs may also desire to avoid financial risks such as energy price risks (see van de Velde et al. 2008a, pp. 59–65 and 2008b, pp. 62–63 as well as Chap. 7), which are usually covered by PTAs via a public service contract.

On the other hand, licenses for commercial services will hamper PTAs from controlling services unlike the regime of a direct contractual relationship with detailed obligations for the operator.[36] Here the PTA may wish to secure and control a level of service that aligns with its own interests. Of course, even in CCL procedures the quality offered by operators must fulfill the minimum quality required by the PTP as determined by the PTA. Failures in its delivery may also be identified by the PTA; however, the PTA may then only inform the LA, without any possibility to directly regulate the operator.

---

[34] Such a regulation can be seen, e.g., for British railway franchises (see Nash and Smith 2006, p. 3 and p. 9), where operators pay a franchise fee to the PTAs for commercial services.

[35] See Sect. 4.4.2 for more details on the level of freedom.

[36] See Sect. 4.4.1 for the pros and cons. See also van de Velde et al. (2008a, pp. 72–80) for an overview of possible contractual instruments, regulations and case studies.

4.7 Conclusions

Chapter 4 has analyzed the institutional framework for public transport services by bus and how the classification of a specific service as commercial or non-commercial depends on the local conditions and the scale of costs and revenues. The results showed that the level of minimum quality standards imposed on operators by PTAs is also a decisive parameter and exerts a major influence on the classification of services as commercial or non-commercial. When PTAs decide to decrease or increase the minimum quality standards for a specific service, ceteris paribus, the services are more likely to be commercial or non-commercial, respectively.

In summary, the survey of the co-existence of commercial and non-commercial services raises doubts about the feasibility and ease of using this dichotomic system. This applies especially to a market organization and an awarding procedure that differ fundamentally across the types of services. A clear classification of services is important information for operators and authorities when developing their strategies for the market. The potential for uncertainty identified at the threshold is one of the main pitfalls of this system.

Nevertheless, the current framework enables operators to bridge the gap if PTAs fail to devote sufficient effort to the level of quality of their local public transport, and/or if the sum of fare revenues is high enough to enable commercial services. This possibility for operators to be involved in the market for commercial services represents an important advantage of the existing framework, since, based on the minimum quality level, operators are free to attract new customers for public transport (and increase their profits) via an entrepreneurial search for optimal solutions and higher quality levels. The co-existence of commercial and non-commercial services is a tool for PTAs to organize their local markets according to their objectives.

Chapter 5
The Practice with Different Institutional Models Within the Framework

5.1 Introduction

As already explained in the essay presented in Chap. 4 the regulatory environment for all sectors of public transport in Germany was changed during market reforms at federal and state level in the mid-1990s. The political objectives at the national level were to introduce competition and thus enhance quality and efficiency. One of the main amendments of the market reforms concerning the German Passenger Transport Act (*Personenbeförderungsgesetz* – PBefG), which covers all non-railway services, i.e. light rail and bus, was the introduction of a definition of non-commercial services (see § 13a of the PBefG) in addition to the existing framework for commercial services. Unlike commercial services which are based on market initiative, non-commercial services are characterized by authority initiative and an obligation to tender them. Despite the new definition, most market participants continued to classify their services as commercial.

While discussions regarding competitive measures have subsided in favor of tendering for the rail sector (see e.g., Beck 2011a), this issue is still unresolved for the bus sector. The main question throughout the past decade is whether or not to classify services as non-commercial with an obligation to tender supplementary direct subsidies. As a result, competition has been used very selectively by both authorities and operators. Although competition for public transport services has always been legally possible in Germany,[1] and the number of cases has increased in recent years, the total volume remains low in comparison to the market as a whole.

Given the importance of bus transport services for the entire public transport market and the intense discussion on whether or not there is an obligation to tender, it is useful to analyze the conversion of market participants' opportunities to act in practice as described in Chap. 4. Thus, the essay presented in this Chap. 5 identifies the market models used to introduce competition and assesses their successes and

[1] In eastern Germany since reunification.

A. Beck, *Competition for Public Transport Services*, Contributions to Economics,
DOI 10.1007/978-3-7908-2802-3_5, © Springer-Verlag Berlin Heidelberg 2012

pitfalls in a case study analysis. The past century's institutional changes are also explained to provide adequate background.

Section 5.2 begins with a description of the development of regulation for market entry in Germany prior to the market reforms in the mid-1990s in order understand the motivation behind the market reform and to provide insights into the force of habit still in place. Section 5.3 outlines the legal changes, followed by an overview of the transition period and the legal debate about public transport authorities' (PTAs) obligations to tender. Section 5.4 presents today's situation, explaining the two major concepts of introducing competition applied in Germany. It also focuses on the problems and obstacles perceived by PTAs during the introduction of competition. Section 5.5 assesses the range of possibilities for market participants. Section 5.6 concludes with intermediate results and a long-term outlook.[2]

To ease understanding, especially for those readers who skipped the analysis of the regulatory framework presented above, there is some overlap between Sect. 5.3.1 and Sect. 4.2. Furthermore the List of Abbreviations included in the first few pages of the dissertation as well as the Glossary and the List of the Acts of Law included in the back are intended to ease comprehension of specific terms for readers not familiar with the regulatory framework of German public transport by bus.

5.2 The Situation Before Market Reform: Where are we Coming from?

German public transport has always faced strict regulation by law (see Köberlein 1997, pp. 137–139).[3] As a result of the rise in competition from motor vehicles after World War I, efforts were undertaken to regulate public transport by bus to strengthen the state-owned railway monopoly. Initial limitations on competition for public transport by motor vehicles in Germany appeared in 1928 in the decree *Verordnung betreffend Kraftfahrzeuglinien* (see Werner 2001, p. 16) and in the law *Kraftfahrtliniengesetz*. From then on, operators required a license to provide public transport services by motor vehicle. If an application to operate a new bus route competed with existing rail or bus public transport services, the licensing authority (LA, responsible for granting licenses to operate these services) was required to reject the application during the license term.

[2] This Chap. 5 is based on Beck (2009c) which presents the results of an analysis completed in spring 2007.

[3] In fact, the first documents on transport regulation date back to the year 1230.

After World War II, as in other regions worldwide,[4] Germany's public transport continued to face diminished passenger numbers because of a further increase in motorized private transport. To sustain a minimum level of public transport, an increasing multitude of compensatory payments (subsidies) were legislated in succeeding decades, financed by a variety of local and regional authorities and federal and national grant systems.[5] All subsidies were included in the accounts of the operators as regular turnover and not as subsidies.[6] Therefore, public transport services remained formal commercial operations.

Prior to the market reforms of the mid-1990s, the public transport sector in the western part of Germany lacked any clear regulatory framework regarding subsidies paid to non-railway services of bus and light rail.[7] Even in the early 1990s, compensatory payments were usually made without a specific legal basis that might oblige the operator to provide a particular service as defined and controlled by a PTA. Subsidies, especially those paid by municipalities or rural districts, were often granted without a contract (and without any specific, detailed control mechanism regarding the service paid for). Subsidies were frequently granted, especially by municipalities or rural districts, without a public service contract (see Beck 2007, p. 425). The increasing deficits of municipal operators were compensated by the municipal shareholder. Where there was no municipal operator, private bus operators and, within regional bus services, Deutsche Bundesbahn, the national railway operator, and/or public operators owned by federal states, provided public bus transport services and received licenses authorizing them to operate these services. Although possible under existing public transport law within the process of renewing the license to operate a bus route, competition via competing applications by competing operators rarely occurred.

In addition to regional routes run by railway operators owned by municipalities or federal states, almost all regional and long distance public rail transport services within western Germany were operated by the Deutsche Bundesbahn, which was administered as a national public authority. Subsidies for most services were paid by the federal government.

Within the new federal states in the former German Democratic Republic – GDR, the previously nationally-owned enterprises (the so-called people's enterprises) for public transport services usually remained public property until after reunification when they became owned by the respective municipalities. Nevertheless, several private operators moved in. Several years after reunification, in 1994 the Deutsche Reichsbahn, the public national railway company of the former GDR, merged with

[4] See e.g., Hermans and Stoelinga (2005, p. 293) confirming the same for The Netherlands.

[5] An outline of the current financing structure for public transport services by bus, which has not experienced major changes compared to the situation prior to market reform with respect to complexity, is presented in Sect. 4.3.1.

[6] According to experts interviewed (e.g., Engelbert Recker, expert formerly responsible for public transport at the German Rural District Association – Deutscher Landkreistag).

[7] According to experts interviewed.

the Deutsche Bundesbahn, the railway company of the former Federal Republic of Germany (FRG). In the mid-nineties, the main problems and obstacles regarding the multitude of financing instruments and lack of control by state authorities for public transport services (see Chap. 4) were the same in the new federal states as in western Germany. Until the market reforms were introduced, almost all privately-owned public transport operators restricted their business to public bus transport. Most such companies remained small, with up to 20 buses, while a few grew to 200 buses. The major players were the public companies, Deutsche Bundesbahn, and municipal operators such as Hamburger Hochbahn AG and Berliner Verkehrs-betriebe AG.

5.3 Transition

5.3.1 Market Reform in the Mid-1990s

Deutsche Bundesbahn had a long history of increasing costs and deficits since World War II. The federal government made many attempts to restructure the system of financing, according to Köberlein (1997, pp. 245–246), the first reform occurred in 1961.

By the early 1990s, Deutsche Bundesbahn's deficits, increasing annually, together with its growing debts, prompted discussion about undertaking a market reform within the public transport sector. As discussed in Sect. 4.2, Regulation (EEC) No 1191/69 and its revised version, Regulation (EEC) No 1893/91, encouraged more competition for subsidies in the EU. Their upcoming implementation in Germany's legal framework also prompted the debate. Within this discussion process, the federal states also asked for a new regulation on public transport services, arguing that in existing public transport law, the monopolies of existing operators were strictly protected (see Werner 1998, pp. 2–3).

The requested market reform came into force on January 1, 1996. The federal constitution, railway law and public transport law were amended and a new Law on the Regionalization of Public Transport (*Regionalisierungsgesetz* – RegG) was introduced. As part of the transfer of responsibilities and following the aims of the principle of subsidiarity, the federal states took over regional and local public transport. Only a few regulatory responsibilities remained at the national level, particularly in the railway sector, and Deutsche Bundesbahn's organizational form changed from a public agency to a public limited company (Deutsche Bahn AG), which today is still fully owned by the federal government.

One of the major regulatory impacts of market reform was the obligation for authorities to introduce competition to the regional passenger rail services market and at the same time to the market for public transport services by bus. For the latter the adjustment of the regulatory framework was characterized by three main changes: (1) an obligation for PTAs to define a level of minimum quality of services; (2) a reorganization of the role of authorities within the public transport sector; and (3) a definition for non-commercial services where subsidies must be tendered.

The first change, the introduction of the obligation for PTAs to define minimum (quality) standards in public transport service, requires local PTAs to fix these standards in a local (public) transport plan (PTP). Within the non-railway sector which operates in accordance with the Passenger Transport Act, these minimum quality standards are the basis for the relevant LA when awarding licenses to operate a specific route.

The second main change, the reorganization of the role of the PTAs, let them become responsible for providing services in conformance with general interests. According to § 1 of the RegG, PTAs now determine and secure an adequate minimum level of public transport services for the citizens in their territory and are responsible for providing services of general interest. Together with the amendment to the national law, the federal states (the *Länder*) modified their own public transport laws, fulfilling the legal framework. Almost all federal states assigned the PTAs duties for public transport by bus and light rail (non-railway services) to the rural districts or larger district-free cities. The PTAs' responsibility for subsidized regional railways (heavy railway services) varies between the federal state level (Bavaria) and the rural district level (North Rhine-Westphalia) (see Werner 1998, pp. 3–6).

The third main change, that tendering is necessary for non-commercial services where subsidy by PTAs is required to secure an adequate level of services, generated intense debate. Although the simple definition, laid down for non-railway services in § 13a of the Passenger Transport Act (*Personenbeförderungsgesetz* – PBefG), seems to be quite clear, this debate ensued among lawyers about whether or not a legal obligation to tender applied to subsidized German public transport services, given this new definition. The general distinction according to the PBefG is summarized as follows:

Distinction between commercial and non-commercial services according to the revised Passenger Transport Act

- Licenses for *commercial* operations (according to § 13 of the PBefG) will be granted for routes where a commercial operation is expected by the operator without further subsidies. Nevertheless, subsidies for fare reductions, e.g., for schoolchildren, are seen as part of regular revenues and not as part of general subsidies on commercial operations. For "commercial" operations, competition is possible in the form of competition for a license to operate those routes/lines or services. The licensing authority then has to grant the license to the operator offering the best quality to passengers, resulting in a quality competition.
- Licenses for *non-commercial* operations (according to § 13a of the PBefG) are licenses for lines or services where supplementary direct subsidies paid by PTAs are necessary to deliver the minimum quality level determined by the PTA in its PTP. These compensatory payments have to be tendered by the respective PTAs.

The effects of market reform on the introduction of competition were heterogeneous. Within the sector for subsidized railway services on regional and suburban lines (non-commercial heavy railway services, regulated by the Common German Law for Railways [*Allgemeines Eisenbahngesetz* – AEG]), the introduction went smoothly (see Beck 2011a). PTAs have since been allowed to order subsidized railway services from railway companies, for example, via tendering. Infrastructure access shall be non-discriminatory. A commercial railway service may be provided by any interested railway company without a specific regulation on market entry (no exclusivity) if there is sufficient track access (open market).

Within public transport services by bus and light rail (non-railway services market), regulated by the Passenger Transport Act, incumbent operators' positions remained protected to a large extent. A license is still required for commercial routes/lines. This protects the owner against competition during the term of approval. Only in the renewal of a specific license can competitors apply to operate lines or services if they are deemed to be commercial. If a competitor can offer better services with respect to quality (including fare levels), the licensing authority must approve the application instead of the incumbent's. Although possible, only a limited number of cases of competition occurred as a result of this amendment.

The distinction between commercial and non-commercial services and the models used to introduce competition for public transport services by bus led to more discussions and legal proceedings. The major transitional landmarks to date are evaluated in the following Sections, which examine the experiences in the transition period until the mid of the 2000s. In Sect. 5.3.2, the models of two regions, among the first to tender non-commercial services by bus, are described and the effects of introducing competition are evaluated. These are (1) the suburban area of Munich and (2) the suburban area of Hamburg. As two major legal proceedings in Germany affected all the efforts to introduce competition to a large extend, the main juridical landmarks of the discussion on whether or not an obligation to tender exists will also be evaluated in Sect. 5.3.3 thereafter. These legal proceedings also had a significant impact on the legislative procedure for the (EC) No 1370/2007 on the EU level.

5.3.2 Introducing Tendering: Initial Successes and Pitfalls

5.3.2.1 Suburban Area of Munich: One of the First to Tender

One of the first regions using tendering in bus services after market reform was the suburban area of Munich.[8] On September 19, 1996, this region published its first call for offers in the *Official Journal of the European Community* for route 838 from

[8] This section is based, inter alia, on BMVBS (2005, pp. 275–305), also called the FoPS study.

Fürstenfeldbruck to Dachau. The tendering procedure was carried out by Münchner Verkehrs- und Tarifverbund GmbH (MVV).[9] The route began operating in January 1997.

The MVV was founded as a public transport association (planning agency) in 1972 by operators supported by the federal state of Bavaria, the city of Munich, and the eight suburban districts in the greater Munich metropolitan area. In the suburban areas where the tendering takes place, 457 buses were operating in 1972.[10] In 1996, the MVV changed from a classic public transport planning agency to an agency performing a supplementary function as a regional PTA.[11] Since 1996, tendering in the MVV area has only occurred for bus services in the suburbs of Munich where the MVV acted as a tendering authority for the suburban districts.[12]

The suburban districts try to bring about competition with a sense of proportion to their areas.[13] The aim is to secure chances for small- and medium-sized (SME) bus operators. Therefore, tendering is used only when prior negotiations with the existing operators on those routes have been insufficient. Thus, the suburban districts expect to reduce costs and increase quality in transport services.[14] Newly established routes can be tendered at any time.

Market access changed with this new awarding policy applied since 1999. Prior to revision of the awarding policy, agreements for subsidies between operator and public transport authority were automatically extended. Now, the extension of the gross-cost contracts must at a minimum be negotiated obligatorily. The reliable option of tendering the related services strengthens the PTAs bargaining position. This may be the reason why the negotiating parties have achieved satisfactory results in most cases and tendering has rarely been used.

The division of the tendered volume into relatively small lots emphasizes the aim to support SMEs. The FoPS study showed that between 1997 and 2002 the number of operators in the suburban area of the MVV increased from 46 to 55 (+ 20%), with SMEs benefiting from the tendering processes each time.[15] In recent years the number has decreased, but never below 46.

According to FoPS the awarding policy of the suburban area of Munich reduced production costs per vehicle kilometer by 7% in the period 1997–2000 for all negotiated and tendered services. In the same period, net subsidies after deducting fare revenues per vehicle kilometer dropped by 14%. Regular cost savings were used by the PTAs to install new routes and a higher quality of services (for example,

[9] See MVV (1996).

[10] See MVV (2010).

[11] See BMVBS (2005, p. 276).

[12] See MVV (2005a, p. 1), MVV (2005b) and BMVBS (2005, pp. 275–276).

[13] See Landkreise im MVV (1999).

[14] See Arbeitsgruppe Verkehrsverträge und Qualitätsmanagement (2002).

[15] See BMVBS (2005, p. 296).

new buses were obligatory in every tendered service). This may also have resulted in increased revenues from passengers, which explains the net subsidy effect.[16]

Tendering shows a significant reduction in production costs by 28% on average according to FoPS, compared to production costs before tendering. For negotiations of sequential contracts, a reduction of production costs of 3.1% on average was observed compared to production costs before negotiation. A price treaty within existing contracts led to a reduction of 6.7% on average, compared to the operators' charge before the treaty. Although the reduction of production costs achieved by tendering often includes other positive effects (i.e. cost-reducing effects due to the optimization of routes and timetables carried out by the MVV in the course of the tender process), the tendering effect is classified as stronger than the effect of negotiations or price treaties within existing contracts according to FoPS.[17] Until June 2006, only a small percentage of the total vehicle kilometer volume within the suburban MVV area was tendered, with no major change to date. The volume in 2006 was around 8.3 million vehicle kilometers tendered via 51 procurements with 54 lots in total. Some routes have since been tendered a second time. On average, each tendered network consists of only one bus route and accounts for 152,844 vehicle kilometers and 2.7 vehicles in total.[18]

The results of the suburban Munich's awarding policy show a reduction in production costs and a reinforced position of SMEs simultaneously. Until spring 2007 only two major international companies were engaged within the regional market of public transport services by bus: Deutsche Bahn AG (DB), with its long history of activity within the region, and Veolia, formerly Connex. Within 10 years of the enactment of competition policy, no other global players have entered the regional market.

The mostly positive results of tendering beg the question why the suburban districts have not yet obliged the MVV to tender all bus services. Although competitive awarding fulfills the goals of the awarding policy (securing quality and a market share for SMEs, reducing the need for subsidies), at least in comparison to negotiations or price treaties, no district has yet passed a resolution to use tendering. Whether to tender remains an open question at the onset of talks between operators and the MVV. Nevertheless, the Munich area is one of the leading regions in competitive tendering in Germany and gives interesting positive results.

---

[16] See BMVBS (2005, p. 292).

[17] See BMVBS (2005, p. 302).

[18] Own calculation on the basis of the publications of the MVV in the Supplement of the Official Journal of the European Union up to June 30, 2006. A more recent analysis, including more recent data, appears in Part III.

5.3.2.2 Hamburg Area: How Tendering was Affected by Competition for Exclusive Rights

One of the first instances where a PTA attempt to tender was countered by a market initiated application to operate commercial services took place near Hamburg. Here, the tendering procedure for non-commercial operations of bus line 235 within the southeast suburban area was affected. The acting PTAs were the federal state of Hamburg and the suburban districts of Stormarn and Herzogtum Lauenburg. The proceeding was carried out by the PTA, Hamburger Verkehrsverbund GmbH, responsible for the metropolitan area of Hamburg.[19] Line 235 accounts for 450,000 vehicle kilometers and around 7,000 passengers annually and was previously operated by the municipal operator Verkehrsbetriebe Hamburg Holstein AG (VHH).

The proceedings began with an invitation for tenders published on September 10, 2003 EU-wide. The start of operations was planned for June 13, 2004, with a contract term until June 2009.[20] Three bids were placed by November 27, 2003, the deadline. The only criterion for the acceptance of the tender for the gross-cost contract was the price for operating the route, as long as several minimum quality criteria were met, such as low floor buses.

While checking the bids received, the HVV discovered that the municipal operator VHH, the incumbent, had also applied for a commercial license to operate on the route with comparable quality features. According to the Passenger Transport Act (§§ 8 [4] and 13 of the PBefG), commercial approvals have priority, and thus the LA had to favor this application and refuse all other applications for non-commercial services on that route. Therefore, the tendering process was terminated within the binding period without any awarding.[21] When it eventually, became clear that no other competing operator attempted to initiate a competition for commercial services, the LA accepted the VHH offer.

Although the rural district of Herzogtum Lauenburg, mainly affected by these operations, was pleased to save ~ €500,000 of compensatory payments which were expected for the contract term of 8 years, the application for a commercial license to operate effectively sabotaged the tendering for line 235. On the other hand, VHH was able to serve these transport services for a further license term. According to experts interviewed it is quite possible that this was a strategic move by VHH to counter the introduction of tendering in the Hamburg area. It has never become public whether VHH reckoned with the acceptance of deficits just to save the service itself.

This case reveals a major difficulty when PTAs conduct tendering for non-commercial lines: operators can and do hand in countering applications to operate commercial routes or services. If they do so, the PTAs lose direct control over the operator through a public service contract. The result, however, has a positive impact on PTAs' budgets by reducing subsidy payments.

---

[19] The HVV was established in 1965 and is the oldest public transport association (Verkehrsverbund) of its kind.

[20] See HVV (2003).

[21] See HVV (2004).

5.3.3 *Is There an Obligation to Tender or Not? The Judicial Point of View*

As can be seen above, initial experiences with tendering procedures were positive from a PTA point of view, particularly with respect to the need for supplementary direct subsidies. Even in cases where operators countered tendering procedures by applications to operate commercial routes, the reduction to zero in subsidy payment was a major success from a PTA point of view. These economic effects supported political decisions to introduce authority initiated competition through the use of tendering.

However, after 1996, an intense legal debate took place about whether or not there is an *obligation* to tender for subsidized public transport services. Within the non-railway industry, an amendment to the law in the mid-1990s resulted in a new § 13a for non-commercial services. The services had to be awarded according to Regulation (EEC) No 1191/69. Advocates argued that the EU law required tendering (or awarding through the use of comparable competitive procedures) of most public transport services in Germany. Moreover, LAs were required to check whether applications to operate commercial lines were subsidized, including subsidies for fare reduction, and were required to refuse applications when finding a subsidy payment.[22]

Eventually, two major path-breaking decisions were reached: the Altmark judgment of the European Court of Justice in 2003 and the judgment of the German Federal Administrative Court in 2006. Both influenced the awarding policy of most PTAs and altered the discussion with respect to the awarding of public transport services at the EU level. The end result was (EC) No 1370/2007 which became effective on December 3, 2009. The importance of the legal decisions for the public transport sector as a whole in Germany as well as on the EU level, is analyzed next.

5.3.3.1 Be Aware of the Granting System: The Altmark Decision

In 1994 the license of the operator Altmark Trans to operate several commercial lines in the rural district of Stendal within the federal state of Saxony-Anhalt was renewed by the LA in charge.[23] Within this procedure, the LA rejected the license application of the municipal operator Nahverkehrsgesellschaft Altmark. The latter then filed suit against the LA at the regional administrative court, arguing that the license for Altmark Trans was illegal with respect to the subsidies paid by the rural district of Stendal, according to the European Treaty.[24]

---

[22] See Werner et al. (2004).

[23] For more details see van de Velde (2005, pp. 491–493).

[24] See press note of the European Court of Justice (2003) and Ronellenfitsch (2004).

After several stages of appeal, the Federal Administrative Court of Germany finally consulted the European Court of Justice about whether or not the subsidies paid by the rural district of Stendal to Altmark Trans were illegal according to the European Treaty. On July 24, 2003, the European Court of Justice found that subsidies for non-commercial operations in public transport accord with European law when four minimum criteria are fulfilled[25]:

Four criteria of the Altmark decision

1. Clear definition of services and public financial support to be paid
2. Statement of objective and transparent criteria before approval proceedings
3. Public financial support at maximum equal to cost surplus required through non-commercial needs defined by PTA
4. In the event of waiving of tendering, financial support is based on the expected costs of an average, well managed firm

The Federal Administrative Court had also asked the European Court of Justice whether German authorities could rule that commercial operations did not fall under the jurisdiction of Regulation (EEC) No 1191/69. In the same decision the European Court of Justice ruled that German authorities were indeed allowed to make this exception for selected public transport services.

After the Altmark judgment, many German public transport operators declared that waiving of tendering was possible by using a market-oriented direct awarding, according to the fourth criteria of the Altmark decision.[26] In the following years, many PTAs entrusted numerous public transport operators with public transport services, waiving the possibility of tendering, and a few others chose tendering. Competition for licenses to operate commercial lines or services (CCL) became another option for some market participants. In the meantime, the legal discussion in Germany focused more on permission to operate commercial lines, still debating whether or not a legal obligation existed to tender public transport services.

5.3.3.2 No Obligation to Tender: The Federal Administrative Court Decision

Several German administrative courts made judgments concerning the obligation to tender with respect to the distinction between commercial and non-commercial

[25] See Altmark Trans judgment of the European Court of Justice, ruling C-280/00, July 24, 2003, and Werner (2004).

[26] See the press note of the VDV (2004), the Association of German Transport Undertakings.

services.[27] In most lawsuits, a competitor disputed the approval of a license to operate commercial lines granted to an incumbent operator. The main objection was to subsidizing lines or services classified as commercial. Several administrative courts judged that subsidized public service operations had to be tendered irrespective of whether the services were granted by general subsidies or by subsidies for reduced fares. At the same time, several administrative courts in other regions of Germany decided that there was no obligation to tender for subsidized bus lines.

Finally, on October 19, 2006, the federal Administrative Court of Germany ruled that there was no obligation to tender. The public transport sector by bus is exempted from Regulation (EEC) No 1191/69 by German law. LAs are therefore not allowed to check the corresponding system of subsidies (including assessing whether subsidies are paid in accordance with EU discretionary clauses); instead the analysis must be carried out by the European Commission.[28]

The background to such lawsuits is the claim by the medium-sized private operator, Hülsmann, that the federal state of Lower Saxony approved a license to operate commercial routes for the municipal operator Emsländische Eisenbahn without checking the granting system. Hülsmann claimed that deficits will always be taken over by the municipal owner. Accordingly, the LA is not allowed to provide Emsländische Eisenbahn with a license to operate commercial lines. In contrast, the federal Administrative Court returned a verdict that a municipal operator can operate commercial lines and that the LA is not allowed to check the granting system.

In summary, the two court decisions remanded the decision on tendering financial subsidies to the PTAs. With respect to the award of financial subsidies in-house, no legal obligation to tender currently exists. The expected economic advantages and disadvantages, together with political and/or social criteria, remain the only decisive criteria for the PTAs. Even the new regulation (EC) No 1370/2007, which went into effect on December 3, 2009, enables PTAs to award services directly in many cases.

5.4 The Current Situation and Perspective: How to Introduce Competition?

Following the decision by the German Federal Administrative Court described above, there is no judicial obligation to tender, nor is there a prohibition to do so. Besides the lively discussion among lawyers, two federal states (*Länder*) decided to introduce competition in their territories and establish an adequate legal framework

[27] See Landsberg (2003).

[28] See the judgment of the Federal Administrative Court of Germany (*Bundesverwaltungsgericht*), ruling BVerwG 3 C 33.05, October 19, 2006.

to organize the market and the role of market participants, but their concepts differed. The federal state of Hesse decided to tender all public transport services on the basis that all services must be classified as non-commercial, while the federal state of Saxony-Anhalt decided not to support the use of tendering in favor of promoting CCL procedures. All other states waived declaring any clear preference for a market model on the state level, including even Schleswig-Holstein, where tendering takes place in the Hamburg area; Bavaria, where tendering takes place in the Munich area; and Lower Saxony, where numerous CCL procedures promoted by PTAs had to be observed. Instead, decisions to introduce competition and to select a market model are left to local PTAs.

Therefore, Hesse and Saxony-Anhalt were the only two of 16 *Länder* which clearly support the introduction of competition within the non-railway industry and both established a full market reform for the regulatory framework on the state level on their own. As these models have been a major subject of discussion among market participants in the past decade, they will be described in this Sect. 5.4.

For Hesse, the numerous cases observed up to spring 2007 allow a meta-analysis of the successes and pitfalls on a state level, complemented by other experiences. The analysis of commercial services in Saxony-Anhalt focuses on the Wittenberg Model since it was the major case up to spring 2007. This analysis is complemented by related experiences on commercial services in Gifhorn, Lower Saxony.[29]

5.4.1 Clear Decision to Tender: The Case of Hesse

5.4.1.1 The Introduction of Tendering

Like all other federal states in Germany, Hesse, with its main city Frankfurt (on the Main), established a system of public transport authorities in the mid-1990s. Two main *regional* PTAs are responsible for fares, planning, and awarding of subsidies for public transport services in regional rail and bus routes: the Rhein-Main-Verkehrsverbund GmbH (RMV) (greater Frankfurt area) and the Nordhessischer VerkehrsVerbund[30] (NVV) (greater Kassel area). Responsibility for local public transport services has been given to the PTAs at city or rural district levels, of which the most important is Lokale Nahverkehrsgesellschaft Frankfurt am Main mbH traffiQ (traffiQ) within the city of Frankfurt.[31]

The former principle of producing *and* controlling public transport by a municipal firm and direction by politicians of main aspects of public transport services via a

[29] An additional quantitative analysis of entry barriers for CCL procedures appears in Part IV.

[30] Nordhessischer VerkehrsVerbund – Verkehrsverbund und Fördergesellschaft Nordhessen mbH (NVV).

[31] See Law for the Advancement of Public Transport Services in Hesse (Gesetz zur Weiterentwicklung des öffentlichen Personennahverkehrs in Hessen).

supervisory board was considered obsolete by Hesse's ministry for transport. Functions and responsibilities have been clearly assigned by the market reform in Hesse in the early years of the past decade. Since then, it is the PTAs' task to define the size and quality of public transport services and to ask operators to concentrate on their responsibility to produce them.[32]

Hesse decided to tender all public transport services and published its first tender announcement in 2002. After debates had begun in 1999, the ministry of transport and the PTAs had a formal discussion on how to introduce competition. They fixed their agreements within a document entitled, "Eckpunkte für den Wettbewerb".[33]

Their aim was to use competitive instruments to make public transport more efficient and to provide higher quality for lower subsidies. While introducing competition, supporting needs are considered necessary to secure the structure of SMEs particularly within the bus sector. The transport ministry therefore expected the PTAs to develop competition at their supervisory level in three steps as follows[34]:

Steps to Introduce Competition for Public Transport Services in Hesse

1. Pre-competition phase, tasks for PTAs: no tendering, development of tenderable networks suitable for small- and medium-sized operators, definition of quality standards, preparation for competitive awarding to begin by December 2004, (re-)negotiation of directly awarded contracts to avoid these contracts preventing the introduction of competition, and to secure quality standards
2. Transition phase, tasks for PTAs until 2009/10: tendering public transport services is divided into almost equally allocated volumes per year with even spatial distribution (RMV started the first tendering in 2002)
3. Competitive phase, beginning 2009/10: awarding public transport services only through tendering

After the Altmark judgment in 2003 and on the basis of a legal study (see Werner et al. 2004), the government of Hesse passed a resolution to tender all services (Güttler Erlass I) to avoid legal uncertainty.[35] The decree defined all routes within the federal state as non-commercial lines, resulting in the need to tender these services instead of using competition for commercial lines. The resolution emphasizes that tendering for regional bus (and train) services is the norm within

[32] See Rhiel (2005).

[33] See HMWVL (2002).

[34] The steps are described for regional public transport services by bus. Urban public transport was allowed to follow later and is not described here.

[35] See HMWVL (2004).

Hesse. Temporary solutions to reduce transition problems are possible (e.g., direct awarding of urban bus and tram services to a municipal operator), but are not the norm.

Based on initial experiences, Hesse later adjusted several details of its awarding policy. The major economic aspects were:

- Tendering procedures must follow common competitive awarding principles based on the German procurement decree VOL/A[36] (a.o. resulting in an EU-wide call for tenders)
- Direct awarding to reduce possible transition problems is allowed, but requires a concept to introduce competition
- PTAs control whether offers include discriminatory public support from third parties (e.g., subsidies for municipal operators from their owner)

Note that Hesse's ministry of transport attempted to support the successful implementation of tendering in public transport by giving the PTAs more detailed instructions. Unlike most of the other federal states, Hesse has now a clear regulatory framework on the state level to structure the roles between local PTAs, regional public transport authorities, and operators.[37]

In 2005 Hesse made further adjustments to formalize the customer-producer relationship between PTA and operators.[38] A new system of financing established by an amended law reduces the multitude of instruments for public funding to two instruments:

- The PTAs' running costs are financed by several-year budgets; incentive payments (bonus and malus, based on quality criteria) encourage a stronger dedication towards higher quality of public transport services at the PTA level
- Subsidies for infrastructure investments (e.g., renewal of rail stations, building new light rail tracks, bus stops, electronic vehicle tracking, and automatic ticketing machines) are paid only to the companies which offer their infrastructure to other companies without discrimination

Although the amended law strengthens the customer-producer relationship which in turn facilitates the use of tendering, it does not focus on the introduction of tendering.[39] Rather, it optimizes the relationship between the federal state, PTAs, and the operators.[40] Hesse's new public transport law is one of the most progressive in Germany, particularly for public co-funding.

---

[36] See Official German Contracting Terms for Award of Service Performance Contracts, Part A (*Verdingungsordnung für Leistungen, Teil A*—VOL/A).

[37] See Rausch (2004).

[38] See Law for Public Transport in Hesse (Gesetz über den öffentlichen Personennahverkehr in Hessen – ÖPNVG).

[39] This was accomplished by means of a decree as described below.

[40] See HMWVL (2005).

5.4.1.2 Enhancing the Hesse Model

The clear decision to declare all services as non-commercial was considered superior by the experts I interviewed. Market participants questioned whether tendering really led to positive results in all aspects. Yet, private operators, in particular SMEs, were afraid of losing market share to municipal operators (subsidized by their owners) and to global players. The pressure group of the German private bus operators, the *Bundesverband Deutscher Omnibusunternehmer* (bdo), consequently ordered a report to recommend the best competitive market system for the German bus market, based on the experiences of competitive market systems elsewhere in Europe.[41]

The report, published in 2005, concluded that tendering does not lead to higher quality and lower subsidies in public transport. It found that tendering in Denmark and Sweden resulted in a tendency to a strong concentration (oligopoly) on the operator side, while the market shares of SMEs decreased significantly. The report also found that municipal operators expected to discriminate against private operators in competitive awarding through their owners' support. Therefore, tendering resulted in greater public influence in the public transport market (socialization). It recommended a competitive market organization according to the experiences of Great Britain and Finland while retaining the main aspects of the existing German market organization.

The report represented a major landmark in the discussion in Germany about the awarding policy of Hesse. From the private operators' view, it supported their critical arguments against tendering, particularly their criticism regarding the reduced freedom of operators to design services within the gross-cost contracts used in Hesse, which they said led to a lower quality of public transport services and reduced passenger numbers. The report also confirmed private operators' fear of losing market share in the course of the tendering process.

Despite the market participants' arguments against tendering, Hesse's ministry of transport confirmed its awarding policy in 2006. Accounting for the status of the negotiations at the EU level on the new regulation for awarding public transport services that year and based on further experiences in tendering, the ministry passed a second decree in February 2006 (*Güttler Erlass II*).[42] This decree confirmed awarding through tendering, and altered a few minor details of the market model. The main adjustments to the existing awarding policy were:

- Networks to be tendered shall be divided into lots of around 700,000 vehicle kilometers per year to improve the chance of small and medium-sized operators being able to compete[43]

[41] See Beuven et al. (2005).

[42] See HMWVL (2006a).

[43] For example, the average volume of all 23 lots tendered up to June 30, 2006 by the RMV was 797,413 vehicle kilometers per year, with some lots of up to 1.8 million vehicle kilometers (source: own calculation based on public announcements by RMV in the Official Journal of the European Union).

- Bidders' calculations are provided in a detailed spreadsheet and placed in a sealed envelope as an attachment to the offer; if the PTAs doubt whether an offer contains sufficient returns, they may open the envelope to avoid dumping offers
- The minimum time between acceptance of a tender and commencement of operations shall be six months to enable a smooth start for a new operator
- Within urban areas, a transition period enables direct awarding in favor of municipal operators according to the amended proposal of the European Commission; but applies only to licenses with termination dates in 2006 and 2007

Hesse has continued its competitive awarding policy despite the controversy[44] and the lack of a definitive decision by the EU regarding the obligation to tender. The main results of the tendering procedures and major events in market developments are examined next.

5.4.1.3 Results, Successes, and Pitfalls of Tendering in Hesse

While conducting tendering for regional, suburban and some selected urban bus services,[45] Hesse experienced several positive results in the starting phase of competitive tendering until 2006. Rausch (2004, p. 321) points out that high quality with a simultaneous clear reduction in subsidies was achieved; the level of competition was high for the first tendering procedures, with 6–8 bidders. He detected a positive, winning situation for private operators which were mostly SMEs. Abnormally low bids by municipal operators observed in several of the first rounds of tendering resulted in an obligatory check whether discriminating public support from third parties was given (see *Güttler I Erlass*, explained above). According to Hesse's transport officials, over 20% of the total bus volume within that state had been tendered by May 2006. PTAs realized savings of up to 30% in terms of Euros paid per vehicle kilometers, resulting in a reduction of public subsidies by €20 million annually.

A major case deserving mention due to its innovative procedure and positive results in quality and environmental matters is the tendering of bus route bundle contracts within the city of Frankfurt on the Main. This city was the first major one to introduce tendering in Germany. A remarkable success story is the procedure that included environmental incentives to reduce emissions. Some details are described in the following box[46]:

[44] See Sterzenbach (2006).

[45] Note that the procedures conducted in Hesse show similarities to those conducted in Sweden and Denmark (e.g., use of gross-cost contracts).

[46] For details, see see van de Velde et al. (2008b, pp. 25–27).

The case of Frankfurt on the Main (Germany): Tendering with environmental incentives

This procedure was conducted by traffiQ, the organizing authority responsible for local public transport services within the city of Frankfurt on the Main. traffiQ successfully tendered a 6-year gross-cost contract with environmental incentives for a sub-network (3.3 million vehicle kilometers per annum operated by 50 vehicles) in 2006. One main policy aim was to reduce air pollution by demanding high anti-pollution standards in order to fulfill the European anti-pollution regime. The operator of this bundle now uses vehicles already fulfilling the ambitious EEV-standards (EEV – Enhanced Environmentally Friendly Vehicle, an EU emission standard) for gas emissions, which is a higher standard than requested by national German law. Despite this increase in quality, traffiQ was able to significantly reduce supplementary direct subsidies.

In the starting phase until 2006, the SMEs located in Hesse, were the obvious winners of the awarding policy. The bids of private bus operators, acting individually or in cooperation, were accepted for 48% of the 36 million vehicle kilometers tendered. The national operator DB won 19%, losing a significant market share of regional public transport services by bus. Municipal operators and the state-owned Hessische Landesbahn, won 17%. Veolia which entered the market through the acquisition of the local private bus operator Alpina, won 16% of the total volume tendered.[47]

Alpina's market share included its successful bid for the *Bündel A* network in Frankfurt on the Main, where strong environmental constraints (such as the EEV standard) were part of the procurement terms as mentioned above. *Bündel A* was one of the largest volumes tendered in German urban public transport services by bus. Until 2007 Frankfurt has carried out three procurement procedures. In these proceedings, there were 25 inquiring companies and 9 bidders. According to von Berlepsch (2005), Frankfurt experienced significant efficiency gains based on this intense competition.

Compared to the other federal states, Hesse has tendered the highest volume in public transport services. On the basis of the procurement policy existing in 2006, 120–130 million vehicle kilometers per year were expected to be tendered within a few years. Despite this interesting volume, global players have not yet played a significant role in the starting phase of the regional market, instead appearing to prefer acquiring firms to secure a sufficient starting position, with e.g., Arriva acquired the bus operator Sippel Group, with 200 buses and 700 employees, one

[47] See HMWVL (2006b) and HMWVL (2006c).

of the largest SMEs in Germany. Sippel, situated in Hofheim (Hesse), has won several networks via competitive tendering. Abellio, a large German player with an international investor, acquired Verkehrsgesellschaft Mittelhessen, a successful joint venture company comprising several SME bus operators that won several tendering procedures in Hesse. Other global players, although engaged in public transport services in Germany, cannot be regarded as active in the local public transport market in the starting phase. It seems as if the aim to support local private operators has been successful in the early years of competitive tendering in Hesse until 2006; Chap. 8 analyzes whether a change has since been observed.

Further activities by larger players are only seen in the case of municipal operators. Besides Verkehrsgesellschaft Frankfurt, the municipal operator of the city of Frankfurt on the Main, Hamburger Hochbahn AG (HHA) entered the regional market. HHA's bid was accepted for the urban bus network of Fulda. HHA also acquired 49% of the municipal bus operator of Wiesbaden, the newly established operator WiBus. The following box demonstrates some hazards of early entry in this case.

The case of Wiesbaden (Germany): Pitfalls of market entry

When HHA initially began operating in Wiesbaden, the level of service was low.[48] HHA used second-hand buses from its Hamburg operations that did not provide sufficient motorization for the local topography. Operating staffs were poorly trained, lacking any local knowledge. Several buses broke down which had a negative impact on schedules. Once the initial problems with vehicles were solved, operations began to run smoothly, and Wiesbaden now has some of the most modern rolling stock in Germany. This shows that even a large municipal operator like HHA can encounter self-imposed difficulties entering a new market.

One of the major examples of unsuccessful participation in procurements is Kraftverkehr Kinzigtal GmbH (KVK).[49] Although competition in procurements in Hesse is strong and market participants expect several calculations to be at zero profits, the KVK case is the first where winner's curse in tendering of public transport services by bus in Germany became public until spring 2007.[50]

---

[48] See Beck (2006, p. 29).

[49] See Burmeister (2006, p. 8).

[50] Winner's curse results in below normal or even negative average profits for the winning bidder due to the failure to account for the adverse selection problem inherent in winning a tendering procedure. A detailed explanation appears in Sect. 7.4.

The case of Kraftverkehr Kinzigtal (Germany): Winner's curse

KVK, a subsidiary of the municipal operator, Hanauer Straßenbahn AG (HSB), won several tendered bus networks with offers calculated below operating costs. It remains unclear whether KVK was unable to calculate properly (missing capabilities) or whether it bid with so-called strategic prices to be able to enter the market.

However, KVK suffered significant losses from its new networks and thus experienced winner's curse. It then decided to assign two networks, including all duties listed in the underlying public service contracts, to the operator ÜWAG Bus GmbH by September 2006. KVK had to transfer the gross-cost contracts for the regional network Linienbündel Hünfeld (running until 2011) and the urban network Linienbündel Bad Hersfeld (running until 2013), including 53 employees and 37 buses. ÜWAG Bus GmbH will receive several million Euros from KVK (and the KVK owner) to balance the expected deficits on those networks.

To sum up the results until spring 2007, the goals of Hesse described above appear to have been realized: introducing competition via tendering had positive results from both a PTA and passenger point of view. Despite some increases in quality and environmental standards, PTAs realized significant savings in subsidies.

From an operator's point of view the results are diverse. Although the SMEs feared losses in market share, they were able to realize a significant increase during the starting phase. The main incumbent, DB, lost market share. The activities of global players are still limited, but the level of competition remains high. At least one case of winner's curse has occurred, which can be considered normal when introducing competition to a former monopolistic market. Therefore the Hesse model is seen as an interesting example on how to introduce competition for public transport services by bus.

5.4.2 *Decision to Promote Competition for Commercial Services: Saxony-Anhalt*

5.4.2.1 The Introduction of Competition for Commercial Services

Saxony-Anhalt, with its capital Magdeburg, is one of the new federal states in eastern Germany. Different to most of the other states in Germany its population density is low, with less than 130 inhabitants per square kilometer, and the density is expected to decrease considerably in the years to come.[51] At the same time, a

[51] See MBV ST (2005, p. 17).

decrease in the number of schoolchildren, the main users of public transport in the suburbs and the rural areas, and a massive increase in the number of senior citizens is expected, which will lead to higher costs for the public transport system. Recently, Saxony-Anhalt took some interesting steps to promote competition in public bus transport services to improve efficiency without using the classic tendering method. In the following the famous Wittenberg Model, named after the rural district of Wittenberg where the model was introduced first and the adjusted model of market organization at state level are described below.

According to the new law for public transport services for Saxony-Anhalt, amended in 2005, the federal state is now only responsible for organizing and financing regional railways.[52] Responsibility for organizing and financing public transport services by bus and tram (light rail) is given to the rural district levels which act as PTAs (including district-free cities). They may also establish financing schemes that still enable commercial services in their area of responsibility. Regional PTAs, such as the RMV in Hesse, have not been established and thus, PTAs for bus and tram services exist only at the local level. The new law also adjusted the multitude of financing instruments in Saxony-Anhalt and implemented incentives.[53] The subsidies for public transport services by bus and tram used to be based solely on structural components and were paid to both PTAs and operators. Now the subsidies from Saxony-Anhalt are based both on structural and success figures. Local PTAs receive payments directly and are requested to secure non-discrimination by deciding independently on an appropriate financing system to support operators. The sum is adjusted every year according to the financial support for public transport services received from the German government's Regionalisierungsmittel fund. Saxony-Anhalt uses the following formula to distribute the funds among the local PTAs:

- Number of passengers (success factor): 40% weighting, divided among the PTAs according to the number of passengers per PTA (not including schoolchildren)
- Timetable kilometers (service provision factor): 25% weighting, divided among the PTAs according to the number of timetable kilometers per PTA
- Plain (structural factor): 30% weighting, divided among the PTAs according to the area per PTA
- Tram (light rail factor): 5% weighting, divided among the PTAs according to the length of light rail network per PTA

Further support for cost-intensive infrastructure investments, e.g., light rail tracks, is provided in the form of additional subsidies. The extra subsidies for

[52] See Law for Public Transport in Saxony-Anhalt (Gesetz über den öffentlichen Personennahverkehr im Land Sachsen-Anhalt – ÖPNVG LSA).

[53] See MBV ST (2005, pp. 9–10) and § 8 to § 9 of the ÖPNVG LSA.

students, historically paid according to a formula based on the number of passenger kilometers per operator,[54] can be changed to other financing instruments, e.g., a lump sum payment, upon request of the PTA. This new financing structure is much simpler to understand for newcomers than the usual financing structure for public transport services described in Sect. 4.3.1.

According to the regional transport plan for Saxony-Anhalt, competitive structures within public transport services are part of the financial objective to increase efficiency.[55] Nevertheless, PTAs at rural district and city levels are asked to design their financing support systems (subsidies) for public transport services following German and European procurement laws without a clear obligation to tender. PTAs are asked to avoid overcompensation by establishing incentive payments to operators, for instance, based on experiences and data from company benchmarking surveys.

Saxony-Anhalt's ministry of transport also established recommendations (*Handreichungen*) for establishing financing structures which refer only to commercial operations. Further recommendations for conducting procedures for competition for licenses to operate commercial lines or services are included. To date, Saxony-Anhalt has not supported the awarding of non-commercial services via tendering. The quality competition, usual in the competition for commercial services, is seen as more appropriate to local requirements than price competition through tendering.[56] The PTAs are asked to design the introduction of competition to support operators' initiatives and secure a market structure comprised of private operators.

In January 2006, the rural district, Wittenberg, announced a competition for a license to operate commercial lines under the new awarding policy of Saxony-Anhalt. Operations were to commence in December 2006. In 2006, approximately 170 public transport operators provided services in Saxony-Anhalt.[57] With the exception of Veolia which began operations in regional railways, the interest of global players was and has remained low.

All in all, Saxony-Anhalt attempted to support the successful implementation of CCL in public transport by giving the PTAs more detailed instructions on how to act when there was competition for commercial services. Furthermore, and unlike most of the other federal states, a clear funding structure explains the streams of public co-funding, including the incentive mechanisms. Like Hesse, discussion on the pros and cons of supporting CCL procedures still remains lively. The results, successes and pitfalls experienced in Saxony-Anhalt are examined in the next section.

---

[54] See § 45a of the Passenger Transport Act.

[55] MBV ST (2005, pp. 4–7, p. 34 and pp. 81–82).

[56] See MBV ST (2006).

[57] See http://www.sachsen-anhalt.de/LPSA/index.php?id=oepnv, retrieved November 11, 2006.

5.4.2.2 The Wittenberg Model

As described in Chap. 4, competition for licenses to operate commercial lines or services (CCL) in Germany is legally based on market initiative. Here operators are free to submit their bids for a license providing them with a temporary exclusive right granted by the LA.[58] Nevertheless, PTAs may decide to promote this type of competition in a progressive manner to encourage numerous operators to submit bids.

Other than Hesse, which supported authority initiated tendering, Saxony-Anhalt decided to support CCLs. Here the rural district Wittenberg and the ministry of transport of Saxony-Anhalt were trying to restructure the CCL procedure with a new model for quality competition. In this model, the rural district established several quality criteria in its local PTP. In coordination with a specific scheme for subsidy payments these relatively detailed criteria were obligatory for operators in that CCL procedure[59]:

- A list of schools where public transport service is obligatory for operators
- Maximum waiting times for schoolchildren at bus stops
- Serving every village with over 200 inhabitants at least once or twice daily
- At least 30-minute frequency within the city of Wittenberg (approximately 50,000 inhabitants)
- 80% of all buses not older than 12 years
- A description of qualifications of bus drivers and cleanliness of buses

The suburban district used the existing regulatory framework on the national level to select the best bus operator and initiate the quality competition based on a CCL.[60] Operators could apply for three different networks: two regional networks, (1) one with around 1.7 million and (2) the other with around 0.9 million vehicle kilometers per year, and (3) one network in the city of Wittenberg with around 0.6 million vehicle kilometers per year.[61]

The rural district did not expect any applications by operators under the old financing scheme. Therefore, it developed an additional system of financial liquidity for transport services for schoolchildren for the winning operator.[62] The new scheme included a lump sum payment of €85,000 per year for the network of Wittenberg and €120,000 and €95,000 per year for each regional network. For participation in the local mobility service bureau, operators received an additional lump sum payment of €10,000 per year. The operators were also entitled to receive the following subsidies (incentive payments) to support an adequate service to

[58] For more details on the regulatory framework, see Sect. 4.3.2.

[59] See Landkreis Wittenberg (2005a, pp. 23–36) and Landkreis Wittenberg (2005b).

[60] See § 13 PBefG and Sect. 4.3.

[61] See Landkreis Wittenberg (2005a, p. 15).

[62] See Landkreis Wittenberg (2005c, p. 1).

be delivered to passengers. The sum of these compensatory payments was based on the lump sum payment of the last few years and the expected regional demographic development.

- €0.90 per passenger, not including schoolchildren, within the regional networks
- €0.40 per passenger, not including schoolchildren within, the city of Wittenberg
- An additional €0.40 per passenger after 6.00 p.m. to support demand responsive systems at these times
- An additional €0.40 per passenger on weekend days before 6.00 p.m. within regional networks to support demand responsive systems at these times
- Further payments to support cooperation concerning fares, e.g., tariff associations

During the license term, the sums to be paid to operators were calculated on the basis of data they furnished to the PTA. These figures were checked (quality standards stipulated in the local public transport plan had to be met) by means of several reports submitted to the suburban district:

- Report of timetable and timetable kilometers delivered
- Report on tickets sold
- Report on the number of passengers transported after 6:00 p.m. (and before 6.00 p.m. on regional networks)
- Confirmation/non-confirmation of all school directors about sufficient provision of public transport services for their pupils by the operators according to the quality criteria of the suburban district[63]
- Copies of a complete version of all complaints by passengers and the operators' responses
- Auditing of all reports by a chartered accountant

The district was allowed to check the proper use of the subsidies paid at any time including unannounced visits to operator offices.

To avoid overcompensation with too high profits for operators, three main mechanisms of ex-post control were designed: (1) the necessity for operators to request for permission for fare increases, (2) the option of the PTA to request a reduction in fares, and (3) the possibility for the PTA of reducing subsidy payments to operators by up to 20%. Nevertheless, questions arose whether PTAs have sufficient calculatory capabilities to identify overcompensation. Furthermore, a PTA might experience a hold-up problem when an operator asks for a fare increase to sustain its level of services without losses.

The district published a call for applications for licenses to operate its commercial services in the *Supplement to the Official Journal of the European Union* on January 13, 2006.[64] To ensure transparency, a detailed description of the rating

[63] See Landkreis Wittenberg (2005b).

[64] See Landkreis Wittenberg (2006).

system and a catalog of further information was sent to interested operators after March 1, 2006. The main criteria for selecting the best operator in the validation procedure starting on June 30, 2006 were:

- Number of services used to transport schoolchildren
- Number of services within regular public transport
- Quality of network (based inter alia on kilometers within timetable and number of bus stops served)
- Fares
- Participation in the local mobility service office

On the basis of this validation scheme, the license to operate a network was granted to the best bid offering significant quality improvements to passengers. In October 2006, the rural district accepted the offer of the consortium, Neuer Wittenberger Busverkehr, led by Vetter, the largest SME bus operator from the new federal states with around 190 buses in 2006. Vetter was supported in that consortium by three small regional operators. Operations began on January 1, 2007. At least 20 operators showed interest in participating in this competitive procedure.[65] By 2005, the routes in the rural district were covered by seven small private operators (the incumbents of those operations).[66] Only two are members of the new consortium. No global player or municipal operator submitted an application, which suggests that such a model might support local SMEs.

To minimize the legal risks which may arise from the new awarding system and the new financing instruments used, the European Commission was notified about the Wittenberg Model by the rural district Landkreis Wittenberg, the federal state of Saxony-Anhalt and the national government by the end of 2005. After checking whether this system of awarding licenses in public transport combined with the specific financing scheme was forbidden according to the EU Treaty, the European Commission approved the financing scheme on May 16, 2006. Although it noted several critical elements, approval was given, corresponding to the EU's White Paper.[67]

All in all the Wittenberg Model shows interesting aspects on how to introduce competition in the public transport market by promoting market initiatives by the PTA. A high degree of freedom to design the service is given to operators. Moreover the system attracts SMEs. The competitive procedure is based on a quality competition mechanism to increase the level of quality provided to passengers and increase passenger figures. Furthermore, it is based on a fixed public budget instead of a price competition to reduce public co-funding.

However, the model has also come in for its share of criticism. Apart from some weak regulations to avoid overcompensation, there is no flexible control

[65] See European Commission (2006).

[66] See Landkreis Wittenberg (2005a, p. 10).

[67] See European Commission (2006).

mechanism based on a direct contractual relationship between the PTA and the operator for the 8-year period of operation as is usual for tendering procedures.

With respect to public co-funding of public transport, a clear commitment by the PTA is necessary, as no flexible contract clauses are foreseen. If there is need to reduce public transport services more than expected in the local PTP, e.g., in the event of lower financial support by the federal state (resulting, for example, from reduced public funds from the national government), this can only be fulfilled by direct negotiations with the operators. This may then result in an unfavorable negotiating position for the rural district if questions arise about whether the PTAs have sufficient analytical capabilities to negotiate “at eye level”. Even a limited change of services, without a sufficient change of return to the operator, is only possible through negotiations, and is not typically found in public service contracts, based on an amendment clause with fixed parameters. A change of operator during the license term is usually impossible. Increasing costs for input factors, especially energy and personnel costs, and reduced financial support by the suburban district which are not sufficiently covered by increases in fares may be significant risks for operators. Nevertheless, they may favor the high freedom provided when comparing CCL procedures to the usual tendering procedures.

Notwithstanding these critical aspects, the federal state of Saxony-Anhalt expects its form of quality competition to be as efficient as a price competition via tendering. Furthermore, the Wittenberg Model is deemed a best practice model by the Bundesministerium für Verkehr, Bau und Wohnungswesen (BMVBW, the national ministry of transport) and has been recommended to other municipalities throughout the country.[68]

5.4.2.3 A Related Experience in Gifhorn, Lower Saxony

Different to the Wittenberg Model, where the CCL procedure was more or less initiated by the PTA, one of the most important real market initiatives in recent years is the Gifhorn case. Here a competing application was submitted by a private operator against services thus far provided by a municipal operator. This was one of the first instances in which an SME won a significant share of services in such a procedure.

The suburban district Gifhorn is located in the federal state Lower Saxony, where the Landesnahverkehrsgesellschaft Niedersachsen mbH (LNVG) is responsible for acting as the LA. The state concentrated the responsibility in the hands of the LNVG formerly distributed among several regional authorities. Unlike Hesse and Saxony-Anhalt, a clear commitment to introduce competition or a comparable market reform determining the roles and tasks of market participants has not been observed in that federal state.

---

[68] See MBV ST (2006).

In 2005, the municipal public transport operator, Verkehrsgesellschaft Landkreis Gifhorn mbH (VLG), applied to renew several licenses to operate commercial bus lines within the suburban district of Gifhorn. As in previous years, VLG expected the licenses would be regranted. This time, however, the private, medium-sized bus operator, Omnibusbetrieb Hülsmann GmbH (Hülsmann), and its subcontractors applied, too. Hülsmann was able to submit a better bid with respect to quality (for example, fixed cycle operations and 60-minute frequency on some lines that had been operated at a 120-minute frequency by VLG). LNVG, acting as LA, accepted Hülsmann's bid on April 29, 2005, because it was a better offer in terms of quality provided to passengers. Hülsmann commenced operations on July 15, 2005 and is authorized to provide services until 2013.[69]

As a consequence, the municipal VLG, owned by the suburban district Landkreis Gifhorn, lost 20% of its total volume of vehicle kilometers. Furthermore, Hülsmann cherry-picked only the most profitable lines in the suburban district network. Since VLG was left with several completely unprofitable routes, some less profitable ones, and a problem of overcapacity, the sum of subsidies paid to VLG by Landkreis Gifhorn rose sharply. Furthermore, VLG's subcontractors faced possible termination of their contracts, including risks arising from pay-back obligations for subsidies granted by the federal state for buses that were now superfluous. Other potential obligations were likely to result from the need for immediate staff cuts.

The suburban district initiated several discriminatory actions against the new operator, such as the decision to establish new transport services for schoolchildren instead of using the services now operated by Hülsmann. Most were soon forbidden by court order. After losing a major lawsuit filed by the suburban district, VLG gave notice to terminate its relationship with the three subcontractors who were now also subcontractors of Hülsmann. After waiving to compete against VLG in future competitions for licenses to operate commercial lines or services, VLG withdrew its terminations against the three. Finally, the suburban district and VLG gave up their legal battle against Hülsmann and accepted the new reality.

Notably the next year, VLG won a new CCL procedure within the suburban district of Landkreis Gifhorn. That procedure was not initiated by Hülsmann, but was instead initiated by the DB subsidiary, Regiobus Braunschweig.

The Gifhorn case again demonstrates the risks and benefits described for the Wittenberg Model. As in Wittenberg, an increase in the level of quality was observed for the Gifhorn case. Nevertheless, there are reasons to prefer this real market initiative model. Activities of authorities to design the service and regulate the awarding mechanism are restricted to a minimum compared to the Wittenberg Model and, even stronger, to the Hesse model. The freedom of operators to design the service is higher, due to a less-detailed PTP of the rural district and a limited

[69] See Burmeister (2005, p. 16).

validation catalog of the LNVG compared to Wittenberg. Furthermore firms in Gifhorn are able to focus on the profitable lines of the network only.

Nevertheless, the suburban district Gifhorn was not prepared for the situation arising from the competitive application of Hülsmann, and was thus affected far more negatively by the pitfalls of a CCL procedure than Wittenberg. Furthermore, and different to Wittenberg, Gifhorn experienced problems resulting from its role as the municipal owner of the incumbent in addition to the problems that encountered by an unprepared PTA.

For example, to regain at least a minimum of control over the routes now operated by Hülsmann, the PTA needed to insert extra clauses in the local PTP after LNVG's approval of the application of Hülsmann, which prolonged the usual decision-making period. Once the LA permitted operating those routes, any detailed control mechanism was virtually impossible, since a private operator now operated the services rather than a municipal one. The old control mechanism provided by the supervisory board of the former monopolistic municipal operator no longer functioned adequately. Because a direct contractual relationship between the PTA and the new operator was not foreseen within the institutional framework for commercial services for the routes now operated by Hülsmann, the suburban district faced diminished control for public transport services.

Moreover, the financial burden for the suburban district rose due to the increasing deficit of VLG from overcapacities and operations restricted to the unprofitable, so-called lemons of the network. While other PTAs might have been satisfied if private companies increased quality levels without the need for further subsidies due to competitive applications against other private companies, Gifhorn experienced financial difficulties due to its ownership of the municipal operator VLG.

5.5 Assessing the Procedural Possibilities

The case study analyses presented in this Chap. 5 provide an overview of the main procedural possibilities developed to introduce competition within the existing legal framework. Based on a long history of regulation, PTAs can now tender their services, as the RMV in the suburban area of Frankfurt did for several lines. PTAs may also decide to negotiate the level of the supplementary subsidies paid directly, with a reliable bargaining position to tender if the results prove unsatisfactory, as the MVV did in the suburban area of Munich. PTAs can now select a procedural framework whereby a CCL is encouraged by the PTA, as in the case of Wittenberg. They can also decide to waive any independent action in favor of a pure market solution, although they might run the risk Gifhorn encountered, where a private operator initiated a competition for commercial lines or services against the municipal operator.

Operators can participate in tendering procedures (RMV and suburban area of Munich), apply to operate commercial lines or services to counter a tendering procedure (suburban area of Hamburg), apply within a CCL procedure initiated by a PTA (Wittenberg Model), or initiate a CCL procedure on their own against another operator (Gifhorn case). The regulatory framework thus provides operators with a variety of procedural possibilities. The different types of contractual relationships discussed above also provide various levels of freedom to design services. Nevertheless, the focus of the discussion of market participants is always on Hesse as this state, in their view, tried to abolish the possibility of market initiatives by operators for commercial services by declaring all services as non-commercial.

To sum up, a PTA needs to make several important decisions about the awarding of services. First, it must decide whether to use competitive procedures. The results achieved so far within competitive procedures in Hesse and in Wittenberg suggest that the introduction of competition would be positive for numerous PTAs in Germany. Nevertheless, some critical remarks have to be made on the pitfalls originating from the legal framework and possible negative economic developments, i.e. the occurrence of a winner's curse and the unanswered question whether an oligopoly structure will develop in the long run.

The intense debate concerning the obligation to tender and the resulting uncertainty have prevented the use of these procedures in most of the regions in Germany to date. However, I believe that this discussion and the lack of a clear regulatory framework for the industry on the national level have enabled the development of many potentially useful procedural models (including several not included in this dissertation).

Should a decision be made in favor of competition, PTAs must then discuss whether to award their services following a strict formal procedure, such as is used for tendering. The case studies described show that competition for commercial services provides an opportunity for positive results from a competitive procedure. Both instruments are possible because PTAs are able to decide whether or not to classify services as commercial or non-commercial and therefore which award procedure should apply due to the PTAs' obligation to fix the minimum level of quality within the PTP.

The bouquet of possibilities within the German market organization provides opportunities for PTAs as well as for operators. While other EU Member States favor only one market model (authority initiated competition *for* the market via tendering as in Sweden and Denmark, or pure market initiated competition *within* the market as in Great Britain outside of London), Germany has introduced parallel authority initiated and market initiated competition within one single market. It will be interesting to see whether this will be preserved with the upcoming adjustment of the national legal framework required to comply with (EC) No 1370/2007. Furthermore, the question arises, whether other states will follow Hesse and Saxony-Anhalt in clarifying legal frameworks and financing structures to promote the introduction of competition by PTAs in their areas of responsibility.[70]

[70] Such recent developments and their effects on the market for commercial services are evaluated in Part IV.

5.6 Conclusions

Germany has a long history of regulation within the public transport market which protected most local incumbents from competition in the second half of the twentieth century. Even the market reforms of more than a decade ago have not significantly changed the situation. Direct awarding to municipal operators and/or the extension of existing authorizations to the former operator without competitive approvals is still the norm. The use of competitive instruments remains an exception. These direct awardings are legal, confirmed by the judgment of the Federal Administrative Court in 2006.

The present debate now focuses chiefly on three issues: (1) how to organize the market, (2) the procedure to be used, tendering or CCL, and (3) how to design competition in detail. The first question indeed is how to organize the public transport market and where to assign PTAs' responsibilities: at regional and local levels (Hesse), solely at local levels (Saxony-Anhalt), or waiving a clear organization of market participants' roles (Lower Saxony). The second question might concern whether to promote tendering procedures (for non-commercial routes), or compete to operate commercial lines or services. Leading private SMEs favor competition for exclusive rights (Gifhorn and Wittenberg), because of the wide (unregulated) operational freedom. In contrast, several major PTAs favor tendering, with a (more regulated) contractual relationship between PTA and operator (Munich, Hamburg and Hesse). The third and final question, which is beyond the scope of this dissertation, is how to design competition in detail with respect to the awarding procedure and the contractual relationship.

Although there is no obligation to tender or even to introduce or promote competition, most market participants expect to see an increased use of competitive instruments by PTAs in coming years. Reduced municipal budgets and decreasing populations, particularly in eastern Germany's rural districts and cities, may in fact lead politicians to favor tendering and similar instruments. Although the question of whether or not to tender from a legal view remains unanswered, economic pressure will no doubt provide the answer in the years to come for several PTAs. Fortunately, policy-makers can then select from the country's experiences as well as best practices elsewhere.

Chapter 6
International Comparisons: Alternatives Beyond Competitive Tendering

6.1 Introduction

The different failures and pitfalls of the specific German model presented in Chaps. 4 and 5 raise doubts about its feasibility and user friendliness. Nevertheless, the variety of opportunities for authorities and operators is a major advantage. When evaluating the international developments on introducing competition to the public transport services market, it becomes obvious that numerous different models to regulate the functioning of passenger transport markets have been developed and introduced. These models have been evaluated by van de Velde and Beck (2010), and the essay presented in this Chap. 6 is based on their findings.

Internationally, most countries and regions contemplating the introduction of competition-based organizational forms for their public transport services market did not focus on deregulated, competitive regimes as introduced in Britain in 1986 (competition *in* the market). In fact, the deregulated British bus market outside London acquired a reputation as an example not to follow. Data in the public domain aggregated at the level of major regions, such as Greater London, Scotland, and the six major conurbations outside London, showed clear differences. While London experienced growth, elsewhere there was a net decline. However, the considerable regional variations were obscured.

Fearful of losing their positions, some transport planners and municipal operators strongly opposed economic deregulation and decentralized market initiatives. Several of the large non-British private transport operators, mainly French transport groups, promoted more controlled competition in the form of competitive tendering of exclusive network and route contracts (competition *for* the market).

Even though cases of successful ridership growth in the UK's deregulated regions were acknowledged within the country, British bus operator trade associations did not lobby to promote deregulated regimes, or facilitate the dissemination of positive news about local successes, primarily because they regarded local performance data as commercially sensitive. As a result, deeper analysis and

A. Beck, *Competition for Public Transport Services*, Contributions to Economics,
DOI 10.1007/978-3-7908-2802-3_6, © Springer-Verlag Berlin Heidelberg 2012

international coverage of the local successes of the deregulated regimes in York, Oxford, Brighton, Nottingham, etc., rarely occurred, and the reputation of deregulated regimes remained contentious.

The rush for competitive tendering was further stimulated by the European Commission's endeavor to introduce a new regulation for the public transport sector that supported competitive tendering of exclusive contracts as the preferred way to organize local public transport markets. This discussion started around 1996 at the European level, and was only finalized in 2007 with the enactment of (EC) No 1370/2007, the Public Service Obligations regulation. While deregulated regimes (i.e. where transport services are initiated by autonomous transport operators) were not foreclosed by the new regulation, the preparatory discussions and reports favored exclusive contracts initiated by public transport authorities and awarded by competitive tendering. The text of the regulation pays little attention to the regulatory needs of deregulated markets. As a result, free competition *in* the market as a radical alternative to competitive tendering *for* the market continued to be perceived as an exception to the rule by lawmakers in both urban and regional passenger transport markets.

Future deregulated regimes however, will most likely assume substantial and expanded roles. This is already apparent for long-distance markets, which are often deemed more suitable for deregulation than short-distance markets. Two European examples are coach passenger transport services (van de Velde 2009) and the international railway markets, once European Directive 2007/58, introducing open-access in international rail passenger transport services and granting such operators cabotage rights, takes effect in 2011.

There is increased development of unregulated minibus services in suburban passenger transport markets in some Eastern European countries. Sweden contemplates introducing a deregulated regime in local and regional bus passenger transport to replace its centrally planned route tendering regime (Lundin et al. 2009), following previous deregulation of its air, coach and rail markets. Germany proposes to liberalize long-distance coach passenger transport services (see CDU et al. 2009). Although the Swedish and German Parliament could reject them, the proposals seem to indicate a change of mind, or a possible trend, towards more market-based regimes on the continent.

An overview of the changes in regulatory arrangements is not complete without observing that many European public transport networks continue to be directly awarded to a publicly-owned operator. Supporters argue that they provide efficiency and service improvements at lower transaction costs than competitive tendering. Various types of performance-based contracts are usually promoted as options to incentivize operators to maintain performance and efficiency.

The developments presented above and the ensuing considerations lead us ask: What institutional alternatives to competitive tendering or comparable arrangements can provide efficiency and service improvements? Based on a comprehensive literature review of current research results, Sect. 6.2 therefore discusses whether the division of competition-based alternatives to competitive tendering is possible and whether direct awarding is an efficient alternative. Following this discussion, Sect. 6.3 then derives three different approaches for a new market initiated regime. Finally, Sect. 6.4 concludes and presents an outlook on future issues.

6.2 Overview and Discussion of International Models

6.2.1 Division of Competition-Based Alternatives to Competitive Tendering – Really Possible?

An issue discussed is whether competition-based alternatives require new forms of authority intervention to guarantee proper functioning of such deregulated markets, and in particular whether regulatory alternatives exist to make this type of deregulation work better than the rather dogmatic fashion by which it was implemented in Britain outside of London. This usually is combined with the question of whether such autonomous market initiatives could or should be more cleverly combined with competitive tendering initiated by transport authorities for some other parts of the markets. Conversely, should there be a possibility for autonomous market entrants to infringe upon competitively tendered or directly awarded concession areas? Or should there remain regimes based upon authority initiative? Would such combined regimes enhance both the market and the tendered part of passenger services?

6.2.1.1 Market Initiative Revisited

There are many examples of market initiated competition in countries which previously introduced such regimes or undertook recent reforms, such as Great Britain and New Zealand. Others, such as Poland, allow some competition on the road, though not always as a conscious choice by lawmakers but rather as a result of not enforcing the existing laws. Moreover, there are countries that can have such competition from legal point of view, though this is by and large not the usual case in practice (Germany).

The chief examples are Great Britain and New Zealand, countries with extensive experience in bus deregulation. Both countries have now introduced legislation to facilitate more coordination between market initiated services, effectively softening some of the dogmatic aspects of their original deregulated regimes. To some extent and under varying pre-requisites, the reforms involve coordination of pricing, timetables and vehicle quality aspects, sometimes upon the initiative of market competitors, and sometimes upon the initiative of the PTA now entrusted with enhanced powers to set the rules for service coordination and quality.

White (2009) expects a possible convergence of practice in the near future between the competitive tendering system in London and the functioning of the regime elsewhere in Britain, especially in England, for the British bus industry. This is due to the potential effects of the Local Transport Act (2008) which gives scope for greater coordination between operators (previously inhibited by competition legislation), and potentially increased use of quality contracts (i.e. competitively tendered route contracts or area franchises as replacements for the deregulated bus market). There will also be some effect of the common regulations at the EU level regarding tenders and contracts.

Gibson (2009) explains the role of the New Zealand Transport Agency, a regulatory and funding entity that supports regional councils when they want to impose greater controls (i.e. rules for private service providers, such as coordinative, integrative or quality requirements) over commercial (non-contracted), and contracted services. The New Zealand Transport Agency is encouraging regional councils to take a strategic approach to the procurement of public transport services as a means of obtaining greater value for (public) money from services. Regional councils may even be free to require that parts or all of their services be provided under contract. Interestingly, New Zealand's Public Transport Management Act of 2008 includes features designed to give regional authorities greater control over urban commercial services, including the ability to specify which services are contracted and the ability to place controls on commercial services. The act also allows regional authorities to access more service data from commercial services.

These developments are akin to Great Britain's Local Transport Act of 2008. Ashmore and Mellor (2009) compared the British and the New Zealand regulatory systems for bus transport services. In their view an eventual move to the regulatory middle ground between a deregulated market for commercial services and a regulated market with tendered services is inevitable over time if public transport targets are to be met. Unfortunately, experience with the new legislation in both countries is not long enough to distill conclusions about effectiveness. New Zealand's recently elected government has signaled more changes to the legislation which are intended to promote and encourage commercial services, almost the opposite of the recently introduced legislation's approach. As a result the effectiveness of the softening of legislation is unlikely to be tested, and it appears that only Great Britain will be able to go ahead and provide evidence on its effectiveness in improving the functioning of deregulated bus markets.

The official proposal above by Lundin et al. 2009 to replace the Swedish route-tendering regime by a more deregulated market initiated regime is also intensely discussed. Moreover, Westin (2009) presents a stepwise approach for Sweden characterized by market initiative, but within a more constraining framework than the more dogmatic version by Lundin et al. Nevertheless, two central elements of the proposal by Westin are that free market initiatives by operators will be introduced and that tendering by PTAs will take place only in addition or as a supplement when it is clear that no sufficient services will be provided commercially. For this purpose, a clear step-wise procedure to invite operators in a formal way will be established. The lesson from Great Britain and New Zealand included appears to be that integration requirements (information, fares, and timetables) to be met by entrants are taken into account from the onset. This goes further and/or is comparable with various aspects of the reforms recently introduced in New Zealand and Great Britain. Should the Swedish proposal proceed, it will probably be the first major example of coordinated deregulation in the developed world.

Other cases of more deregulated regimes could very well emerge in the near future in Europe. Poland and Germany are examples of two countries where free market initiatives are now legally feasible and could potentially play a more important role in the future. Grzelec et al. (2009) presented the Polish case in a paper devising a proposal for an alternative regulatory regime to be applied in that country. The current regime combines various elements varying from "on the road" competition (competition *in* the market) to contracted services (competition *for* the market) and directly awarded services. The paper presents the current regime as inefficient and ineffective and advocates, especially with respect to integration of public transport services, the need for more regulation. The perceived regulatory need has already resulted in greater involvement of local authorities in recent years, but Grzelec et al. believe that this is still insufficient.

For the German market, Sect. 4.3.3 presented above indicates a low level of competition for commercial (market initiated) services. Although legally possible, competitive market initiatives for commercial services are still rare. As we have explained, initiatives are underway to implement a more deregulated regime.

6.2.1.2 Regulation Versus Deregulation

A key question policy-makers face is whether a deregulated or a regulated market would provide better results. It is clear that Great Britain's deregulation has created its own problems. New Zealand shows promising auspicious results, but also a number of setbacks. This includes little competition in tendering and a tendency for incumbents to be successful. Competitive tendering regimes are indeed not without problems. Strongly regulated regimes like Sweden (mainly under tendering) and Germany (mainly without tendering) are good illustrations of these problems. While the British and New Zealand models have moved towards more regulation, other countries are moving towards more deregulation. The question then is: What regulation, and how much, is needed to make deregulation successful?

Based on the limit price approach presented by Bain (1956) and the contestable market approach of Baumol (1982), Cowie (2009) shows empirical evidence for the contestability of the provision of most of the bus services in Great Britain outside London. Since Cowie also shows that contestability is not given everywhere outside London, the issue is whether imperfect contestability is an acceptable market outcome. Therefore, we must recognize that it is very likely that alternatives to deregulation (public production and competitive tendering) will not either work perfectly. When developing a new regulatory framework where market initiatives for commercial services are accepted, necessarily the question arises whether we can accept imperfectly contestable markets.

Another major concern is whether "cherry-picking" (operators select and operate only the most profitable lines and services in a network) will be permitted, meaning that lines in sparsely populated areas, or some off-peak services will be left to public authorities. In consequence, PTAs are asked to award the required subsidies if they deem these services necessary, as in Great Britain outside London. An argument against allowing cherry-picking means accepting the privatization of some profits. In a competitively tendered authority initiative case, these could be used to cross-subsidize non-commercial services. Allowing entry and cherry-picking could also jeopardize the realization of economies of scale as a result of providing all services in one area. It may also open the door to a comparatively very high level of supply of some selected commercial services, e.g., in densely populated areas (too high frequency [mini]buses driving in packs as seen in Poland, or, in Germany, too high quality levels for some routes and blocs of time instead of cross-subsidizing unprofitable services during weekends [see the Gifhorn case in Sect. 5.4.2 above]), which would not necessarily be in the public's best interest. However, some believe that cherry-picking is actually beneficial and necessary to generate stronger incentives for innovation by incumbents, e.g., increasing passenger numbers.

Absent a definitive conclusion, it is generally believed that there should be room for market initiatives even when competitive tendering is the regulatory instrument. Here, the discussion revolves around whether to measure the revenue and passenger abstraction generated by new entrants at the costs of contracts already tendered in the past. If the measurement shows a significant abstraction the question then becomes whether or not to allow cherry-picking in specific cases. Griffiths (2009) has discussed the "not primarily abstractive" test developed by the Office of Rail Regulation for the British railway network in the context of franchising network concessions. The test considers whether benefits to passengers as a result of entry of a new firm operating at its own risk (and without a tendered contract) outweigh the possible disbenefits to taxpayers from increased subsidy requirements for the existing franchise. The test examines the ratio of revenues generated by the entrant to revenues abstracted from the existing franchisee. Essentially, competing services that would be primarily abstractive of incumbents' revenues without compensating economic benefits beyond proposed or potential lower prices for existing customers would be disallowed.

The British experience serves as a cautionary note that competition policy measures which inhibit cooperation between operators may actually create problems, for example, for ticketing and timetables. A PTA may then assume a role of independent coordinator of the commercial interests of individual operators. The main challenge is that a sufficiently well-developed regulatory framework is also crucial.

6.2.1.3 Further Experiences from the Rail and Coach Markets

Deregulated regimes are common in the coach sector. Rail, too, is increasingly being submitted to deregulated open access regimes in Europe. Hence it is interesting to see whether the future opening of the international and some national railway markets in Europe could be test cases for additional deregulation of urban and regional public transport markets in Europe and elsewhere. The difference between short- and long-distance routes in the regulation of scheduled passenger transport should be taken into account here.

Nash (2009), who analyzes the development at the European level, concludes that enforcing and clarifying existing legislation is needed within the EU Member States. He shows that competitive tendering for gross-cost contracts has worked well, yet both franchising and open access for more commercial services show some problems.

The existing open access regimes differ in the extent and ways in which open access is legally feasible, and the current experience is not yet pointing in a single direction. Séguret (2009) evaluates the current open access regime in the German railway industry. Full open access is a legal principle, but in practice the national operator still provides the majority of non-tendered services. Séguret finds that the long-distance market with free access is very dependent on regional traffic markets where tendering occurs and that only a limited number of operators deliver commercial services. Séguret concludes that with a market share of less than 1% 9 years after the first entry, competition in the long-distance passenger transport can hardly be termed a success, although this may change with the market opening in international traffic in Europe in 2010.

Alexandersson and Hultén (2009) analyze the gradual on-the-track competition regime introduced in the Swedish passenger rail market and the reform introduced in 2009 which will gradually liberalize commercial (i.e. profitable) services. The authors show that the existing and the reformed system have their pros and cons, especially with respect to risk and the possibility of developing an oligopoly operator structure. Furthermore, Griffiths (2009) provides some insights about open access in the British rail market which is characterized by authority initiated concessions and a complementary role for open access. He concludes that although open access entry does have some negative effects in terms of a potential reduction in government revenue, the beneficial effects are increasing market sizes and customer satisfaction.

Alexandersson et al. (2009) add some information from the deregulated long-distance coach market in Norway and Sweden. They compare the impacts of these different regulatory systems on the performance of long-distance transport services for rail and coach services. The Norwegian coach market seems to be more developed and efficient compared to the Swedish market, although Norway is characterized by less competition, more coordination between operators and more state ownership.

6.2.2 *Direct Awarding – an Efficient Alternative to Competitive Arrangements?*

Non-competitive options remain essential features of urban public transport, especially in Europe after the adoption of recent legislation facilitating this option.

Thus another question that has to be addressed is: How can policy-makers reconcile the absence of competition with the achievement of more efficiency and performance improvements? Can negotiated performance-based contracts guarantee such achievements? What are the conditions for their success?

Veeneman and de Groot (2009) review recent experiences with direct awards in the three largest cities of the Netherlands, namely Rotterdam, The Hague and Amsterdam. A development towards competition was expected in these cities since the enactment of the Dutch Law on Passenger Transport in 2000 that foresaw competitive tendering. However, as policy on the EU level shifted so as to drop the obligation of tendering for municipal operators, the three cities decided to stay with direct award regimes. Rotterdam chose a conservative model with close cooperation between municipality, regional transport authority and incumbent public operator. The Hague chose close compliance with the evolving legal framework, leading to a more controlled position for the incumbent public operator with a substantial level of cooperation between operator and regional authority. Amsterdam chose to decouple the responsibility of the municipality as owner of the operator and that of the regional transport authority as client for its services. Veeneman and de Groot show that each model has its advantages and disadvantages, without stating a clear preference.

Gorter (2009) identifies organizational models for awarding local public transport services in Germany, directly depending on the local needs and organizational possibilities. He finds that each region has its own individual model. Gorter identified the so-called Querverbund-model as a significant preserver of direct awarding. For a municipal operator, this model enables the cross-subsidization of public transport services via the financial benefits resulting from reduced corporate tax payments. This is due to interconnected associations with profitable public companies, such as municipal energy suppliers.[1]

Van de Velde et al. (2009) examine the direct award contracting experience of the Dutch ministry of transport in the Dutch railway sector. They show the different contracting approaches adopted since the initiation of railway reforms in 1996. After a strong deregulation, an attempt to introduce substantial financial incentives failed. Policy reconsideration then led to a more cooperative approach between the players, together with a contracting based on an incremental, continuous improvement, with no immediate financial incentives at first. This approach proved more successful than the previous approaches.

Saito (2009) describes the experience of Japanese railways characterized by long-term monopoly rights for private vertically integrated railway operators. Contracts and competitive awards are absent, yet the sector is characterized by high performance and profitability. Currently 87.5% of rail passenger transport in major metropolitan areas is provided by profitable private railway companies, which are trying to increase their profits by diversifying into other markets.

[1] See also Sect. 4.3.1.

Saito looks at the effects on the Japanese passenger rail market of a slight (fare) deregulation applied in 2000 and 2002. He discusses the growing role of vertical disintegration between operation (private) and infrastructure (authority-owned) when further increases in capacity are only possible with state aid.

6.3 An Attempt at Designing a Market Initiated Regime

Taking up the issues discussed above, we will design a market initiative based regime in the following. When discussing several options it shows that numerous aspects need to be considered when developing a new regulatory framework:

- PTAs should set minimum standards for quality, environmental aspects, personnel, and security; assume infrastructure charges and related costs; take care of a proper existence and functioning of the different relationships between different public bodies, operators and passengers; support transparency and accountability.
- PTAs should define services of general interest and establish a vision for market development through the publication of a general public transport plan, either to provide general guidance, or as basis for more concrete public service contracts.
- Entry barriers for commercial services must be minimized or avoided; the regulatory framework must not discriminate against potential new entrants; no operator should receive any preferential treatment regarding rolling stock investment or compensatory payments for fare reductions.
- From the passenger perspective, integration and cooperation between operators are crucial for delivering appropriate services; PTAs should define the precise role of autonomous initiatives for commercial services in the organization of the market, the extent of minimum standards, and whether they should be voluntary or obligatory; PTAs should define minimum standards and use incentives for cooperation and open integration platforms to implement them; a neutral moderator is preferable.
- Competent, strong authorities with expertise are essential to market success; regulators should thus be equipped with: the skills to fulfil the tasks set, solid market knowledge, adequate funding, personnel and competencies. PTAs should be empowered with the necessary instruments concerning data access, monitoring, etc. as this is perceived to be a crucial aspect to the well functioning of markets and regulation.
- Several other aspects are usually common sense and should serve as minimum standards when introducing market initiatives for commercial services: clarity of policy aims on national and regional levels; full information/transparency for both authority and operator to report patronage and fare revenues; clear minimum (quality) standards; assets (rolling stock) owned by operators and infrastructures (e.g., stations) owned by PTAs; all operators in private ownership.

Model 1: Several contracts in one area + additional market initiative	**Model 2: Market initiative + additional tendering**	**Model 3: One contract for one area + (threat of) market initiative**
▪ Awarding steps: ▫ 1. Authority designs and tenders core-network, including minimum quality standards determined for all services in that area ▫ 2. Market initiative for additional commercial services possible upon own risk of operators ▪ Authority sets concessionary fare schemes, interavailable fares and ticketing, lower fares by operators possible ▪ Discussion club (PTAs, operators, passengers)	▪ Transport plan (only functional) by transport authority ▪ Awarding steps: ▫ 1. Commercial services as market initiative, only clever exceptions and fare freedom ▫ 2. Additional tendering to fulfill transport plan ▪ Concessionary fare schemes and/or superincentives to avoid fare regulation ▪ Maybe some exclusivity linked to headway regulation ▪ Need for quick response to unfair behavior	▪ Awarding steps: ▫ 1. Negotiating contract with incumbent ▫ 2. Threat of competitive tendering if negotiations unsuccessful ▫ 3. Threat of possible commercial entry (if incumbent is not affected negatively) ▪ National body to support transport authorities in contracting ▪ Performance-based penalties and benchmarking ▪ Partnership between transport authority and operator

Fig. 6.1 Main differences between the regimes

PTAs also need different types of awarding instruments, ranging from awarding procedures for market initiatives and competitive tendering to direct awards. Furthermore we suggest that:

1. Policy-makers should design a combination of commercial services and competitive tendering or direct award services (combining these would depend on the particular circumstances).
2. Net-cost contracts are preferable when contracts are to be used and for the usage of additional incentives to induce patronage growth when needed.
3. Caution in using direct awarding is necessary as this should remain an alternative only in very specific cases that should, furthermore, be used with sufficient transparency

Based on these three minimum criteria and the aspects described above, we design three different regimes. Figure 6.1 sketches the main differences between these regimes to be explained below. Only Model 2 can be classified as a true market initiative regime; the others are essentially contracting models with a strong authority initiative, but each also has substantial elements of market initiatives.

Model 1 allows several contracts within one geographic area. The awarding procedure starts with a competitive tendering procedure designed by the PTA for the core network. The quality standards for this network (e.g., direction and number of routes, frequency, and hours of operating services) are set by the PTA as minimum conditions and they are based on its definition of services of general interest. After the tendering procedure, in a second step operators are free to suggest market initiatives for commercial services which are omitted by the winning bidder in the tendering procedure. These services also must fulfill the minimum criteria set by the PTA and the operators are not impeded by exclusivity for commercial services. To enable adequate integration and cooperation, the PTA sets standards for fare rebates, inter-available fares and ticketing. Lower fares by operators are always possible. A discussion club to discuss matters of local public transport between PTAs, operators and passengers similar to the German Verkehrsverbund model is necessary to support integration and build cooperative trust.

Model 2 starts with a public transport plan that contains clear aims (functional design, e.g., 85% of inhabitants of the city can reach the next bus stop by 400 m maximum walking distance). Awarding the services starts with market initiatives for commercial services. Various options for direct on-the-road competition exist. These include headway regulation (minimum intervals between departures of different bus operators at stops), but without eliminating all possibilities for parallel services. Perhaps it is possible to incorporate some exclusivity linked to headway regulation, but this is generally not foreseen in this model. The chief difficulty and regulatory danger is to prevent integration (e.g., by too little regulation), or prevent innovation (e.g., by too much regulation). Nonetheless, a quick response by the regulator towards unfair behavior is critical. Services not provided commercially are tendered in a second step. Concessionary fare schemes and super-incentive contracts are used to avoid other forms of fare regulation.

Model 3 foresees only one contract in one geographic area. The first awarding step is negotiating a contract with the incumbent in order to avoid high transaction costs, and to secure the incumbent's knowledge on how to operate the services in question, or accommodate its high level of quality in the past. In a second step, if negotiations are unsuccessful, at any time the PTA can decide to use competitive tendering. This represents a threat for the incumbent. A further threat during the contract term is the possibility of market initiatives for commercial services. Authorities may only deny such initiatives if the incumbent is affected negatively (measured by the non-primarily abstractive test as described by Griffiths 2009) in order to secure commercial stability for the services in question and reduce risk costs to be calculated by the incumbent. Based on the approach used in New Zealand, a national body supports PTAs in negotiating contracts. The contractual relationship between operator and authority is characterized by a partnership of trust with performance-based penalties and benchmarking.

For these models and similar plans, policy-makers need to ask the following questions about intervention: Are they willing to prevent or correct a possible market failure? Will they enable a commercially viable market for operators via market initiatives? How will they realize their policy aims? The answers will depend upon the authorities' own decisions about other aims and policies as well as external factors. Furthermore, regulators must learn to recognize the problems that might arise from the parallelism of commercial and non-commercial services, and how to resolve them. Whether or not exclusivity should be envisaged is obviously an issue. In some circumstances, especially when some exclusivity is guaranteed, it may be necessary for authorities to have a view on what is and what is not a commercial service from an operator viewpoint.

6.4 Conclusions

Although some major international models have been discussed here, we conclude that there is no single, definitive approach to follow. In fact, each model has some drawbacks, and we identify new topics for additional research. Even our own attempt to design a market initiated regime shows that several approaches are conceivable to enhance the engagement of operators. Nevertheless, the proposed approaches make clear that market initiatives and their competitive threats can be implemented in frameworks that foresee the reasons to (1) tender a network first, (2) tender the residual non-commercial services subsequent to market initiatives for commercial services, or (3) negotiate a direct awarding with the incumbent.

Too often, optimality is assumed (perfection of the authority's actions in managing a competitive tendering regime), or expected to accept a regime as a good regulatory option. The real world is, however, imperfect. Authorities and markets fail. Hence, policy-makers must determine whether a sub-optimal level of free market results is acceptable, given that competitive tendering as an alternative is also sub-optimal in practice. This holds especially for cherry-picking, which is becoming more relevant for allowing market initiatives in markets formerly subject to exclusivity. We suggest that the real effects of this scenario on the ability to utilize economies of scale, support innovation and increase ridership should be evaluated in detail.

Moreover, public transport plans established by PTAs in several of the presented and discussed regimes, provide guidance for the free market. Various forms of the rules of the game, also termed controls, can be combined to improve market outcomes, and this feature appears in recent amendments to the more deregulated regimes. But granting such guidance and control powers to transport authorities also opens the door to a growing influence on service design and a reduced level of market initiative. Thus, the challenge is to organize such intervention without having monopolizing service design offend up on the side of the authority, and to design this regime to optimize its effect on market synergies.

The results also point to other recommendations for further studies on market regimes. As indicated, more information about the performance of market initiative regimes is needed. Several sources provide information at a national level, but the data tends to mask local successes. Analysis of the successes and their causes in both authority initiated and market initiated regimes would enrich the debate on how to make economic deregulation a success. It would be useful to detail the innovations suggested and implemented in deregulated market regimes. A comparative analysis of market initiatives could assist regulators to enhance social welfare and quality for passengers. In order to deepen such examinations, the following essays focus on the experiences of the two sub-markets for commercial and for non-commercial services in Germany.

Part III
Competition for Non-Commercial Services

The next three chapters fully discuss the competition for non-commercial public transport services by bus. Chapter 7 provides insights about the awarding structure, barriers to entry and potential risks. Chapter 8 evaluates the experiences of authorities, operators, passengers and employees throughout the tendering process and after awarding. Chapter 9 explains the results of my analysis of tender prices. Where appropriate I provide case studies throughout to ease understanding of specific aspects.

Chapter 7
General Conditions Surrounding Non-Commercial Services

This section begins with a description of tendering's basic structure and awarding schedule. Section 7.2 then focuses on barriers to market entry and the relevance of uncertainty. In Sect. 7.3 I examine the structural differences of risk factors and typical forms of risk allocation based on a study of 34 public service contracts in Europe. Section 7.4 expands the discussion on revenue risk with respect to Germany. I conclude with a summary of the main economic effects of risk within tendering procedures in Sect. 7.5.

7.1 Introduction: Basic Structure for Tendering Procedures

Germany's tendering procedures are generally structured in three phases as shown in Fig. 7.1. In the *preparation phase*, the PTA develops the tendering documents. These contain necessary information on the services being put out to tender (e.g. passenger figures) and the tendering parameters, contractual conditions and responsibilities, deadlines, etc.

The *tendering phase* begins with the official announcement of the public tender, which usually appears in the *Official Journal of the European Union*. Interested parties submit applications to the PTA and receive the tendering documents for a fee. The conditions stated in the tendering documents, primarily those for the public service contract, regulate both the tendering design and the characteristics of the principal-agent relationship between the PTA (principal) and the operator (agent). The documents set the required services and provide other relevant information – for instance, about potential demand – which will form the basis for bidders' calculations. These conditions usually cannot be altered after the tender has been announced. Submitting a bid obliges the bidder to provide the contractually-agreed services upon award of the contract.

A. Beck, *Competition for Public Transport Services*, Contributions to Economics,
DOI 10.1007/978-3-7908-2802-3_7,

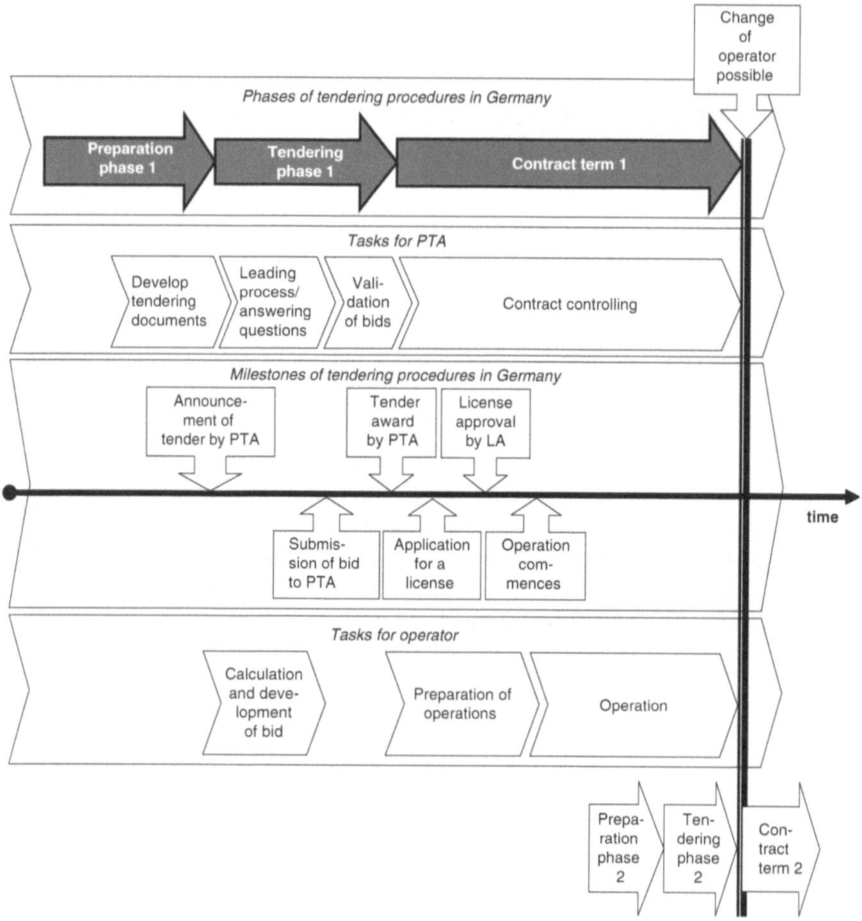

Fig. 7.1 Schedule of tendering procedures (Own figure based on van de Velde et al. (2008a, p. 41))

Interviews with experts confirm the PTA's role as auctioneer[1] in pursuing the objectives of encouraging competition, minimizing any required supplementary direct subsidies, and securing sufficient quality. Usually, the PTA selects the lowest offer or bid, provided it does not fall short of the minimum quality set by the PTA in the tendering document; normally, bidders must at least match the existing quality. The awardee then applies to the LA for a license to operate non-commercial services (see also Sect. 4.3). Upon approval, actual operation commences at the beginning of the contract term, being the third phase of the procedure. The PTA is responsible for implementation of the contract and for monitoring the operator's

[1] See Sect. 4.5.1 for more details on this classification.

obligation to fulfill the contract during the contract term, which usually coincides with the license term of these services. During this term, the operator monitors the granting of compensations set by the contract (see Sect. 4.4.1).

In the final step and throughout the term of a contract, the PTA's focus turns to mitigate information asymmetries and their negative effects. The goal is to provide incentives to operators to guarantee high-quality transport services, e.g., a bonus-malus payment scheme for punctuality.

7.2 Barriers to Market Entry

7.2.1 General Remarks

The economic literature contains many definitions of barriers to entry. Initial research was done by Bain (1956). Fisher (1979, p. 23) defines the term: "A barrier to entry is anything that prevents entry when entry is socially beneficial but is somehow prevented." Demsetz (1968, p. 56 f.) provides insight that using tendering is favorable for those cases where exclusivity for providing a service enables the use of significant economies of scale and several candidates exist for providing the services. Inspired by Demsetz (1968, pp. 55–65), the model developed by Laffont and Tirole (1993, pp. 309–318) shows that in general increasing the number of bidders will increase the winning bidder's productivity in a tendering procedure, what then will favor the price realized by the auctioneer. Wilson (1977, pp. 511–518) shows that increasing the level of competition for a first price auction will enhance the situation of the auctioneer: the higher the number of bidders, the more likely the result of the auction will be close to the real value of the object of the auction. Moreover, McAfee and McMillan (1987) provide evidence that by increasing competition and encouraging more aggressive bidding prices will drop to competitive or very at least efficient levels.[2]

The ultimate aim of increasing competition within tendering procedures for non-commercial services from a PTA point of view is to reduce the need for subsidies. As an auctioneer determining the tendering conditions, the PTA is able to influence the intensity of the competition by setting participatory conditions that ensure as many bidders as possible. Conditions that prevent potential bidders from submitting bids are barriers to market entry.

[2] The same is indicated by Bester (2003, p. 12).

7.2.2 Relevance of Uncertainty and Risk for Public Service Contracts

McAffee et al. (2004, p. 465) define newcomers' disadvantages compared to the incumbent's position as market entry barriers. They emphasize that if there are sunk costs in the market, these barriers include "uncertainty about market conditions." If the level of uncertainty is (significantly) lower for the incumbent than for the newcomer, this also can be classified as a "disadvantage" because newcomers must reckon with higher risk costs than the incumbent. While new players can reduce their level of uncertainty with careful analysis, the cost of research, i.e. sunk cost, is also a barrier. Finally, sometimes a group of smaller barriers together "may constitute a significant entry barrier".

Analyzing tendering procedures for public transport services by bus it becomes obvious that these procedures differ by numerous aspects that might influence the level of competition. There are several factors that influence sunk costs, for instance, the volume of the service in question (e.g., in terms of vehicle kilometers to be provided per annum), and the level of risk to be borne by the operator.

A key concern with respect to risk is contract duration which is usually 6–8 years in Germany. In general, a longer term tends to increase uncertainty about the development of costs and revenues during the contract duration. Williamson concludes (1976, p. 81): "The upshot is that, although franchise awards can be reduced to a lowest bid price criterion, this is apt to be artificial if the future is uncertain and the service in question is at all complex. Such awards are apt to be arbitrary and/or pose the hazard that 'adventurous' bids will be tendered by those who are best suited or most inclined to assume . . . risk."

Economic theory generally assumes a higher risk aversion of the agent than of the public principal. By assuming risks, the PTA (principal) – a public entity that is generally assumed to be risk-neutral – may prevent bidders (agents) from calculating high risk premia. This holds especially for aspects affected by external factors beyond an operator's sphere of influence. Stanley and van de Velde (2008, p. 23) stress for public transport services "the general proposition that risks should be allocated to the party most able to manage those risks". However, in a time of budgetary constraints and a global recession, more PTAs prefer that operators assume these risks.

It can be argued that a higher level of risk would not per se reduce the number of bidders if they calculate an adequate risk premium to be paid by the PTA, but this argument applies only under the assumption that all operators are symmetric bidders and thus have the same level of risk aversion. The argument fails to apply if the risk attitude of bidders is probably different, as already discussed for asymmetric bidders by McAfee and McMillan (1987).

For Germany it can be supposed, that the risk attitude of bidders is probably asymmetric. Here small- and medium-sized private operators compete against global private operators (like Veolia Transport or Keolis), when only the size of the latter's capital is sufficient to bear the higher levels of risk. Moreover, all private operators compete with public entities like DB or Hessische Landesbahn. Economic theory usually assumes a risk-averse attitude for private companies and a risk-neutral attitude for public entities like DB. Based on interviews held with operators, I assume all (potential) bidders are risk averse since all public bidders in practice act similarly to private operators (especially DB with its aim of becoming a private firm by going public). Note, too, that the degree of risk aversion among potential bidders remains unknown ex ante.

Hence, if the conditions in the tendering documents entail a high overall risk for potential bidders and the bidders are risk averse, this scenario is likely to deter some parties from entering into competition. Fulfilling the participation constraint of a higher number of potential bidders then leads to a higher level of competition. Preston et al. (2000, p. 111) emphasize that the risk aversion of bidders in British rail franchising procedures increases the need for subsidies by increasing the risk premium to be calculated by the remaining bidders. An optimal auction or tender accordingly reduces bidders' insecurity in order to reduce the risk premium. I have reached the same conclusion based on interviews and discussions with bus operators active in Germany.

7.3 Risk Factors in Public Service Contracts

Contracts for public transport services allocate various financial risks among the contracting parties. Moreover, many incentive mechanisms can also be added, such as quality incentives, which again influence the risk level of the parties. Many contracts spell out the operator's level of risk in a more or less clear manner. Based on an evaluation of 34 public service contracts in Europe, the next sections will describe these risk aspects in more detail. My aim is to develop a catalog of risk components to facilitate assessing the possible risks assumed by operators when concluding a public service contract.[3] The categories presented below form the basis for identifying the influential factors discussed in the essays presented in Chaps. 8 and 9.

7.3.1 Definition of Risk Components

The two major risk components in the public transport sector are *cost risks* and *revenue risks*. *Cost risks* can be divided into two main sub-components:

[3] Section 7.3 is based on research conducted as a researcher for van de Velde et al. (2008a) and (2008b).

Main components of cost risks for public transport services by bus

1. Operational cost risks: Who carries the risk of possible operations costs variations? If operational costs are higher/lower than forecasted at the beginning of the contract, which contracting party will support the additional loss or receive the additional benefit? These risks (and chances) can be divided between:

   (a) External risks: Risks that cannot be influenced by the operator (e.g., flooding of streets in case of natural disaster), or that can only be indirectly and slightly influenced by the operator (energy price, price of materials, labor costs)
   (b) Internal risks: Risks that can be directly influenced by the operator (some operational costs, maintenance costs like production process decisions, vehicle maintenance, etc.)

2. Investment risks: Who bears the risk of property and value of assets (infrastructure and vehicles), which also relates to the residual value of the assets at the end of the contract period (market exit risk)

Revenue risks can also be divided into two main sub-components:

Main components of revenue risks for public transport services by bus

1. Risk from passenger revenues: Who bears the risk related to the amount of revenue expected from passenger receipts? If passenger revenues are higher/lower than expected at the beginning of a contract, who benefits from the additional profit or incurs the additional loss?
2. Risk from public entities' revenues: What is the design of subsidies from public entities? Are they lump sum payments or are they varying? In case of varying payments, these risks (and chances) can be sub-divided between:

   (a) Varying volume risk: Payments display the cost structure with respect to input factors (e.g., payments per vehicle kilometers or payments per seat kilometers provided to passengers), or simply to costs of production; this risk is thus limited to a varying volume ordered by the PTA p.a. during the contract period, but its variation is usually limited by a specific bandwidth
   (b) Incentive risk: Public payments include (additional) incentives; the stimulus varies according to specific objectives regarding quality (e.g., punctuality), or output figures (e.g., number of pupils, increase in passenger figures per year)

Again these risks can be divided between internal and external risks. If the operator is able to directly influence the risk out of varying passenger revenues and public payments (e.g. level of maintenance of vehicles in order to enhance bonus-payments for punctuality) this risk is classified as internal. But the operator may also have to bear external risk factors such as reduced number of pupils due to demography.

Note: Other components of revenues that usually contribute only slightly to sales for public transport operators, e.g., revenues from advertising in and on buses, revenues from shops at bus stations, are not included in this analysis.

Several aspects can simultaneously affect both, the costs and the revenues of the operator. This holds, e.g., for energy prices that affect the costs for diesel fuel for operators, and, at the same time, affect the passenger revenues due to an increasing number of passengers opting not to use their cars. Another major aspect is the operational and/or organizational complexity of the service in question. Here risks may result from new large and/or complex networks, new untested vehicles, unclear market organizations, etc.[4]

Along the schedule of the tendering procedures (see Sect. 7.1), the realization of risk can occur either in the *tendering phase* or in the *contract term*.

Tendering Phase

- Inadequate data, e.g., bad data quality on passenger figures in a net-cost contract, plan production processes, etc.
- Contract with high risk level
  - Extent to which PTA assumes external risks
  - Type of contract (gross-cost, net-cost, etc.)
  - Level of additional incentives

Contract Term

- External risks
- Internal risks
- Incorrect calculations by operator

Based on the categorizations presented, some types of risk allocation are defined in the following.

[4] Bräuer et al. (2005) show that PTAs should avoid introducing mechanisms which are overly complex.

7.3.2 Typical Types of Risk Allocation and Contract Forms

Risk can be allocated and shared in various ways between the PTA and the operator. A basic classification of contracts forms according to risk allocation is the following:

Typical contract forms

- Simple *management contract* (M): the authority bears both, the production cost risk and the revenue risk, the operator bears none
- Simple *gross-cost contract* (GC): the operator bears the production cost risk, the authority retains the revenue risk
- Simple *net-cost contract* (NC): the operator bears (the balance of) both risks – the cost risk and the revenue risk, the authority none

Figure 7.2 shows a simplified representation of some of the possibilities using this traditional distinction. As illustrated, many intermediate forms of risk sharing can in fact be imagined.

An alternative way to arrange the typical contract forms according to the risk level to be borne by the operator along a continuum is shown in Fig. 7.3. Without taking incentives into account, in general management contracts create a rather low

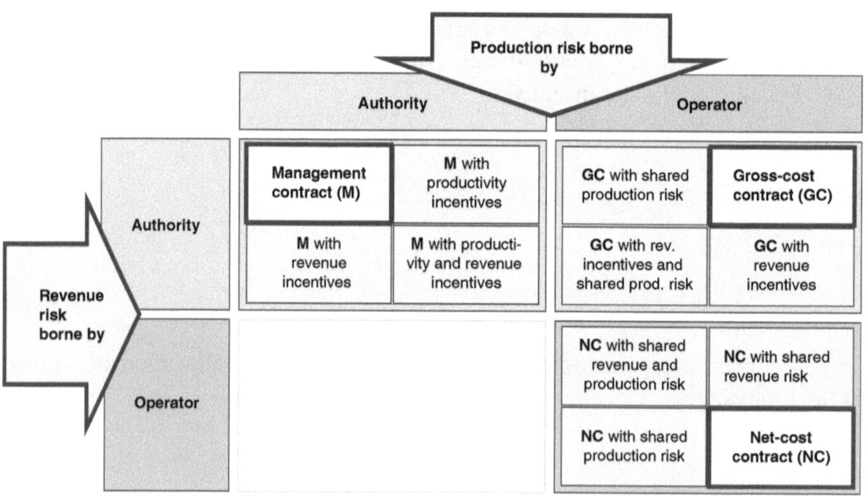

Fig. 7.2 Extended typology of contracts according to risk allocation (This figure was developed by Didier van de Velde (see van de Velde et al. 2008a, p. 61))

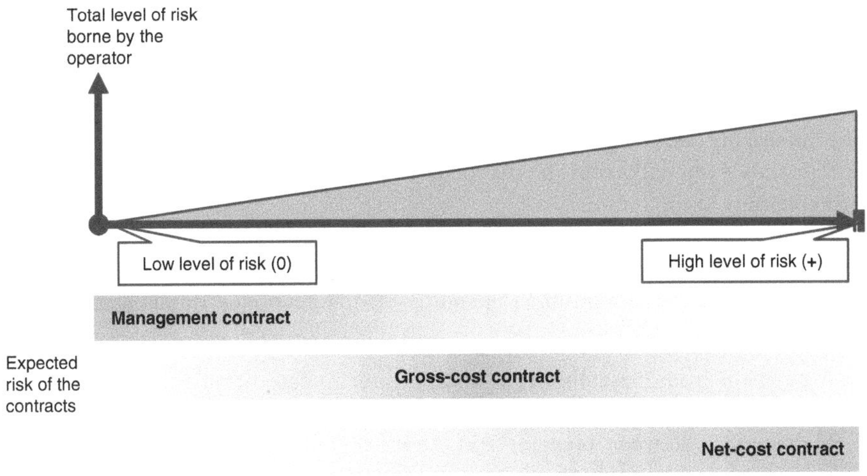

Fig. 7.3 Risk continuum

level of risk; net-cost contracts create a rather high level of risk and gross-cost contracts fall somewhere between. To date, only different types of gross-cost and net-cost contracts have been tendered in Germany. Management contracts are widely used in France (see Lyon as explained by van de Velde et al. 2008b, pp. 56–49).[5]

The risk allocation chosen leads to a specific contract payment between PTA and operator. In a management contract, the payment represents a management fee for the management of the network, in a net-cost contract the payment represents the balance between costs and revenues and in a gross-cost contract, the payment represents the expected production cost for the services contracted (always including a risk premium and the usual profit margin). By allocating only the production risk to the operator in a gross-cost contract, PTAs bear the revenue risk.

Van de Velde et al. (2008a, p. 62 and 2008b) give various examples for incentivized gross-cost contracts in Europe. For example, London uses 700 gross-cost contracts, one for each bus line. The contracts include additional production incentives or penalties based on a so-called "Quality Incentive Contract". Operators are able to earn +15% over the contract price in bonus payments. Penalty payments cannot exceed 10%. Stockholm uses gross-cost contracts for route bundles where quality incentives can be up to +/– 23% of the contract price based on monitoring punctuality and customer perception of service, a substantial incentive for operators to improve service quality.

Elmshorn in Germany and Halmstad in Sweden use gross-cost contracts with passenger incentives. These are actually mixed forms of gross-cost and net-cost contracts with shared additional fare box revenue. For example the operator in

[5] As management contracts are not used in Germany, we will not discuss them here.

Elmshorn receives 35 Euro cents per additional passenger based on an average calculation for the first year of operation.[6] In both Elmshorn and Halmstad the operator is also responsible for significant planning and development of the service. This is essential for the balance of the responsibility and incentives in the contract. The increasing use of gross-cost contracts with shared passenger incentives in Europe may eventually blur the distinction between gross-cost contracts and net-cost contracts in the future.

In contracts where the operator bears both types of risks, such as in net-cost contracts, the payment represents the expected balance of production costs minus revenues, plus a risk premium. Depending on the economic circumstances, this payment can either be:

- A payment from the authority to the operator in case of an expected need for public co-financing (similar to non-commercial services in Germany)
- No payment between operator and authority when revenues are expected to balance costs (similar to the threshold discussed in Sect. 4.6 and to commercial services in Germany)
- Payment or franchise fee from the operator to the authority when there is an expected surplus from service operation

An advantage of using net-cost contracts is the direct incentive for operators to invest in further quality improvements in order to increase both number of passengers and passenger revenues (and their profits).[7] But problems can arise if the operator's power to influence passenger figures in the short or long term is limited. For example, passenger demand can be influenced more significantly by the existence of a competing operator in the same area, or external factors, i.e. parking policy changes or car usage costs, than by the operator's service improvements. It is no surprise that many net-cost contracts tend to assign service design responsibility to the operators. An example of a tendered net-cost contract described by van de Velde et al. (2008a, p. 63 and 2008b, pp. 86–87) is the urban bus system in Sundsvall (Sweden). It is described in the following box.

Case study Sundsvall (Sweden): Pure net-cost contract

In Sundsvall they used a pure net-cost contract without additional passenger incentives. Nevertheless, if the level of increasing passenger figures per year drops below 2%, the operator must increase its marketing effort up to a maximum of 4% of subsidies. The service design for the first year is defined by the authority and can only be redefined by mutual agreement. For the remaining contract period, the operator is free to revise the service, but cannot

[6] See Sect. 4.4.2 for a more detailed explanation of this case.

[7] See e.g., Beck et al. (2007) confirming this aspect for regional rail passenger services in Germany.

reduce the seat km (kilometers offered to passengers) beyond the initial service level. The network design must always meet the specific accessibility criteria defined in a functional way by the authority in the contract: (1) 80% of the inhabitants must live within at least 400 m from a bus stop; (2) 90% of the inhabitants must live within at least 600 m from a bus stop; and (3) the network must be coordinated at defined locations.

The easiest way to avoid an incalculable risk to the operator and to reduce the risk premium to be paid by the authority might be a management contract without incentives, whereby the PTA bears both production and revenue risks. Nevertheless, it might be useful to select either a gross-cost contract or a net-cost contract to take full advantage of the optimizing efforts of the operator.

The use of financial incentives is only recommended if the operator has a sufficient level of influence on the realization of the chance (or risk). Furthermore, rationally acting operators will always weigh the balance between the costs of meeting certain requirements and the cost of any fine or penalty for poor performance, especially towards the end of the contractual period, since the operator will see little or no return from the effort necessary to meet the requirements (especially if the contract is not renewed). This is one reason why it is necessary for the PTA to set the appropriate level of possible penalties or rewards while bearing in mind the height of a risk premium.

Throughout Europe many contracts fall between gross-cost contracts and net-cost contracts. In general there are gross-cost contracts with very strong additional passenger incentives and net-cost contracts with shared distribution of additional fare box revenue, as indicated above, or commercial net-cost contracts. When revenue risk (net-cost contract) is used as the sole incentive, it might be sufficient only if there is a high enough level of revenue contributions to cover the additional production costs (e.g., due to additional quality provided to passengers). Furthermore, a high level of operational freedom of operators is necessary to enable them to acquire new passengers by adjusting the service.

Thus the PTA's task is to calibrate incentives to generate the desired behavior of the operator and avoid misleading incentives; however, the task can be difficult for PTAs which lack experience.

7.3.3 Risk Sharing

Absent the general classification of different contract types according to risk types, various ways to arrange the allocation of risks per risk type between contracting parties include:

- Full allocation of the complete risk (e.g., the revenue risk) to one of the contracting parties: the full divergence between the expected amount of costs and/or revenues and the realized amount is borne by the operator or the authority
- Shared allocation of risk: a specific percentage of risk (e.g. 50%) allocated to each party
- Shared allocation of risk with thresholds: Similar to shared allocation, except that the agreed sharing varies with the size of the divergence; usual examples are:
  - Cap regulation (e.g., 100% of increase to be borne by operator up to a maximum penalty of €1 m, higher penalties will experience a 50/50 sharing between operator and PTA)
  - Minimum threshold (sharing of risk only when the increase/decrease of a specific parameter exceeds a threshold of e.g. +/– 20%)

In the case of net-cost contracts, there are actually two aspects of risk sharing. Here sharing may be based upon an allocation of both cost and revenue risks in a single unit based upon the expected operational deficit (expected total costs of production minus expected passenger revenues). Alternatively, it may be based upon an allocation based upon two risk units, one related to cost and the other to revenue. This distinction is important when different thresholds are defined for risk sharing for both components.

An example is the delegated management contract awarded by Santiago de Compostella in Spain (see van de Velde et al. 2008a, p. 64 and 2008b, pp. 78–80). Here the authority has awarded a delegated management contract based on a quality tendering. This contract is an intermediate contract between gross-cost contract and net-cost contract, where the authority and the operator share the extra fare box revenue (50/50) and publicity revenue (70/30) for 10 years with the possibility of extension if the operator meets specific requirements for improving demand (passenger-km) and quality. Different to this, e.g., Winnes (2007) shows an example for the PTA Verkehrsverbund Rhein-Neckar GmbH (VRN), which obliges the operator to assume the full risks of revenues *and* costs, including risk for external factors.

7.4 Revenue Risk and Winner's Curse: A Cause for Debate in Germany

Whether or not operators should bear the revenue risk for the service in question has been a subject of major discussions in Germany. Although tendering, in other words, buying services in an auction, has become more common in recent years, numerous occurrences of winner's curse have been reported by Beck (2006) in bidding for items of uncertain (common) value, for the public transport industry. These have occurred due to overestimated revenues, but also due to underestimated costs. Such an occurrence then results in below-normal or even negative average profits for the winning bidder due to bidder's failure to account for the adverse selection problem inherent in bidding on alternatives of uncertain value.

A prominent example for net-cost contracts in Germany was reported for the rail firm FLEX AG, which operated the Hamburg-Flensburg(-Padborg) rail network in 2002/2003. It went bankrupt after several months of losses during summer 2003 due to the occurrence of a winner's curse with respect to revenues (see Wewers 2004).

Due to its importance for the analysis of risk factors and the influence of uncertainty on market results, we will discuss this matter in greater detail in the following two sections. First, we provide a brief overview of common value auctions and the winner's curse. Based on these explanations the second section will analyze the surrounding conditions as observable for net-cost contracts in Germany.

7.4.1 Common Value Auctions and Winner's Curse

When there is uncertain value of an object at the time of the auction, bidders only have an estimate or some privately known signal to correlate with the true value. This signal may be an expert's estimate or the bidder's own calculation. Nevertheless, the object's real value is the same for all bidders, but unknown at the time of bidding. This is called a common value or mineral-rights auction (see Wolfstetter 1999, p. 225 and Krishna 2002, p. 4). Outer Continental Shelf oil-lease auctions and UMTS auctions are typically modeled as pure common-value auctions.[8]

Suppose that all bidders are risk neutral and each maximizes the expectation of the true value of the object. While the ex post value is common to all, it is unknown to any particular bidder ex ante. Assume that the object is sold using a sealed-bid first-price auction (like it is usual for tendering procedures) and that all bidders are symmetric and follow the same strategy. If, for example, bidder 1 in fact is the winner, this reveals that the highest of the expectations of the true value of any other bidder (bidder 2, bidder 3...) is less than his own expectation. As pointed out by Krishna (2002, p. 85), this announcement immediately leads to a decrease in his own estimated value.

A bidder failing to fully account for this and bidding an amount which is close to his own (first) estimation, would presumably, upon winning, pay more than the object's estimated worth. The result is negative profits, because the estimate is an overestimate conditional on the event of winning (see Kagel and Levin 2002, p. 2). The lesson is that bidders may need to "shade" their bids well below their initial estimates to avoid the winner's curse and to address uncertainty as described by Davis and Holt (1993, p. 288).

Taking these considerations into account, theory predicts raising revenue for the seller (or decreasing need for supplementary direct subsidies for the PTA) by increasing the amount of public information. Hence, providing more information

[8] Capen et al. (1971) were among the first to identify the winner's curse for oil-lease auctions.

on the item being tendered by the PTA should reduce uncertainty due to a reduction of the interval of private estimations, reduce the risk of the occurrence of a winner's curse and improve the auction's results for the PTA.

7.4.2 Revenue Risk: A Relevant Issue of Winner's Curse in Germany

From the bidders' perspective, the revenue potential of a particular route is determined by the demand potential and the fare. Since the fare structure, including the type of ticket, is directly or indirectly stipulated or at least influenced to a large extent by the transport associations and/or tariff networks (*Verkehrsverbünde*), the cases examined in Chaps. 8 and 9 below assume that the operator usually cannot influence the fare structure directly. Consequently, the fare revenue potential is affected to a large extent by external factors that the operator is unable to affect, such as demand potential, which is mainly influenced by population density, quality of alternative means of transport, profitability of fares,[9] and the like.

In addition, Germany's established procedures of revenue-sharing in transport associations and/or tariff networks are often confusing and opaque for new companies (as are the conditions for entering the Verkehrsverbünde). Generally, only the incumbent obtains detailed information, which gives him an information-based competitive edge (see Schmidt et al. 2004 and Stammler and Pulkkinen 2008). Limiting the extent and quality of information it provides to the PTA allows the incumbent to discriminate against its competitors, because the PTA usually provides this information to newcomers with the tendering documents. Further potential for discrimination arises with the distribution of tickets (selling fee by seller, point in time of liquidity settlement, etc.), which is e.g. a common practice of DB for rail services and which also affects fare revenues (see Eisenkopf and Grotemeier 2009).

The fare revenue potential can thus be compared approximately to the common value approach in auction theory explained above. If a bidder is subjected to revenue risk he is faced with what is known as the winner's curse in public transport, meaning that winning the call for tenders is bad news because it is highly likely that the winner has miscalculated the expected fare revenue.

Newcomers tend to form their expectations about fare revenue potential primarily on the basis of the information made available by the PTA in the tendering phase. Thus, as already depicted above, the more information about demand potential made available (in other words, the smaller the interval of private estimations on the demand potential), the lower the uncertainty about the (expected) fare revenue potential, and the lower the risk premium needed in the

[9] Note that the profitability of fares is determined by multiplying the types of ticket selected by passengers by the number of users of each type of ticket.

event of a tender assigning the revenue risk to the operator. The incumbent operator's information advantage concerning the demand potential and the profitability of fares should be viewed critically, since it can lead to a bias of the bidders' initial conditions. In general, bidders assess the information provided by the PTA as more reliable, and ideally, the PTA has furnished prospective bidders with a comprehensive report on demand potential as part of the tendering documents.

Nevertheless, net-cost contracts tend to provide better incentives than gross-cost contracts. Here the operator's revenue is at least partly connected to the quality of its performance in the passenger market.

7.5 Conclusions

The cases above concern pure expenses and revenues related to the production and sales of passenger transport services. Divergence between expectations and realizations of the totals represent risks. Different contracts allocate these risks in different ways. Allocation creates incentives for the parties bearing the risks. This may ensure a more favorable value, e.g., by lowering costs and increasing revenues while respecting the contractual requirements pertaining to service definition and quality. The PTA must decide how to allocate the risks appropriately.

Again, risk can have a negative effect on the contractual outcome, especially when using competitive awarding:

- The higher the risk, the higher the risk premium the operator will calculate (increasing the subsidy to be paid by the PTA)
- A very high level of risk may result in a greater danger of insolvency for operators in case of a full realization of the risk
- The higher the risk, the lower the number of bidders (high entry barriers)

Schematically, risk can be classified into three types:

Three classifications of risk

- *Low risk*: Predictable for operators and/or not critical for operators in case of realization; operators will calculate a low risk premium
- *High risk*: High uncertainty and/or critical for operators in case of realization; operators will calculate a high risk premium
- *Unbearable risk*: Unpredictable and critical for operators in case of realization; risk not bearable for operators (market entry barrier, operators will not submit a bid)

On the other hand, the PTA should include incentives to encourage the operator to perform well and to take full advantage of the operator's potential to optimize. Gross-cost contracts (where the production risk is borne by the operator), for example will encourage the operator to optimize the operation as far as possible within the framework of the existing contract because this directly increases profits.

PTAs must be aware of the trade-off between the positive effect of incentives and the negative effect of risks in these incentives. In principle, the question is: When will the operator calculate a risk premium lower than the positive effects from using incentives? The question is difficult to answer with inadequate data, and hence I focus in the following sections on the risk effects that are currently measureable: level of competition measured by the number of bidders per procedure, and in the case of tendering of non-commercial services, the price to be paid by the PTA.

Chapter 8
Experiences with Competitive Tendering of Bus Services

8.1 Introduction

After a long transition period with only a few isolated cases of competitive tendering for public bus transport services in Germany, numerous such procedures have taken place in recent years. The question arises whether the introduction of competitive tendering has produced the desired effects from the PTAs' perspective and what impacts can be observed for other market participants.

The main aims of tendering procedures from a PTA's view are a decreased level of subsidies and an increased level of quality provided to passengers. Other objectives of PTAs in Germany are to sustain a sufficient market share of small- and medium-sized enterprises (SMEs) and to secure sufficient social standards for employees, both for political reasons, a.o. due to the high influence of SME pressure groups and unions. From an economic view, a high degree of competition and low entry barriers are necessary to achieve a sufficient level of quality by operators and reduce the subsidies paid by PTAs. The essay presented in this Chap. 8[1] therefore assesses whether PTAs have been able to fulfill these somewhat contradictory goals when introducing competition and whether they have simultaneously succeeded in limiting the negative impact on market participants. My objective is to determine whether the results in Germany are in line with results in other parts of the world presented by a variety of papers (e.g., Hensher and Wallis 2005).

Another aspect to remember is the low share of tendering procedures in Germany. Although PTAs are able to monitor contract compliance in non-commercial services more effectively via the direct contractual relationship than is possible with commercial services (see Sect. 4.4.1), it is rare that services are classified as non-commercial and tendered out (see Sect. 4.3.4). Therefore it is necessary to

[1] This Chap. 8 is fully based on an analysis completed in 2009, see Beck (2009e, g and the journal arcticle Beck 2011c).

A. Beck, *Competition for Public Transport Services*, Contributions to Economics,
DOI 10.1007/978-3-7908-2802-3_8, © Springer-Verlag Berlin Heidelberg 2012

analyze whether German PTAs experience negative results from competitive tendering procedures, which could explain their limited use.

Due to data constraints and a lack of economic research on this subject, analyzing the competitive market for non-commercial public transport services by bus in Germany is a difficult task. Internationally, and following the liberalization trends in the late 1980s, several articles have analyzed competition for public bus transport services beginning in the 1990s. The first researchers studied the level of competition in Britain, New Zealand and Scandinavia where competition was introduced at a very early stage, stating the factors influencing competition and the processes' results. For example, White and Tough (1995) compare the results of tendering gross-cost versus net-cost contracts in Britain and provide evidence that net-cost contracts lead to a significantly lower number of bidders and higher prices "as the risks are clearly greater" (White and Tough 1995, p. 282). Unfortunately, their database consisted only of non-commercial services tendered by authorities outside the London area. Alexandersson et al. (1998) show first effects for Sweden with respect to patronage, providing evidence that the decline of demand experienced in the early years is not a result of introducing tendering or of deregulation. They conclude that it probably relates to the deep recession at that time and the increase in fares due to the introduction of a value added tax on public transport tickets.

Tendering models for (non-commercial) bus services have been analyzed in numerous international articles. Alexandersson and Pyddoke (2003) evaluate the results of 15 years of competitive tendering in Sweden, indicating a long period of decreasing costs and a substantial change in operators' structure which benefited the PTAs. Hensher and Wallis (2005) present a meta-analysis of international studies on competitive tendering, a.o. showing a significant price reduction in the first tendering round, but also some price increases thereafter.

The influencing factors for the London bus tendering model have also been examined. Amaral et al. (2006) confirm that the price decreases as the number of bidders increases. Cantillon and Pesendorfer (2007) identify problems with price discrimination and strategic pricing by bidders in the multi-unit auctions conducted in London. Amaral et al. (2008) give an analysis on collusion for the London bus tendering model as well as for the French model. Their analysis is based on the unsuccessful French model, where the three main operators had to pay a penalty of more than €12 million for collusive strategies in 2005. The paper provides evidence that transparency, the discretionary power of public bodies and the level of competition are key factors to prevent collusion and corruption. They show that the London model was able to realize better performance indicators than the French model due to a tendering strategy that sufficiently recognizes the three key factors.

Mathisen and Solvoll (2008) focus on the development of the market structure when competition was introduced in Norway, confirming a negative correlation between the number of operators per region and the introduction of competitive tendering. Furthermore, they show that the number of private and local public companies decreases while the number of foreign private and non-local public companies increases. A recent evaluation of the results of introducing tendering in Israel by Sharaby and Shiftan (2008) confirms increasing quality levels and decreasing prices.

German studies on competitive tendering for public transport services by bus are rare. While the issue of the German rail franchise has received increased attention (e.g., Beck 2009a; Lalive and Schmutzler 2008a, b, and Peter 2008), only a limited number of quantitative economic papers on competitive tendering for bus services have been published. In particular, there is no comprehensive survey of the results of competitive tendering in Germany for the period between the 1996 market reform and 2008. Examining the results of different studies and verifying the results against my own database, the present Chap. 8 tries to fill this gap and provides an overview of the state of the art regarding competitive tendering of bus services in Germany and related experiences.

Germany's development of competitive tendering has been influenced significantly by the market reform of the mid-1990s and a specific regulatory framework. Based on the results presented in Part II and Chap. 7, Sect. 8.2 illustrates central market developments in the main regions where tendering has taken place so far. The investigation of the results of competitive tendering is divided into a survey of previous studies and a current study based on an empirical analysis of my own database. Section 8.3 presents the main characteristics of these sources of information. The results of the investigation are discussed in Sect. 8.4. Section 8.5 provides an overview of the key findings and conclusions. To ease understanding there is some overlap between this section and Part II. Moreover, the List of Abbreviations, the Glossary, and the List of the Acts of Law are intended to ease comprehension of specific terms for readers not familiar with the framework of German public transport by bus.

8.2 Market Development and Background

By the end of 2009 only four regions had experienced a high number of tendering procedures for public transport services by bus: the state of Hesse, where the largest volume has been put out to tender, the Mannheim area, the Hamburg area and the Munich area. In most cases, only rural or suburban services were affected by tendering using gross-cost contracts.

In the wider Bielefeld area (state of North-Rhine Westphalia) several individual tendering procedures were initiated, although numerous procedures had to be terminated before selecting the winning bidder due to competing market initiatives for commercial services. Other individual cases of tendering were identified in other regions, but no other clusters of cases. Based on the overview in Fig. 8.1, the following sections explain the major characteristics of the awarding policies in the main areas until 2009 and describe how competition was introduced.

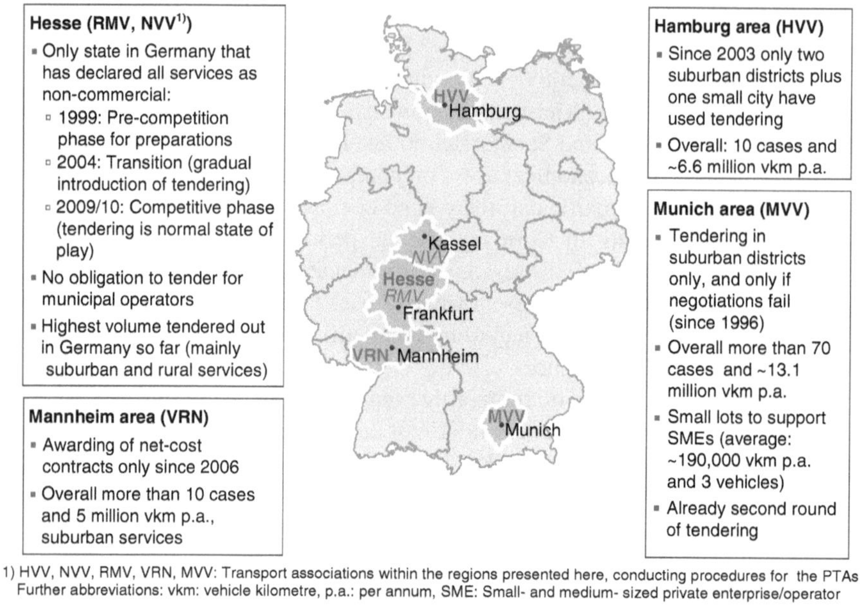

Fig. 8.1 Main regions of competitive tendering in Germany

8.2.1 State of Hesse

As explained in Sect. 5.4.1, the federal state Hesse established a system of PTAs in the mid-1990s.[2] Two main *regional* public transport authorities were founded: the Rhein-Main-Verkehrsverbund GmbH (RMV) (greater Frankfurt on the Main area) and the Nordhessischer VerkehrsVerbund[3] (NVV) (greater Kassel area).[4] Responsibility for *local* public transport services is assigned to local PTAs at the city or rural district level. The most important of these is the Lokale Nahverkehrsgesellschaft Frankfurt am Main mbH traffiQ (traffiQ), which is responsible for local public transport services in the city of Frankfurt. Hesse was the first and only federal state to make a clear decision to tender all public transport services. After debates on this topic began in 1999, Hesse's ministry of transport and the PTAs drew up an agreement in 2002 on how to introduce competition.[5] The aim was to use

[2] There is considerable overlap between this Section and Sect. 5.4.1. Readers familiar with the latter may skip this Sect. 8.2.1.

[3] Nordhessischer VerkehrsVerbund – Verkehrsverbund und Fördergesellschaft Nordhessen mbH (NVV).

[4] Additionally the Hessian rural district of Kreis Bergstraße is part of the Verkehrsverbund Rhein-Neckar GmbH (VRN).

[5] This agreement is entitled "Eckpunkte für den Wettbewerb"; see HMWVL (2002) for more details.

competitive instruments to make public transport more efficient and to provide higher quality for lower subsidies. When introducing competition, specific support was seen as particularly important to secure the structure of SMEs. The state called on PTAs to develop concepts about introducing competition at their supervisory level and foresaw three stages for developing these concepts[6]:

- *Pre-competition phase:* Tasks for PTAs: no tendering, development of tenderable networks suitable for SMEs, definition of quality standards, preparation for competitive awarding to begin by December 2004, (re-)negotiation of directly awarded contracts to avoid these contracts preventing the introduction of competition and to secure quality standards
- *Transition phase:* Tasks for PTAs up to 2009–2010: tendering all public transport services divided into almost equally allocated volumes per year with an even geographical distribution (the RMV first initiated tendering in 2002)
- *Competitive phase:* Starting in 2009–2010: awarding public transport services only via tendering

In 2004 the federal government of Hesse finally passed a resolution to tender all services to avoid legal uncertainty.[7] The decree defined all routes as non-commercial, resulting in the necessity to tender these services instead of using competition for commercial lines or services. Thus, Hesse's ministry of transport attempted to foster the successful implementation of tendering by providing detailed instructions to the PTAs.

Lively discussion on the pros and cons of this bold step towards competition continued, both in Hesse and throughout Germany.[8] Based on further experiences with tendering and initiated by court decisions, e.g., the 2006 decision by the German Federal Administrative Court, Hesse's ministry of transport then changed several details of its awarding policy. None of these amendments altered the obligation to tender all public bus services where the PTA is not the owner of the (municipal) operator, and consequently all such services were expected to be tendered by the end of 2010. Direct awarding which is now used in numerous urban areas is still possible for municipal operators. However, Frankfurt am Main decided to tender its public bus services, the only major German city to do so.[9] In Hesse, usually first-price auctions in gross-cost contracts similar to the Scandinavian model are used in tendering procedures.

---

[6] The steps are described for regional bus services. Urban public transport services were allowed to follow later and are not described here.

[7] This resolution is the so-called Güttler Erlass I; see HMWVL (2004) for more details.

[8] See Rausch (2004).

[9] For a more detailed explanation of tendered route bundle contracts in Frankfurt am Main, see van de Velde et al. (2008b, pp. 25–26) and Rehn and Valussi (2005).

8.2.2 Mannheim Area

In the Mannheim area, the Verkehrsverbund Rhein-Neckar GmbH (VRN) is the public transport association that carries out the majority of awarding procedures for public transport bus services. Unlike other regions, the VRN has conducted several tendering procedures in its area of responsibility in a total of three different states: Hesse (the rural district of Kreis Bergstraße only), Baden-Württemberg and Rhineland-Palatine.[10]

Unlike the tendering procedures in the Munich area, the Hamburg area, and in Hesse, which are generally characterized by services classified as non-commercial by PTAs and by the use of gross-cost contracts, the VRN selected a different measure. Services are normally classified as commercial. Consequently competitive procedures for commercial lines or services have to be carried out. Only if revenues generated from fares (including compensatory payments for fare reductions) are not sufficient to cover operating costs are they classified as non-commercial. In this case, the VRN initiates a competitive tendering for net-cost contracts. Operators therefore have to bear the revenue risk here at all times. This system is similar to the theoretical approach described in Sect. 4.5.2.

8.2.3 Hamburg Area

Only a few of the PTAs in the greater metropolitan area of Hamburg in the state of Schleswig-Holstein decided to tender: the suburban districts of Stormarn and Herzogtum Lauenburg and the city of Elmshorn.[11] All tendering procedures were carried out by the Hamburger Verkehrsverbund GmbH (HVV).

The first call for tenders was published in 2003. Although preparing for competition is seen as a central obligation of all operators (see HVV 2005), only 10 procedures with a total of 6.4 million vehicle kilometers per annum has been put out to tender in that region to date. Like the MVV, the HVV supports PTAs in negotiating direct awarding and in conducting tendering procedures (see HVV 2007).

8.2.4 Munich Area

As explained in Sect. 5.3.2, some of the first German regions to use tendering after market reform in the mid 1990s were the suburban districts of Munich in the state of

[10] See http://www.vrn.de/ueberuns/vergabestelle retrieved August 20, 2009 and Winnes (2007).

[11] See Sect. 4.4.2 and Sect. 5.3.2 for a more detailed explanation of the Hamburg area.

Bavaria.[12] The first call for tenders was published in 1996[13] and the procedure was carried out by the Münchner Verkehrs- und Tarifverbund GmbH (MVV); the MVV has since conducted all tendering procedures for the PTAs.

The suburban districts, acting as competent PTAs, attempt to foster competition in their areas in moderation.[14] The aim is to secure opportunities for SMEs. Tendering is therefore used only when prior negotiations with the existing operators on those routes have yielded insufficient results.[15] Newly established routes can be tendered at any time. The division of the tendered volume into relatively small lots underscores the aim of supporting SMEs.

Market access has changed since this awarding policy was introduced in 1999. Prior to revision of the awarding policy, agreements on direct subsidies between operator and the PTA were automatically extended. Now, at a minimum, the extension of the gross-cost contracts must be negotiated. In most cases, the negotiating parties achieve satisfactory results. Previously, tendering was used for a limited volume of services. The realistic opportunity to tender services if negotiated results are not satisfactory may have strengthened the bargaining position of PTAs, and enabled satisfactory bargaining results. The Munich area so far is the only one in Germany in which a second tendering round occurs in numerous cases after the end of the first contract term.

8.3 Description of Database

The analysis of the effects of competitive tendering on public transport services by bus in Germany consists of two parts. First, a survey of previous quantitative studies summarizes the results of competitive tendering. Second, an analysis of what I term database I[16] of tendering procedures is presented, with a particular focus on entry barriers. The characteristics of data sources are described in the following two sections.

---

[12] There is considerable overlap between this Section and Sect. 5.3.2. Readers familiar with the latter may skip this section.

[13] On September 19, 1996, the first call for tenders was published in the *Official Journal of the European Community* for route 838 from Fürstenfeldbruck to Dachau, which began operating in January 1997. A more detailed case study on tendering in the Munich area appears in Schenck et al. (2003) and in van de Velde et al. (2008b, pp. 62–64).

[14] See Landkreise im MVV (1999).

[15] See Arbeitsgruppe Verkehrsverträge und Qualitätsmanagement (2002).

[16] Chapter 9 gives the results of a different database II, also consisting of tendering procedures.

8.3.1 Characteristics of Previous Studies

Quantitative studies on the results of competitive tendering in German public transport services by bus are rare. Up to July 2010, only the results of Beck et al. (2006),[17] BSL (2008), Augustin and Walter (2009), and Conpronet (2009) have become public.[18] Table 8.1 shows that the focus is on Hesse because most of the services put out to competitive tendering so far are located in this federal state.

The study by Beck et al. (2006) shows that within the Munich area a remarkable number of 54 lots has been tendered since 1996. The database consists mainly of gross-cost contracts, with a contract term of 6–8 years. The validation of bids submitted is conducted mainly according to the price.

The average volume of the procedures analyzed by Beck et al. (2006) is 361,728 vehicle kilometers per annum (vkm p.a.), while the databases compiled by BSL (2008) and Augustin and Walter (2009) show higher volumes on average. Within the database of Beck et al. (2006), the average volumes per area show a large spread between the area of the Münchner Verkehrs- und Tarifverbund GmbH – MVV (153,703 vkm p.a.) and the area of the Rhein-Main-Verkehrsverbund GmbH – RMV (795,652 vkm p.a.), as well as the area of the Hamburger Verkehrsverbund GmbH – HVV (675,000 vkm p.a.). Most services tendered are rural and suburban services; where the national railway operator Deutsche Bahn AG (DB) is the main operator. It is the main incumbent in all studies via its regional acting subsidiaries within the DB Bahn Stadtverkehr enterprise.

8.3.2 Characteristics of Database I

Database I was composed in 2008 for the analysis in this Chap. 8 and contains n = 113 lots tendered in 2003–2008, mostly services in rural or suburban areas. Although responsible PTAs are obliged to release a minimum amount of information to bidders (see § 17 VOL/A), complete data for tendering procedures, results and official statistical data are not available. Hence, the number of variables with sufficient data is limited.

Database I was developed from publications by PTAs in the *Official Journal of the European Union*, complemented by information from reliable publications using (1) well-known information systems specialized in public transport in Germany (Newstix, convia, and the Gesellschaft zur Information des Verkehrsgewerbes); (2) expert interviews with market participants involved in the respective

[17] This study was published as three separate articles: Beck and Wanner (2007), Wanner and Zietz (2008) and Beck and Wanner (2008). These publications are the basis of this analysis. The full version of the study, conducted by Beck et al. in 2006, remains unpublished.

[18] Note that of the four studies mentioned only the Beck et al. study is based on full data access provided by PTAs.

Table 8.1 Overview of main characteristics of databases used in previous studies

Studies	Location of observations	Observations	Main statistics	Relevant characteristics	Prior operators (figures in% of total vkm p.a.)
Beck et al. (2006)	Bavaria (Munich area only, conducted by MVV) (~67% of all observations, ~28% of sum of vkm), Hesse (Frankfurt am Main area only, conducted by RMV) (28%, 63%), Schleswig-Holstein (Hamburg area only, conducted by HVV) (5%, 9%)	81 tendered lots, results of questionnaire of n = 30 operators and further general data from HVV, MVV and RMV (e.g., from RMV vehicle database)	Observations for period 1997 to 2006, average volume per lot: ~7.3 vehicles and 361,728 vkm p.a., contract duration: 6 to 8 years on average	Rural and suburban services, gross-cost contracts only, validation: mainly according to price	Mainly DB (79%), some municipal (4%), some SMEs (12%, mainly services already won in first tendering, now tendered a second time) and newly established services (5%). Real SME market share including services operated as subcontracts (mainly for DB): ~40%
BSL (2008)	Hesse (Frankfurt am Main area only, procedures conducted by RMV and local PTAs)	60 tendered lots, results of questionnaire of n = 15 operators and further general data from BSL databases	Observations for period 2002 to 2007, average volume per lot: ~680,000 to ~760,000 vkm p.a., contract duration normally ~8 years	Rural, suburban, and some urban services, primarily gross-cost contracts, validation: mainly according to price	Mainly DB (63%), several municipal (27%), SMEs (4%) and global players (6%), adjusted for services based on subcontracts. The "real" market shares are: DB 38%, municipal: 20%, SMEs: 39% and global players: 3%

(continued)

Table 8.1 (continued)

Studies	Location of observations	Observations	Main statistics	Relevant characteristics	Prior operators (figures in% of total vkm p.a.)
Augustin and Walter (2009)	Baden-Württemberg (~2% of all observations where data was raised), Bavaria (29%), Hesse (61%), North-Rhine Westphalia (1%), Rhineland-Palatine (1%), Schleswig-Holstein (6%)	Sample includes 196 line bundles (lots)	Observations for period 1997 to 2009, average volume: ~11 vehicles per lot, ~472,959 vkm p.a., mean contract duration ~6 years	Rural, suburban, and some urban services, primarily gross-cost contracts (over 90%)	Mainly DB (51%), some municipal (26%) and private operators (23%, note that this analysis doesn't foresee a distinction between SMEs and global players)
Conpronet (2009)	Only Hesse (full area)	Sample includes 157 line bundles (lots)	Observations for period 2003 to 2008, average volume per lot: 573,885 vkm p.a	Rural, suburban and some urban services, primarily gross-cost contracts	Mainly DB (43%), several municipal (32%), SMEs (21%) and global players (4%)

cases,[19] and (3) the database of awarding procedures of the Consultancy BSL Management Consultants.[20]

Database I only includes tendering procedures for regular non-commercial line operations conducted by PTAs with reliable and sufficient data and therefore does not contain all tendering procedures that took place in Germany during the study period. Subcontracts and exclusive school transport services are not included. Nevertheless, the tendering procedures studied show a high level of representativeness for all competitive tendering procedures in Germany as data of all main PTAs conducting tendering in Germany are picked up into the database. Moreover, the characteristics presented below resemble the other quantitative studies above. Prior to entry into database I, reliability was validated, usually by double-checking against other sources, and incomplete or questionable information was identified and checked against other published information and/or additional results from expert interviews. With this methodology, only publicly announced and/or confirmed tendering procedures were included in database I.

The level of competition is measured by the dependent variable *number of bidders* per tendered lot.[21] Table 8.2 shows that the average level of competition is 6 bidders. The number of bidders per tender ranges from 1 to 19, with a standard deviation of 3.02. The wide distribution may indicate that some tendering conditions prevent individual inquirers from submitting bids and raises the issue of the existence of market entry barriers.

Several factors might influence the level of competition in a specific tender procedure. The table shows the influencing factors (independent variables) for which sufficient data with respect to the quality (especially number of observations and reliability) are available and which, according to experts, are expected to have a major influence on the level of competition. These variables are: (1) the volume of the tendered lot (measured by *vehicle kilometers per annum per tendered lot [vkm p.a.]* and *number of lines per tendered lot*[22]), (2) place in time (measured by *start of operations [year]*), (3) classification of the incumbent (measured by different dummy variables for *incumbent type*), (4) distribution of revenue risk among the contracting parties (measured by the dummy variable *type of contract*) and (5) location of the services tendered out (measured by different dummy variables for *state*). Data for price escalation clauses and other factors identified as possible sources of risk in Sect. 7.3 are not available.

[19] Interviews were arranged with responsible leaders and/or executive officers in charge of conducting tendering pocedures. The sample of individuals contains representatives of the major PTAs that have conducted numerous tendering procedures, including the HVV, the MVV, the NVV, the RMV, the traffiQ and the VRN, as well as operators and consultants.

[20] Special thanks to all individuals and institutions that provided data for this study.

[21] Note that in Germany one tender is usually divided into two or more lots to support SMEs. Operators are then able to bid for one or more lots (or batches).

[22] The number of lines tendered per batch also serves as a measure of complexity.

Table 8.2 Criteria on data included and descriptive statistics for database I

	Observations	%	Mean	Maximum	Minimum	Standard deviation
Number of bidders	113		6.23	19	1	3.02
	102		*6.26*	*19*	*1*	*3.05*
Vehicle kilometers	113		594,440	3,300,000	21,800	544,898
p.a.	*102*		*547,017*	*1,839,275*	*21,800*	*445,470*
Number of lines	24		4.42	17	1	3.89
Start of operations (date)	81			14/12/2008	29/06/2003	
Start of operations	113			2008	2003	113
(year)	*102*			*2008*	*2003*	*102*
Incumbent	63	100.00				
	63	*100.00*				
Municipal	9	14.29				
	9	*14.29*				
Private SME	16	25.40				
	16	*25.40*				
Subsidiary of DB	38	60.31				
	38	*60.31*				
Global player	0	0.00				
	0	*0.00*				
Type of contract	102	100.00				
	102	*100.00*				
Gross-cost	91	89.22				
contract	*91*	*89.22*				
Net-cost contract	11	10.78				
	11	*10.78*				
State	113	100.00				
	102	*100.00*				
Baden-	4	3.55				
Württemberg	*4*	*3.92*				
Bavaria	33	29.20				
	33	*32.35*				
Hesse	63	55.75				
	52	*50.98*				
Rhineland-	3	2.65				
Palatine	*3*	*2.94*				
Schleswig-	10	8.85				
Holstein	*10*	*9.80*				

Figures in italics are generated from a condensed dataset for which regressions were conducted

For a quantitative analysis, a numerical database is necessary. Therefore, all qualitative information collected is classified and operationalized according to a catalog of definitions (for variables where analysis seemed appropriate). A full list explaining each variable appears in Table A.1 in the Appendix Sect. A.1. The descriptive analysis in Table 8.2 above shows that the average volume of vehicle kilometers per annum per tendered lot is 594,440. Assuming 50,000 vkm p.a. per vehicle on average as a typical volume according to experts, this is roughly 12 vehicles per lot. Most of the tendered lots are located in Hesse (56%), followed by Bavaria (29%) and Schleswig-Holstein (9%). 89% of all observations are gross-cost contracts. In most cases (60%), the incumbent is a subsidiary of the incumbent DB.

Note that the empirical analysis is based on condensed data with 102 observations, as complete data were available for most of the variables here (*number of bidders, vehicle kilometers, start of operations [year], and state*).[23] For reasons of comparison, the condensed data appear in italics below for every relevant entry.

8.4 Results and Discussion

The investigation of the results of competitive tendering from the previous studies cited above shows that the following issues were analyzed in detail (see Table 8.3):

- Impacts on unit costs and quality
- Effects on operators, especially with respect to the development of company structures within a liberalized environment
- Level of competition and possible entry barriers

The study of Beck et al. (2006) presents additional results on transaction costs and impacts on operators' employees. In the following, the results from the different previous studies are presented, analyzed and compared to further publications. Some of the results are re-investigated by the current database. Given the limited data available, this verification will focus mainly on the level of competition and possible entry barriers.

8.4.1 Impacts of Tendering on Unit Costs and Quality

The main effects of competitive tendering from a passenger point of view are the impacts on the level of quality. According to Beck et al. (2006), an analysis of the RMV vehicle database shows that this PTA was able to reduce the average age of buses in tendered services from 7.8 years in 2001 (before tendering took place) to 4.4 years by the end of 2005. Services still not tendered show an average age of 7.8 years at the end of 2005. BSL (2008, p. 14) shows that the RMV increased

[23] The dataset is condensed with respect to the low number of observations for the other variables and the correlations shown in Table A.2 in the Appendix Sect. A.1.1.

Table 8.3 Summary of the impacts of competitive tendering

Studies	Impacts on unit cost (€ per vkm paid by PTAs) at average	Impact on company structure (figures in percentage of total vkm p.a. tendered out)	Level of competition	Factors influencing the level of competition
Beck et al. (2006)	Hesse: –31% reduction, Bavaria: –15% reduction, Schleswig-Holstein: no data. Taking inflation into account, prices per vkm for PTAs were stable for observation period of ~10 years, average unit costs (price basis: 2005): €1.84 per vkm	Increase of market share of SMEs to 60%, market share of global players and DB: 21%, municipal operators: 19%, positive impact on probability to win for SMEs by using bidding associations	7 bidders on average, varying between 1 and 14 bidders per tendered lot	No reduction in bidders over time, no entry barriers identified at a significant level, operators are developing instruments to minimize costs for market exit
BSL (2008)	"Clear reduction in unit costs" (no figures), with an increase in costs per unit in recent years	Market share of SMEs varying between 36% (services tendered out by RMV) and 27% (services tendered out by local PTAs), decreasing in recent years due to take-over's of SMEs by global players and a sharp increase in share of success of global players and DB to up to two-thirds in 2007, declining market share of municipal operators	6 bidders on average (no results on variation published)	No entry barriers identified, but reduction of average number of bidders over time down to 5 observed for 2007
Augustin and Walter (2009)	No information	Sharp reduction in market share of DB by –41% down to 30%, reduction of share of municipal operators by –31% down to 18% and sharp increase in	5.1 bidders on average, varying between 1 and 14 bidders per tendered lot	Reduction from 6.4 bidders on average in 2005 to 3.5 bidders in 2008, correlation for probability of operator change at a significant level identified

(continued)

Table 8.3 (continued)

Studies	Impacts on unit cost (€ per vkm paid by PTAs) at average	Impact on company structure (figures in percentage of total vkm p.a. tendered out)	Level of competition	Factors influencing the level of competition
		market share of private operators (no distinction between SMEs and global players) by +126% up to 52%		for number of bidders (positive coefficient), several structural coefficients significant: contract term in years (positive c.), number of vehicles per lot (positive c.), number of lines per lot (negative c.), start of operations (year) (negative c.)
Conpronet (2009)	"Clear reduction in payments by PTAs" (no figures), with an increase in costs per unit in recent years	Sharp reduction in market share of DB by –40% down to 26%, reduction of share of municipal operators by –28% down to 23%, sharp increase in share of global players by 675% up to 30% and stabilization of share of SMEs at 21%	5.4 bidders on average	Conpronet only highlights that their analysis indicates that DB and SMEs do have high success rates within small lots, while municipal operators and global players do have high success rates for lots with large volumes in vkm

quality standards gradually since tendering was introduced, e.g., by reducing the maximum age of vehicles from 12 to 8 years and by requesting air conditioning and more ambitious emission standards. Significant positive impacts are also identified by Beck et al. for the minimum quality standards set for emissions (air and noise pollution)[24] and air conditioning at the MVV, where PTAs achieved 76% of vehicle kilometers tendered out with new buses.

Moreover, as shown by Freitag (2009, pp. 232–236) the MVV was able to increase the vehicle kilometer volume p.a. offered to bus passengers by 26% between 1997 and 2006. Passenger figures increased by 38% in the same period. These positive impacts were due to the contractual standards set by the PTAs, which is in line with the results of introducing tendering elsewhere in the world (see Hermans and Stoelinga 2005, p. 298, for an example from the Netherlands). The results of a questionnaire used by Beck et al. indicate, furthermore, that several operators began to buy vehicles with the (higher) quality standards of tendered services for both tendered and untendered services in order to participate in future tendering procedures. Because of this, tendering standards were then classified as an incentive for innovation for the regional market, an effect confirmed by the results in Schenck et al. (2003, p. 18). This development can be risky for operators if the PTA decides to change quality requirements in its tendering procedures, but is positive for passengers on routes not yet tendered. Despite the significant quality improvements achieved, due to the use of gross-cost contracts, these developments are almost totally authority initiated. Incentives from net-cost contracts, where the operator bears the risk and the chance of changing patronage figures when changing the quality delivered, are usually not observable. The framework selected therefore restricts the impacts of market forces in this market segment primarily to innovations to improve productivity (and reduce costs), without using the market forces for product innovations to increase passenger figures.[25]

With respect to the sharp increase in quality standards, the question is whether the introduction of tendering also leads to an increase in unit costs, or if operators are able to compensate with efficiency gains in an increasingly competitive market environment. As observed in several other states worldwide (see e.g. Alexandersson et al. 1998; Amaral et al. 2008; Hensher and Wallis 2005 and Sharaby and Shiftan 2008), the Beck et al. study shows an average cut in unit costs for PTAs. Prices measured by € per vkm dropped by minus 31% for Hesse (range: minus 23% to minus 40%) and minus 15% for Bavaria (range: ~0% to minus 42%). The Bavarian data includes 11 lots tendered again after the first

[24] These minimum quality standards are higher than the ones set by national law. From an economic perspective such standards are positive due to their high accuracy with respect to reduced noise and air pollution compared to other regulatory instruments, e.g., increased gasoline taxes (see Brenck et al. 2008, pp. 439–440).

[25] Although other aspects, e.g., the scheduled frequency, the level of punctuality or the friendliness of the bus driver, would have been more important to analyze for their impact on the passenger market, sufficient data can only be obtained for aspects directly vehicle-related.

contract term ended (second tendering round). The results of the second tendering round show a stabilization of unit costs. Overall, the PTAs included in the Beck et al. study realize savings of ~ €93.1 million for the full contract period for the lots tendered in Hesse and ~ €8.7 million for Bavaria (price basis: 2005), showing high efficiency gains that obviously overcompensate the costs of quality improvements realized.[26] No data on observations in Schleswig-Holstein was available.

The results of other German publications confirm a "clear reduction in unit costs" due to the introduction of tendering (first tendering round). For the bus services tendered in the city of Frankfurt am Main, von Berlepsch (2005) and Rehn and Valussi (2005) confirm the significant savings achieved even with an increased level of quality. Berschin (2003) shows unit cost reductions of around minus 25% in an analysis of 17 observations. For the state of Hesse, Rausch (2004) confirms "high quality for clearly reduced prices (subsidies)." Achenbach (2006) shows efficiency gains in prices to be paid by PTAs of €0.50–0.75 per vkm, and consequently expects savings of €15–25 million per annum for all public bus services to be tendered by the RMV. All of the studies show a high level of savings achieved so far, and simultaneous quality improvements are observed in most of the cases.

The study by Beck et al. shows average unit costs on the basis of 2005 prices of €1.84 per vehicle kilometer (range: €0.73–3.92). Interestingly, sufficient results are also achieved from a PTA point of view in cases with a low number of bidders (even with only one bidder), which leads the authors to conclude that the expected and not the achieved level of competition is crucial for the unit costs offered by operators. Their analysis of a possible correlation between prices and vehicle kilometers per annum per lot shows that the distribution of unit costs diminishes as the vehicle kilometer volume per lot increases up to ~1 million vehicle kilometers per annum per lot. All lots with a greater volume than one million vehicle kilometers per annum show unit costs between €1.59 and 1.85. Experts explain this result by an increasing opportunity to balance efficient and non-efficient lines when the volume of the tendered lot increases. This applies particularly to opportunities to optimize circulation plans, blocks, and schedules (minimization of dead mileage). As none of the factors analyzed in the empirical investigation (quality aspects such as low floor-buses, age of vehicles, etc.) shows a significant correlation with prices, I conclude that the operators' opportunities to optimize circulation plans are probably the most important factor influencing unit costs, although more research is needed on this subject.

The development of inflation-adjusted prices per vehicle kilometer for PTAs over time shows stable results for the Beck et al. study's observation period of ~10 years, although the authors originally hypothesize an increase in prices after market consolidation. In contrast, the BSL study (2008, p. 22), based only on figures provided by the RMV, shows that in the period 2003–2005 the average unit

[26] In Bavaria (MVV suburban area) these efficiency gains were almost fully reinvested in an increased vehicle kilometers p.a. volume offered to passengers, which might explain the significant increase in passenger figures observed there (see Freitag 2009, pp. 232–238).

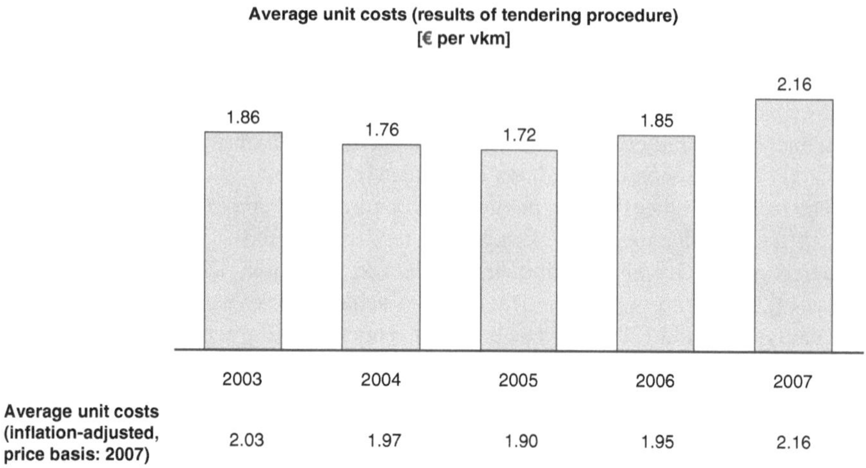

Fig. 8.2 Development of unit costs within the RMV

costs decrease from year to year, while the average prices realized in 2006 and 2007 increase (see Fig. 8.2). These findings are confirmed by Conpronet (2009). Some experts (and to some extent BSL 2008 and Conpronet 2009) believe that these recent results are the real unit costs and that the prices between 2003 and 2005 are strategic prices, whereby operators accept a loss in order to increase their market share, or to enter the market for the first time. Recent developments in Hesse where operators obviously experienced the winner's curse confirmed such assessments.[27] However, none of the studies analyzed here confirms the assumption of strategic prices through empirical investigation. Such an analysis might be appropriate for further research.

In an analysis of the efficiency gains for PTAs from competitive tendering, expenses related to carrying out both the tendering process and contract management during the contract period need to be considered. Beck et al. concludes that these transaction costs for PTAs are relatively low at only ~5% of the efficiency gains realized by the RMV for all contracts tendered (gains for full contract period) or ~2% of the costs to be paid by PTAs for the specific services in question for the full contract period.[28] Similar results presented by Berschin (2003, p. 198)[29] indicate that the transaction costs that arise for tendering do not overcompensate the realized efficiency gains.

[27] See Beck (2006, pp. 29–31) for the relevance of winner's curse in public transport. Recent examples are the termination of a specific contract by Abellio (NedRailways) and the insolvency of several operators such as Werner or Kraftverkehr Kinzigtal due to losses in operations launched as the result of tendering procedures. The Kraftverkehr Kinzigtal case appears in Sect. 5.4.1.

[28] This is an analysis based only on gross-costs. Due to the lack of appropriate data, it was not possible to carry out such an analysis on a net-cost basis, where the difference in administrative costs between direct awarding and competitive tendering for PTAs has to be analyzed. This would probably lead to different results.

[29] For Hesse, Conpronet (2009) assumes higher administrative costs on the PTA level, while also claiming that these costs are not transparent.

8.4.2 *Effects of Tendering on Operators and Employees*

Liberalizing activities are usually viewed with skepticism by employees, who fear worsening working conditions or salaries. Beck et al. show that salary levels stabilize at the level stipulated in the collective labor agreement for private operators, but the level is well below that for public operators such as DB and municipal operators. Furthermore, the results of a questionnaire show that the workload for employees increases after winning a tendering procedure. The question arises whether future tendering procedures will lead to further negative impacts on employees. To avoid diminishing social standards, the RMV and the MVV have established skill-based standards and implemented instruments to ensure that salaries remain at the level of collective labor agreements for private operators. The finding that wages are decreasing or kept stable differs from other international studies. For example in the railway sector, wages have tended to increase in recent years in Britain and Sweden as good labor grows scarce (see Nash and Nilsson 2009, p. 6). A legal obligation by a PTA that the winning operator must accommodate the employees from the losing operator, as shown for the Netherlands by Hermans and Stoelinga (2005, p. 296), is not observed in Germany, which lacks any such legal obligation.

From an operator's perspective, introducing competition through tendering has led to alternations in firm structure in regions where tendering occurs. All studies analyzed here confirm that the main incumbent, DB, lost a significant market share. For example, Augustin and Walter show a sharp minus 41% reduction in the DB market share down to 30% (figures in percentage of total volume of vehicle kilometers per annum tendered), while private operators (aggregated group of global players and SMEs) are able to increase market share. Municipal operators also lose significant market share.

The Beck et al. study points out that SMEs adapt to the increasingly competitive environment and increase their market share from ~40% (including services operated under subcontracts, e.g., for DB) to 60% (excluding subcontract services). Beck et al. also confirms that the probability of SMEs being able to win a tendering procedure increases if they form a group and submit a joint bid (bidding consortium).

The BSL results differ. Its study on market development in Hesse from an SME perspective shows that 85% of the SMEs have fewer than 16 vehicles. According to BSL, the number of SMEs involved in public bus transport services has declined due to takeovers by global players,[30] concentration on the tourist business, and full market exit (only some SMEs). The number of global players active in Hesse has increased from 0 to 4 (plus DB). BSL points out that after several successes during the initial period of competitive tendering, the percentage of successful SMEs has declined in recent years.

[30] As shown for the Dutch market by Hermans and Stoelinga (2005, p. 300), foreign firms obviously prefer to acquire national firms instead of entering the market via direct bidding in a tendering procedure.

The results by Conpronet (2009) for Hesse confirm that the number of SMEs has declined as well. They indicate a market exit of 20% of SME operators, mainly due to winner's curse and/or firms' small size. After initial successes during the starting phase, market share has declined since 2006 due to losses in tendering procedures and corporate sale. Including subcontracts for existing services not tendered out, SMEs have so far lost more than one-third of their previous market share. DB lost almost 40% of its tendered services, while its success rate is ~25%. Global players increased market share to 30% (within the RMV, to 40%). Conpronet's analysis indicates that DB and SMEs have high success rates with small lots, while municipal operators and global players have high success rates for lots with large volumes in vkm per annum.

In contrast to the other studies, Conpronet compares the development of market shares within the market subject to competitive tendering (*tendering market*) to the development of market shares of *services effectively operated*. Here the *tendering market* represents the market share of licensees. *Services effectively operated* represent the market share of licensees corrected by those services operated by subcontractors. Subcontracts have been an important market for SMEs prior to the introduction of tendering. Conpronet based its investigation on DB figures and its own assessments. Figure 8.3 shows that the real market share of SMEs has decreased sharply for the services effectively operated, while the market share of global players has increased. PTAs need to be careful to avoid the creation of oligopoly structures by sustaining a sufficient number of bidders in their market.

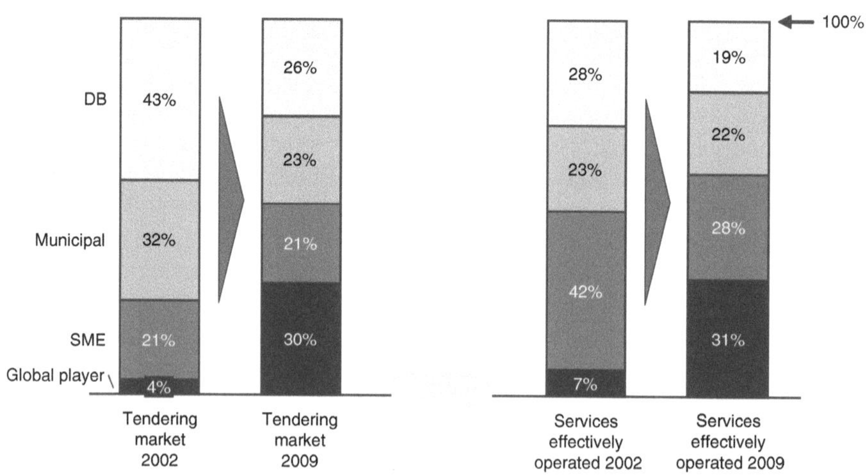

Fig. 8.3 Development of market shares in Hesse (Source: own figure based on data of Conpronet (2009, pp. 50 and 61). Abbreviations: DB = Deutsche Bahn AG (national railway operator, currently biggest operator for regional bus services in Germany), Municipal = Municipal or state owned operators, SME = Small- and medium-sized private operators, Global player = Consolidated operators Veolia, Arriva, Transdev, BeneX, NedRailways (Abellio). Especially Veolia, Arriva and Transdev have also been observed in other EU Member States)

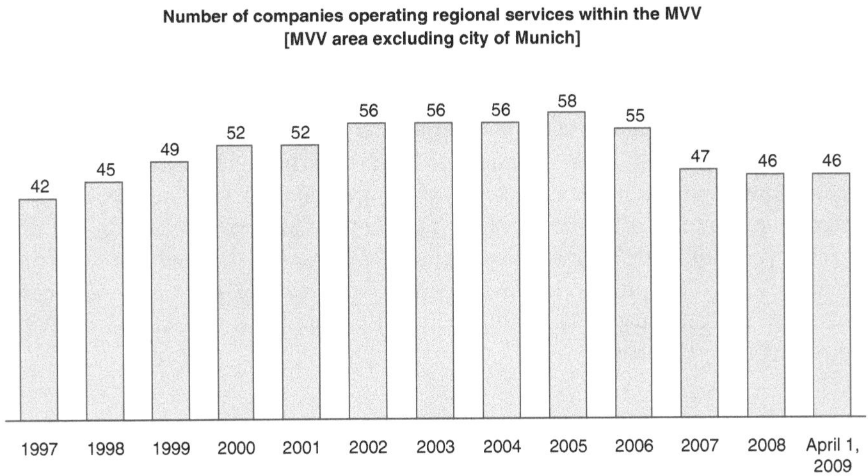

Fig. 8.4 Number of firms in the MVV 1997–2009 (Source: own figure based on data provided by the MVV)

Unlike BSL and Conpronet which focused on Hesse, the FoPS case study presented in Sect. 5.3.2 shows different results for regional services in the Munich area. Here, the small volume per tendered lot has obviously led to an increase in the number of SMEs and only one active global player (plus DB). The FoPS study confirms that between 1997 and 2002 the number of SMEs in the suburban area of the MVV increased from 46 to 55 (+ 20%), with SMEs benefiting from tendering procedures each time (see BMVBS 2005, p. 296). Although the number of operators has decreased, 46 firms are still contractors of the MVV for regional services in the MVV area outside the city of Munich (see Fig. 8.4). Considering the limited volume, this represents a vital and lively market structure.

To sum up, the studies discussed reveal a declining market share of the public operator DB and to some extent, municipal operators. The overall development of the market share of SMEs is unclear. While high success rates are observed in the Munich area, the results from Hesse show that after initial successes in the starting phase, the market share of SMEs declines in recent years. A full market exit by this group of enterprises is not observed in any region so far. As in several other European states (see e.g., Mathisen and Solvoll 2008 for Norway or Alexandersson and Pyddoke 2003 for Sweden), the market share of global players has increased, especially in Hesse. The question arises whether PTAs are able to sustain a high level of competition with numerous competitors, or whether market consolidation will lead to, or already has produced, an oligopoly characterized by a few large operators and bidders and higher prices. The current level of competition will therefore be analyzed next.[31]

[31] The development of prices is analyzed in Chap. 9.

8.4.3 *Entry Barriers Within the Market for Non-Commercial Services*

To reduce the need for subsidies for transport services – permanently, if possible – and optimize the situation from the PTAs' perspective, economic theory recommends maintaining a high level of competition. In view of the complex structure of German PTAs responsible for public transport services by bus and their varying tendering philosophies (Sect. 8.2), it can be assumed that tendering conditions exist that prevent interested parties from bidding. I now investigate the barriers to market entry by analyzing the results of previous studies and verifying the results using database I.

8.4.3.1 Results of Previous Studies

Analyzing the level of competition presented in the previous studies shows different results. Beck et al. shows 7 bidders on average, BSL 6, Augustin and Walter 5.1 and Conpronet 5.4. While the Beck et al. database does not show any significant market entry barrier or influencing factor on the number of bidders, BSL and Conpronet identify a reduction in bidders over time for Hesse. Conpronet identifies 6 bidders per lot between 2003 and 2005 on average, and 4 bidders per lot on average between 2006 and 2009. This development is confirmed by the empirical analysis of Augustin and Walter (negative coefficient for the variable *time*, highly significant), with a reduction from 6.4 bidders in 2005 to 3.5 bidders in 2008.

In contrast to other authors, Augustin and Walter focus on the *probability of an operator change* as an indicator of a competitive market and identify a mean probability of 68.4%. They also present a highly significant influence of the variable *number of bidders* on the *probability of an operator change* with a positive coefficient. Their results show that several structural coefficients have a significant influence on the *probability of an operator change* (and also on the *number of bidders*): operation period measured by *contract term in years* (positive coefficient); size measured by *number of vehicles per lot* (positive coefficient); and complexity measured by *number of lines per lot* (negative coefficient). In their analysis, the type of contract (either a *gross-cost contract* or a *net-cost contract*) and the type of the regulatory framework of a *state* do not show any significant influence on the probability of an operator change. With respect to the influence on operation period, the costs of market exit (residual costs) may also affect the level of competition, since they represent market exit barriers. Beck et al. identified several activities initiated by operators to minimize these costs, including renting instead of building depots, leasing instead of buying vehicles, and so on.

Summing up the previous studies, the level of competition appears to be in decline in recent years. Other factors that influence the number of bidders and the probability of an operator change identified by Augustin and Walter show that activities by PTAs are necessary to secure a sufficient level of competition.

Beck et al. and BSL, however, are unable to identify entry barriers. The question arises whether the Augustin and Walter's results can be confirmed by a different database with current data for the regions presented above and whether a decline in the number of bidders has occurred over time. My analysis of database I aims to verify these differing results in the next section.

8.4.3.2 Analysis of Database I

The empirical analysis of database I, which is conducted using a condensed dataset of n = 102 observations,[32] indicates that several factors influence the dependent variable *number of bidders* at a significant level. My investigation shows contrasting results compared to Augustin and Walter, Beck et al. and BSL (see Tables A.3 and A.4 in the Appendix Sect. A.1). The outcomes for the explanatory variable *start of operations* (year) (negative correlation, highly significant), which confirm the results presented above, show that a significant reduction in the number of bidders per lot has indeed occurred in recent years. It suggests that PTAs should focus on sustaining a high level of competition by reducing entry barriers. Only through this measure can the positive results of competitive tendering be secured in the long run, even though no case of corruption or collusion has become public for the German market.

An entry barrier is identified for the explanatory variable *vehicle kilometers* (negative coefficient). This influence indicates that size is important, which might be especially relevant for SMEs. Further results presented in Table A.4 in the Appendix indicate a negative correlation for the incumbent type *municipal*. With respect to only 14.29% of all n = 63 incumbent type observations classified as municipal, this aspect demands additional analysis. Table A.4 also indicates a positive correlation for the *states* where most of the tendering procedures in the dataset have taken place: Bavaria (32.35% of all observations) and Hesse (50.98% of all observations). This might be explained by the fact that regional markets with numerous procedures attract more operators to participate in tendering than those where only a limited number of procedures have been observed, e.g., Schleswig-Holstein. The existence of a satisfactory framework for newcomers like Hesse's (see also Sect. 5.4.1) might also be an explanation.

It is important to recognize that risk also matters. With respect to the positive influence of the independent (dummy) variable *gross-cost contract* (see Table A.3), avoiding revenue risk for operators seems to motivate more bidders to participate in tendering. The simple regression of dummy variables presented in Table A.4 confirms a positive coefficient for *gross-cost contract*. With respect to the low

[32] Each regression is also conducted with the maximum sum of observations (up to n = 113) for the regression-specific explanatory variables, but the results do not show any major differences. The software used is Stata for Windows 9.1. Methods used are the usual ones as explained a.o. by Kohler and Kreuter (2008).

number of only n = 11 *net-cost contract* observations, this aspect has to be analyzed further for Germany. However, it does confirm with the results presented by White and Tough (1995) for the bus industry in Britain.

As shown in Sect. 7.3.2, operators usually have to bear a higher level of risk in net-cost contracts than in gross-cost contracts. Section 7.4 asks if in fact the surrounding conditions are adequate to minimize external risks for operators when concluding a net-cost contract in Germany. Perhaps this is why gross-cost contracts have been used for most of the non-commercial services tendered. The empirical investigation by Beck (2011a)[33] identifies market entry barriers at a 99.9% significance level for net-cost contracts in comparison to gross-cost contracts for tendered lots for rail franchises in Germany. This analysis shows that detailed data on passenger revenues is crucial for reducing uncertainty from the competitor's view. This includes passenger figures, compensatory payments for fare reductions, tariff structures and liquidity management in the transport associations and/or tariff co-operations (Verkehrsverbünde), including their conditions for admission. The transfer of revenue risk therefore entails the risk of winner's curse. Assuming a stochastic revenue function and a risk-averse bidder, the latter will reckon with a risk premium commensurate with the revenue risk. Waiving this risk premium may result in insolvency, as experienced by FLEX AG (see Sect. 7.4).

Nevertheless, net-cost contracts generally provide better incentives than gross-cost contracts, since the operator's revenue is at least partly connected to the quality of its performance in the passenger market. In fact, new forms of tendering and other means of awarding public transport services are being discussed by several European Member States and by the research community in order to improve the quality of operators' performance and thereby establish a stronger relationship to passenger satisfaction (see Chap. 6). To secure a sufficient level of competition, efforts should be undertaken to avoid a high level of risk in these new awarding procedures.

8.5 Conclusions

After the market reform of the mid-1990s and the long transition period with only a few isolated tendering procedures, German public transport bus services have experienced an increasing number of instances of competitive tendering in recent years. Nevertheless, only a limited part of the market has been put out to tender so far. More procedures have been observed only in the suburban areas of Munich, Hamburg, and Mannheim, although usually not within the cities themselves. Hesse is the only state which now tenders almost all regional bus services.

---

[33] This journal article is based on Beck (2010a).

The results of competitive tendering vary. The quality level of the public transport services tendered has improved considerably, illustrated, for example, by the average age of vehicles within the RMV area, which has dropped from 7.8 years to 4.4 years. The same applies to environmental standards, which are better implemented and maintained, a development mainly initiated by increased quality requirements in the contracts tendered. At the same time, PTAs have been able to realize significant efficiency gains, reducing subsidy payments by −15% to −31% on average. Inflation-adjusted prices per vehicle kilometer for PTAs have remained stable over almost a decade, while recent results indicate that unit costs are increasing. Expenses related to the tendering process (allocation, contract management) are relatively low at only ~5% of the efficiency gains or ~2% of the costs of a public service contract for the full contract period.

When tendering was first introduced, many operators feared losing market share. This has been the case especially for DB, so far the main incumbent for the bus services tendered. SMEs increased market share in the initial phase, although their success rates in Hesse have declined in recent years. The few active global players have increased market share.

Employees of operators have experienced a stabilized level of the collective labor agreements on a par with private operators, which is, however, well below the level for public operators. At the same time, the workload for employees has increased after winning a tendering procedure.

The overall level of competition is relatively high, with 5–7 bidders on average. Nevertheless, the analysis shows at a highly significant level that the number of bidders has declined over time, especially in recent years. Entry barriers have been identified at significant levels for several parameters, particularly for the volume tendered out and the revenue risk to be borne by the operator. Reducing these barriers should be a major aim for PTAs in order to secure the positive results of competitive tendering with respect to public subsidies over the long term.

PTAs were able to fulfill their aims to a large extent, thanks to the introduction of competitive tendering which decreased the level of subsidies and increased the level of quality provided to passengers. The market share of SMEs has stabilized in the Munich area, but shows diminishing shares for Hesse in recent years. Finally, social standards have been secured on the level of collective labor agreements of private operators.

Some of the results presented here, such as the decreasing impact on public subsidies, the increasing level of quality, the shift in market share towards non-local operators, the influence of net-cost contracts on competition and the decreasing number of bidders over time, confirm the results of other international studies. Other results, such as the stabilized prices over time, the impact on unit costs, the influence of transaction costs, the success of the MVV to sustain a high number of operators and a high share of SMEs, and the impacts on employees, have not been addressed in other studies known by the author.

Future research should focus on barriers that prevent PTAs from implementing competitive tendering in their regions. As tendering enables authorities to establish a direct contractual relationship and generates several positive economic results with respect to subsidies to be paid and quality delivered, other influencing factors have to be assumed. The analysis shows negative results for some groups of operators and, to some extent, for employees. It appears as though PTAs which do not use tendering prefer to secure the existing market shares of operators and ensure safe social standards instead of reducing subsidies to be paid and increasing the quality to be delivered.

Further research should also be undertaken on the development of unit costs for the years to come and factors influencing the price per vehicle kilometer for PTAs, why this subject will be analyzed in more detail in Chap. 9. Although several entry barriers have been identified, questions remain with respect to the risk resulting from net-cost contracts; the answer will require a sufficiently large database.

Chapter 9
Factors Affecting Tender Prices

9.1 Introduction

Local public transport in Germany is already a costly enterprise. Although European regulation (EC) No 1370/2007 appeared to mitigate the need for restructuring through the possibility of direct awards, the unexpected global recession has been a major factor affecting the public budgetary crisis. Moreover, the nation's constitutional goal to achieve balanced budgets in the period 2011–2020 adds urgency to the need for fiscal reform of public transport.

Expecting diminishing capabilities of public co-funding, the application of instruments to improve efficiency is more important than ever for public transport authorities (PTAs). As mentioned, many international studies confirm significant efficiency improvements when introducing competitive tendering to a previously monopoly situation (see among others Alexandersson et al. 1998, Hensher and Wallis 2005 and Sharaby and Shiftan 2008). Thus, competitive tendering has received increased attention in recent years in Germany, especially where there is no municipal ownership of the incumbent operator. The major areas of competitive tendering activity are the federal state of Hesse including Frankfurt on the Main, and the agglomeration areas of Munich, Hamburg and Mannheim (see Chaps. 5 and 8).

While introducing tendering in a formerly monopolistic market has shown positive results in terms of efficiency and quality delivered to passengers, securing these results in the long run is difficult (for example, see Sect. 8.4.1 as well as Hensher and Wallis 2005). Little is known about the factors that influence tender results in terms of the prices to be paid by the PTA to the operator for the delivery of services (tender prices) and the differences in these tender prices. Knowledge of such factors will enable PTAs to set effective tendering conditions and to secure public transport services in an environment of decreasing public budgets. This essay, based on Beck and Walter (2010), identifies the influential factors and differences of tender prices by analyzing a unique and comprehensive data set of 157 observations for the period 1997–2009 explicitly collected for our research. Rather than developing a cost function for bus operators, we chose to examine the

A. Beck, *Competition for Public Transport Services*, Contributions to Economics,
DOI 10.1007/978-3-7908-2802-3_9,

tendering conditions which will help operators to improve efficiency and reduce costs, if properly set by the PTAs.

We apply several regression techniques to differentiate between a general cost-impact and an efficiency-impact only affecting single observations, for example, potential overcompensations or winner's curses. We also examine whether price and efficiency differences exist between the regions, since market organization and tendering policies differ significantly (see Chaps. 5 and 8).

Numerous papers have analyzed efficiency in public transport services by bus based on operator data (usually annual reports), among them Brons et al. (2005), Dalen and Gómez-Lobo (2003), Farsi et al. (2006) and Walter (2011). Fewer authors have analyzed in detail the factors propelling efficiency (e.g., Miller 1970 for some American cities). Wolanski (2009) compared the efficiency levels of direct awards and competitive tendering and analyzed the causes of efficiency for the Polish market. He found that PTAs will reach optimum efficiency levels when selecting contract terms between 1 and 8 years; assigning a volume appropriate for small- and medium-sized operators (SMEs); and tendering numerous services in one area to support a dynamic market development. Wolanski confirms that tendering of public transport services results in considerable efficiency improvements.[1]

To our knowledge, no efficiency analysis has been published that is based solely on data generated from competitive tendering procedures. By examining efficiency and regional developments, we provide a comprehensive economic analysis that enables PTAs to achieve further efficiency improvements in future tendering procedures.

The remainder of this essay is organized as follows. Section 9.2 describes the key characteristics of the data set and the explanatory variables, and explains our methodology to adjust prices for inflation, regional differences in price levels, and subsidization. Section 9.3 describes the SUR methodology and presents the results of our analyses with a special focus on regional developments. Section 9.4 describes the SFA methodology and the results. Section 9.5 concludes with a discussion and suggestions for future research.

9.2 Data

9.2.1 Database II

Although Germany's PTAs are obliged to publish a minimum amount of information (see §§ 17, 19 [2] and 23 Official German Contracting Terms for Award of Service Performance Contracts, Part A [VOL/A] 2009), comprehensive data on

[1] The results of a comparison of several towns point to lower costs for services provided by private than by public operators. Nevertheless, public operators receiving part of their orders under the direct award procedure are able to tender services at lower than average prices.

competitive tendering, including tender prices, remain unpublished, and official statistical data is unavailable. For these reasons we construct a new database II in three steps to enable sophisticated empirical analysis: (1) identification of all criteria deemed to influence the price; (2) development of a questionnaire; and (3) data collection and verification.

A first catalog of relevant criteria (the criteria that are assumed to affect tender prices) is developed based on a comprehensive literature review and our personal consulting experiences. The criteria are verified via interviews with 30 representatives of PTAs, operators, and consultants involved with competitive tendering of local bus services in Germany. The criteria are re-evaluated in a roundtable discussion with the Arbeitskreis Vergabe (AK Vergabe) der Bundesarbeitsgemeinschaft der ÖPNV-Aufgabenträger in der Bundesvereinigung der kommunalen Spitzenverbände Deutschlands (BAG ÖPNV).[2]

The questionnaire is drafted, again followed by a roundtable discussion with the AK Vergabe, and we pre-test it with several PTAs to identify potential problems and misleading questions. The final questionnaire is distributed to all German PTAs via the BAG ÖPNV.

All major PTAs that have conducted numerous tendering procedures so far have provided data.[3] The final step, the reliability check of the data, identifies and clarifies incomplete or questionable information. Altogether, the database contains quantitative and qualitative data for 232 criteria for n = 157 lots[4] tendered by 16 PTAs in the period 1996–2009. The next two subsections discuss the dependent and relevant explanatory variables, and their designs, calculations, and expected influences.

9.2.2 Dependent Variables

Analyzing the factors with monetary impact in the competitive tendering market requires a sufficiently large and unbiased database. Our questionnaire asked PTAs to provide data on the price per vehicle kilometer to be paid by the PTA to the operator for lot i in the first contract year as a result of competitive tendering on a

[2] The AK Vergabe is the workgroup for awarding within the BAG ÖPNV. The BAG ÖPNV is a joint association of local acting PTAs of the Deutscher Städtetag (German association of cities), the Deutscher Landkreistag (German association of rural districts) and the Deutscher Städte- und Gemeindebund (German association for small cities and towns).

[3] Special thanks to all PTAs that provided data for this study.

[4] Note that in Germany one tender is usually divided into two or more so-called lots to support SMEs. Operators are then able to bid for one or more lots (or batches).

gross-cost basis (p_i).[5] Since our goal is to adjust any peculiarity with influence on the price per vehicle kilometer beyond the influence of the PTAs, we introduce structural and environmental variables which net out such factors. Doing so allows us to identify the true factors of influence of PTAs when setting their tendering conditions, and sets the focus on where the PTAs can directly influence tender prices.

Considering the observed period of 13 years, the effect of inflation is a major bias that requires adjustment. Numerous studies on efficiency in public bus transport services, e.g., Farsi et al. (2006), restrict their reassessment to the consumer price index. To verify whether this index fits with the real development of the operating costs for public bus transport services, we develop our own index I to adjust p_i adequately. The development of this index is based on data provided by the Federal Statistical Office, expert interviews with bus operators, representatives of the bus industry, and PTAs, and complemented by our research into the different regional cost levels that arise from structural differences, such as schemes of public co-funding and wage rates.

We conclude that total costs for an average lot are influenced by: (1) labor costs (LC, primarily bus driver costs); (2) capital costs (VC, primarily depreciation for vehicle investments); (3) fuel or diesel costs (DC); and (4) other costs (OC, primarily administrative or overhead costs). LC_t, VC_t, DC_t and OC_t represent the relevant index values for the public transport industry for a specific year t filled with data provided by the Federal Statistical Office.

Our examination of the collective labor agreements for federal states where tendering data is available shows that labor costs differ significantly between the states due to labor rates and effective hours (we define effective hours as the sum of working hours for which the driver is effectively available). We find that working hours per week range from 38.5 to 40, the amount of leave days per annum (p.a.) range from 20 to 31, public holidays p.a. range from 9 to 13, and we also note the various arrangements for breaks. In addition, salaries per bus driver p.a. at the junior level of seniority, for example, range from €27,135 to €32,540, whereas their development over time was in a similar range between the states. Based on our examination we adjust LC_t by up to 23%, depending on the height of the different weighting factors per state (we develop the weighting factors out of the comparison of the different levels of labor rates and effective hours between the states).

Regarding vehicle costs we find that a system of public co-funding for vehicle investments is effective in Bavaria[6] and North Rhine-Westphalia. Thus, we need to adjust VC_t by up to 50% for these states.

[5] Note that net-cost contracts are made comparable to gross-cost contracts by using their net subsidy payment plus the fare revenues of that batch. Furthermore, note that P_i in Table 9.1, which we define later, differs from p_i.

[6] Bavaria undertook reforms within our observation period, resulting in an abolishment of the subsidies paid for vehicle investments in 2005 which had previously been 50% of the purchase costs.

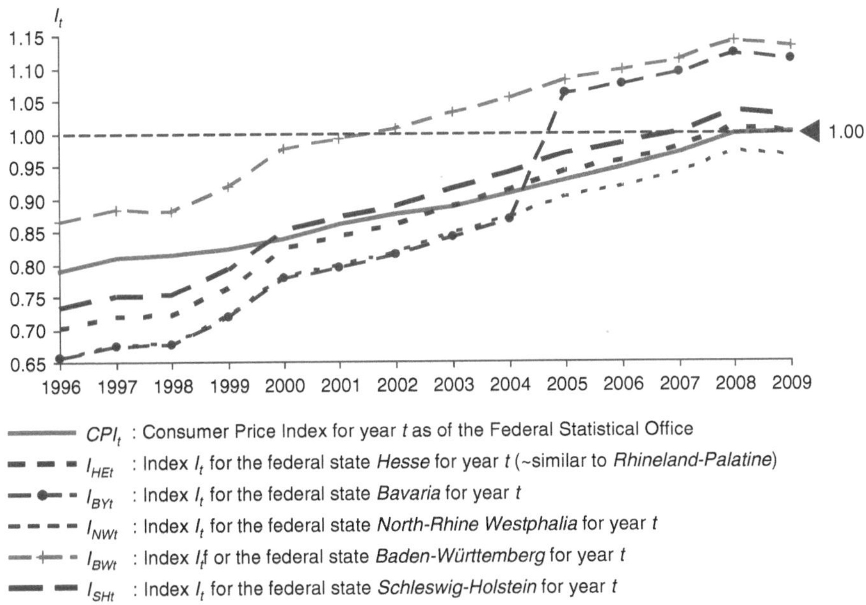

Fig. 9.1 Development of the total costs indices compared to the consumer price index

The index I_{st} necessary to adjust p_i for lot i in state s in year t can be written as:

$$I_{st} = 0.7 \times LC_{st} + 0.15 \times VC_{st} + 0.1 \times DC_{st} + 0.05 \times OC_{st} \tag{9.1}$$

where 0.7, 0.15, 0.1 and 0.05 are the typical shares of total costs for an average lot according to experts and verified by our research. Figure 9.1 shows the real development over time t with I_{HE2009} representing point 1.0 since the analysis is based on 2009 prices.[7] We observe a significant difference between the development of the consumer price index CPI_t of the Federal Statistical Office and the index values I_{st} per state, with a jump of I_{BYt} due to the adjusted public co-funding for vehicles in Bavaria since 2005.[8] Thus, we conclude that an adjustment of tender prices which is solely based on the CPI_t would be inadequate and that tender prices need to be adjusted according to the real development of operators' costs to avoid analytical bias.

[7] Note that the index for Rhineland-Palatine shows values similar to those for neighbouring Hesse; thus, Fig. 9.1 omits the less-relevant Rhineland-Palatinate.

[8] A simple OLS-regression confirms that these index values show a correlation on a high significance level with the real development of the unadjusted prices per vehicle kilometer p_i.

Consequently our analysis below is based on P_i being the adjusted price per vehicle kilometer for lot i originated in state s. We portion the set K of lots ($i \in K$) into disjunct subsets K_{st}, with $\mathrm{U}K_{st} = K$. For every K_{st} there exists a unique I_{st}. The adjusted price P_i for lot ($i \in K$) is then given by

$$P_i = (1/I_{st}) \times p_i \tag{9.2}$$

for every $i \in K_{st}$ for every s and t.

Table 9.1 Descriptive statistics for 157 observations and for main criteria for database II

	Mean	Standard deviation	Minimum	Maximum
Price variables				
Adjusted price per vehicle kilometer (P_i) in €	2.09	0.50	0.81	4.38
Full price p.a. (FP_i) in €	1,059,349	1,366,135	40,299	8,673,811
Variables set by PTA				
Vehicle kilometers p.a. (*vkmpa*)	508,970	599,962	9,200	3,706,757
Number of lines (*linesno*)	4.10	4.06	1	21
Number of vehicles (*novehcl*)	10.43	10.73	1	57
Average vkmpa per bus (*kmpervehcl*)	50,540	23,145	9,200	191,833
Labor agreement standard (*declwage*)	1. no requirements: 50, 2. closure of any labor agreement with employees required: 79, 3. specific labor agreement set as minimum standard: 28			
Average length per bus in meters (*lengthbus*)	12.37	1.44	7	18
Contract term in years (*term*)	6.51	1.83	1	8
Security deposit in percent of FP_i (*deposit*)	3.45	3.57	0	17
Days of submission (*submdays*)	55.65	18.38	25	145
Option for term extension foreseen? (*extopt*)	no: 137; yes: 20			
Renewal of vehicles during term? (*renewal*)	no, not necessary: 122; yes, renewal necessary: 35			
Revenue risk: contract type (*revrisk*)	gross-cost contract: 145; net-cost contract: 12			
Structural variables beyond PTA influence				
Level of experience of PTA for lot *i*: specific number of the lot *i* by the PTA over time (*expr*)	19.01	18.72	1	67
Sum of experience: sum of all lots tendered by the PTA (*exprsum*)	37.01	26.60	1	67
Start of operations (*startoyear*)	–	–	1997	2009
Number of bidders (*bidders*)	5.37	2.74	1	14
Change of operator? (*change*)	no: 43; yes: 114			
Winning bidder SME? (*sme*)	no: 67, yes: 90			
Spatial type of transport service (*spatial*)	1. major city: 8, 2. medium-sized town: 3, 3. small town: 15, 4. suburban: 21, 5. rural: 110			
Federal state (*fedstate*)	HE: 72, BY: 67, SH: 10, BW: 4, NW: 3, RP: 1			

HE Hesse, *BY* Bavaria, *SH* Schleswig-Holstein, *BW* Baden-Württemberg, *NW* North Rhine-Westphalia, *RP* Rhineland-Palatine; variable denotations are presented in italics; a more detailed explanation of all variables is presented in Appendix Sect. A.2.1

As shown in Table 9.1 P_i varies from €0.81 to €4.38. The mean price is €2.09. We also investigate the full price to be paid by the PTA p.a. to the operator per lot *i*, being $FP_i = P_i \times vkmpa_i$, where $vkmpa_i$ is the volume of vehicle kilometers p.a. (vkm p.a.) per lot *i*.[9] The mean value of FP_i is €1.1 m.

9.2.3 Explanatory Variables

To discover the conditions with a significant impact on price, we classify the independent variables in three groups according to the general contract conditions with influence on: (1) productivity of the services from an operational viewpoint; (2) the risk level to be borne by operators; and (3) variables capturing other factors beyond the PTAs' direct influence.

With respect to economies of scale,[10] the chief factor in a contract is the volume tendered out. We theorize that it is a cost-decreasing influence when PTAs are able to increase the volume per lot or the volume per vehicle, e.g., by optimizing the required timetable. An average lot in our database is characterized by a volume of four lines, 508,970 vkm p.a. and 10 vehicles, yet we note much variation. The average *vkmpa* output per vehicle, a simple partial productivity measure, shows a mean volume of 50,540. Other conditions set by PTAs that probably limit operational flexibility of the winning bidder are assumed to have a price-increasing effect, most notably for labor agreements where the requirements set by PTAs are measured by an ordinal increasing scale.

For analytical purposes we assume that different risks also affect price due to the risk premia that operators must calcuate.[11] The average extent of investment risk, measured by the average length per bus per observation, is assumed to have a price-increasing impact as a market exit barrier since operators need to purchase the necessary vehicles. The mean value shows that most of the buses used are standard 12-m vehicles. The risk level for market exit influenced by the contract period set by PTAs in the tendering conditions that is available for depreciation is assumed to have a price-decreasing impact.

Net-cost contracts, where the PTA decides that the revenue risk shall be borne by the operator, are assumed to have a price-increasing impact. We assume the same for the volume of deposits given by operators to PTAs as security. The duration between the date of the public call for tenders and the date of submission set by PTAs is assumed to have a price-decreasing impact. Operators are also assumed to

---

[9] As *vkmpa* we count only those vkm p.a. provided on the specific lines of the batch according to the timetable usually set by the PTA. Other tours, for example, transfer between depot and start of a specific line, are excluded.

[10] Due to missing data for relevant criteria (e.g., length of routes) the analysis of economies of density was not possible.

[11] See Chap. 7 for a detailed discussion on risk.

need a sufficient period to develop a proper calculation; otherwise they must add a risk premium. Contract conditions set by PTAs that presuppose a renewal of vehicles during the contract period are assumed to have a price-increasing impact, also true for contract conditions that foresee PTAs' options to extend the contract period at the end of the contract term.

Variables that are usually beyond the direct influence of PTAs, such as the PTA's level of expertise, time, level of competition, and spatial aspects, are also assumed to have an impact on prices. As mentioned in this dissertation, few PTAs have tendering expertise (the Münchner Verkehrs- und Tarifverbund GmbH [MVV] has undertaken the most tendering, 67 procedures in suburban Munich area since 1996).[12] Previous or a higher experience level is assumed to have a price-decreasing impact, which is also assumed for the start year of operations.

Spatial aspects are measured by classifications of population density and transferred to an ordinal scale. Services in high density (city) areas (low ordinal scale) are assumed to be more expensive in terms of € per vkm than services in low density (rural) areas (high ordinal scale), e.g., due to higher level of average vehicle kilometers per hour possible outside cities. Most of the procedures analyzed are in Hesse (73 observations or 46%), the only federal state to tender almost all bus services, as illustrated in Fig. 9.2 (see also Sects. 5.4.1 and 8.2.1 for the awarding policy of Hesse). This Fig. 9.2 shows, too, that the average volume per lot is far lower in the Munich area than in Hesse.

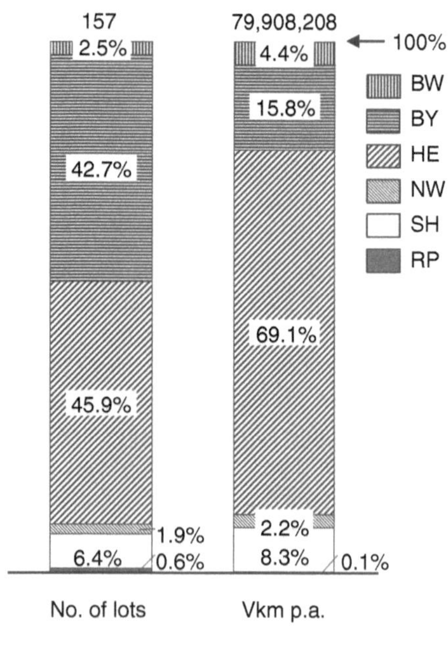

Fig. 9.2 Distribution of number of lots and vkm p.a. by state

[12] These are the sum of all Bavarian observations. To date, no competitive tendering was observed for the Munich city area.

Analyzing the level and structure of competition shows that, on average, five companies submit bids and that the incumbent is unable to regain the services in 114 of 157 cases. SMEs which often claim diminishing opportunities to survive in this market, win 57% of the lots tendered (the highest success rates are in the Munich area).

The number of *bidders* is assumed to have a price-decreasing impact. Indeed, a simple OLS-regression confirms that the number of *bidders* has a clear price-decreasing effect, highly significant on a 99.9% level (see Appendix Sect. A.2.2). Since the variable, *bidders*, depends on contractual and structural factors (see Sect. 8.4.3), we omit it as an explanatory variable.

9.3 Seemingly Unrelated Regressions

9.3.1 Methodology

Simple OLS-regression is potentially able to identify the determinants of prices in competitive tendering. However, after the regionalization of local public transport during railway reform in 1996, the federal states are now responsible for their own local public transport policies, and many responsibilities are delegated to the county or communal levels, thus every state and every region shows its own awarding philosophy.[13]

This has important implications for selecting the proper regression technique. Clearly, the differences in the design of tenders, various price determinants, and other such factors cause us to consider a system of regression equations. In particular some structural factors may only be relevant in specific states or regions. We also bear in mind that our data set could inadvertently neglect some influential factors. The topography of the service area or the overall market organization in a specific state or region may be an example for a cost influencing factor not covered by the data set. Assuming that the error terms of our regression equations are correlated, we first consider selecting the seemingly unrelated regression (SUR) model (Zellner, 1962).[14]

With a slight abuse of notation, the SUR model can be written as

[13] For more details on the regionalization and the current framework see Chap. 4. For examples of different awarding philosophies in the areas analyzed here see Sects. 5.3.2, 5.4.1 and 8.2.

[14] However, we do not assume that there is a spatial dependency measured by distances between service areas that determine tender prices. Hence, we do not pursue the path of spatial econometrics.

$$P_{ri} = \alpha_r + x'_{ri}\beta_r + \varepsilon_{ri} \tag{9.3}$$

where P_{ri} represents the adjusted price per vehicle kilometer to be paid by the PTA to the operator for lot i in region r (which is located in state s), α_r is the region-specific intercepts, x_{ri} is the matrix of explanatory variables with region-specific coefficient vectors β_r and the error term is ε_{ri}. The number of explanatory variables differs between regions, for example, because some variables exhibit no variation in some regions.

In contrast to many applications of the SUR model (see, e.g., Wooldridge, 2002, pp. 143 ff.), it is obvious that the number of observations per equation, hence region, is different in our analysis, because we use tendered lots as observations. Therefore we use the algorithm proposed by McDowell (2004) that allows us to estimate a system of SURs with unbalanced equations using Stata's xtgee command. For this command, the iteratively reweighted least-squares estimator equals maximum likelihood.

9.3.2 Model, Results and Interpretation

Our SUR analysis focuses on: (1) the *Munich area* in Bavaria; (2) *HesseX* (most of the federal state *Hesse*); and (3) *Other regions*. Observations located in the *Munich area* are solely gross-cost contracts tendered out by the MVV. The lots are relatively small with a mean vkm p.a. volume of only 188,733. Observations located in *Hesse* are usually gross-cost contracts. Here, the state obligation to tender out almost all services and the high market volume in terms of vkm p.a. is expected to have a special influence.

In forming the *HesseX* group, we correct the *Hessian* cases by 12 cases located in the Verkehrsverbund Rhein-Neckar (VRN) area and in Frankfurt on the Main (FFM) (*HesseX* excludes VRN & FFM). Unlike the other areas in Hesse, the VRN uses net-cost contracts with a high overall risk level for operators at any time and tenders out only in certain cases, namely if no offers to operate the requested services commercially have been put in place (see Sect. 8.2.2 for more details). Lots tendered out in FFM are characterized by comparatively high volumes (usually at least 40 vehicles), very high quality requirements, and long durations for submission. Furthermore, FFM remains the only major city in Germany using tendering. Therefore the VRN cases and the FFM cases, together with all remaining observations, form the group *Other regions*.

The results in Table 9.2 confirm our hypothesis that different influences are at work in different regions. This finding holds for both significance levels and directions of influences. Regarding the volume tendered out, measured by *vkmpa*, the results confirm economies of scale only on a very low and insignificant probability level of 85.9% and only for *HesseX*. We surmise this is because the average volume of a lot, which is 633,369 vkm p.a. in *HesseX* (range: 61,761–1,839,275), is

Table 9.2 SUR results for exogenous variables on the adjusted price per vehicle kilometer P_i (Altogether we tested 29 SUR models for the three regions presented here; Table 9.2 shows the results for the model with the best fit with respect to e.g. significance levels, number of significant variables, and pairwise Pearson correlation between the independent variables identified. The program code developed for the present analysis is shown in the Appendix Sect. A.2.3)

Region Variable	Munich area	HesseX	Other regions
vkmpa	1.98×10^{-7} (4.76×10^{-7})	-1.67×10^{-7} (1.14×10^{-7})	-9.35×10^{-8} (1.15×10^{-7})
kmpervehcl	-1.19×10^{-5}*** (2.79×10^{-6})	-7.59×10^{-6}*** (2.75×10^{-6})	-1.30×10^{-5}*** (4.70×10^{-6})
lengthbus	0.1388*** (0.0470)	0.1059*** (0.0396)	0.0573 (0.0637)
term	0.0036 (0.0292)	–0.0513* (0.0303)	–0.0219 (0.0656)
extopt	–0.1889 (0.2666)	–0.1033 (0.1412)	0.3976 (0.2424)
deposit			4.2164* (2.4481)
spatial	–0.1855*** (0.0703)	–0.1402* (0.0849)	–0.2130*** (0.0633)
startoyear	–0.0282 (0.0174)	0.0539** (0.0250)	0.0460 (0.0437)
exprsum		–0.0197*** (0.0062)	–0.0013 (0.0253)
Constant	85.8647 (34.6412)	–105.1419 (49.9640)	–89.37328 (86.7471)
Observations	67	60	30
Number of PTAs per group	1	6	9

Significant levels: *** 99%, ** 95%,* 90%, Standard errors in parentheses
Wald chi2: 5,437,55, Prob > chi2: 0.0000

considerably higher than the mean volume in the *Munich area* of 188,732 vkm p.a. (range: 9,200–668,800), but not high enough to be meaningful. On the other hand such an influence might not exist at all, for example, due to the contrary effects of overhead or administrative costs, or might be too low compared to other factors of influence presented in the following section. For *Other regions* the low number of observations might be a reason for an insignificant result.

One clear finding for all three groups is that a higher productivity, measured by the average *vkmpa* per bus (variable *kmpervehcl*), lowers the price significantly. The results show that operator ability to optimize circulation plans, blocks, and schedules (minimization of dead mileage), based on the conditions set by PTAs (timetable, direction of lines, etc.), significantly impacts prices.

Several findings confirm that a higher risk level increases the price to be expected by PTAs, presumably due to the higher risk premia to be calculated by bidders. A first finding is that an increase in the average height of investment risk per bus, measured by *lengthbus*, has a price-increasing impact on P_i. This result is highly significant only for the *Munich area* and *HesseX*. Obviously, larger buses expose the operator to higher investment risks and they also imply higher investments and depreciations. Furthermore, the longer the bus length the higher the maintenance cost (e.g., for cleaning). Again, note that the low number of observations might be a reason for an insignificant result for *Other regions*.

For the contract *term*, where we assume a price-decreasing impact with respect to depreciation possibilities and the level of risk at the end of the contract period due to the remaining resale value (resale risk at market exit), a significant result is confirmed only for *HesseX*. For the *Munich area* the low volume in terms of vkm p.a. per lot (and thus the low investment volume) probably limits such risk in the view of the operators. For *Other regions* the limited variation in this variable (contract term: 5–8 years, compared to 3–8 years, for example, for *HesseX*) could prevent any significant results.

As discussed in Sect. 9.2.3, we assumed that the option for PTAs to extend the contract term has a price-increasing impact, but we find an insignificant level of probability of 89.9% only for *Other regions*. Due to the fact that the price fixed for the first treaty year is usually also used for the optional years (adjusted by the usual price index only), operators claim they must add a risk premium for the years which are the most difficult to assess. They also claim they can only calculate the main contract term for depreciation etc. (excluding the extension option) since this is the only fixed and calculable period. Hence, adding an extension option has no price-decreasing effect, although the depreciation period could be extended. Nevertheless, with respect to quality delivered the option is generally assumed to have positive incentivizing effects.

The significant result for *deposit* for *Other regions* confirms again that increasing the risk for operators, here via a higher security deposit, has an increasing influence on price. For this variable, we note that a missing variation for the *Munich area* and a very low variation for *HesseX* (only two observations with little differing values) impedes an admission of *deposit* into the SUR-model for these two groups.

In addition to contractual conditions influencing the price there are several structural variables beyond a PTA's influence that affect P_i. The results for the *spatial* type of service show a significant decreasing influence for the gross-costs per vkm for all of the regions analyzed. An increasing population density therefore increases P_i, e.g., due to a lower average speed per bus in city areas. Furthermore, several labor agreements foresee a mark-up for employees in urban areas (see e.g., OVN and ver.di 2007 and ver.di hessen 2007).

The coefficient for the start year of operations (variable *startoyear*) has the expected positive sign, although it is only significant for *HesseX*, meaning that prices increase over time. Market participants in Hesse have claimed that the low prices realized by PTAs during the starting phase of competitive tendering were set at strategic levels by global players or were miscalculated. Some cases of the winner's curse became public since (see Sects. 5.4.1 and 8.4.1). BSL (2008) also mentioned that quality requirements have become more ambitious over time in the Frankfurt on the Main area in Hesse, which also could have led to increased costs.

Unlike *Hesse*, prices in the *Munich area* show a decreasing trend, but insignificant on a low level of probability of 89.5%, despite a clear increase in quality standards (since 2002 almost all procedures require new vehicles and a 100% low floor and air conditioning share). Most likely, the increasing experience level of the MVV over time enabled a gradual reduction of prices since the MVV is the only PTA in our database that has conducted more than 23 tendering procedures.[15]

[15] As explained before, the sum of all MVV tendering procedures in our database is 67.

Finally, analyzing the sum of experience of a PTA (the sum of all procedures per PTA until 2009, variable *exprsum*) confirms that a high level of experience of a specific PTA lowers the price. A high market volume with recurring opportunities for operators in a specific region, compared with an increasing experience share for operators, might also affect the price. This result is highly significant only for *HesseX*, but is remarkable since *startoyear* has a positive impact. The *Munich area* with only one PTA could not be analyzed due to the missing variation. Furthermore the high level of 98% pair wise Pearson correlation with *startoyear* impeded an admission of *expr* into our SUR model.

9.4 Stochastic Frontier Analysis

9.4.1 Methodology

So far we have only looked at cost differences due to structural differences, either fully set by external circumstances or set by the PTAs. Cost differences can also be caused by the inefficiency of bus service providers and/or the overcompensation due to a low level of competition. These cost differences are not identical for all firms and operating areas, but are individually specified by, for example, poor bus utilization, excess labor, gold-plating, etc.[16]

The two main methods of scientific efficiency analysis are non-parametric data envelopment analysis (DEA) and the parametric stochastic frontier analysis (SFA).[17] We choose to rely on SFA for two reasons. First, since SFA and SUR are both regression techniques, SUR is much more comparable with SFA than with DEA. For SFA and SUR, we can interpret and compare coefficients and their impacts on dependent variables. Second, the significance of impacts for both can be evaluated by looking at standard errors of the estimations. This is not possible with DEA, because it only looks at the efficiency of observations and does not assume a functional relationship between output and input. In other words, it is impossible to interpret the impacts of structural variables.

The concept of SFA was introduced by Aigner et al. (1977) and Meeusen and van den Broeck (1977) in a cross-sectional model.[18] It is a regression technique that estimates a best-practice efficiency frontier in contrast to average curves set by

[16] When we bear in mind that the winner in a competitive tendering is still the best offer in the market, these inefficiencies occur for all bidders.

[17] See Coelli et al. (2005) for a profound introduction to efficiency analysis.

[18] Given that only 12 second-round batches are included in our data set, we are not able to analyze recurrent tender rounds, and cannot make use of more sophisticated SFA panel data models.

traditional econometrics. In a cost framework, the estimated equation can be written as

$$\ln\ FP_i = \alpha_0 + x_i'\beta + v_i + u_i \tag{9.4}$$

where FP_i represents the full price p.a. to be paid by the PTA to the operator for the i-th lot, α_0 is an estimated intercept, and x_i is a vector of explanatory variables with coefficient vector β. The stochastic term is given by a lot-specific error part v_i, which is independently and identically distributed following a normal distribution $v_i \sim iid\mathrm{N}(0, \sigma_v^2)$, and a lot-specific, non-negative, inefficiency component, which is independently and identically distributed following a half-normal distribution $v_i \sim iid\mathrm{N}^+(0, \sigma_v^2)$. The vector of explanatory variables usually includes outputs, factor prices and control variables, so that the resulting inefficiency component can be interpreted as cost inefficiency. Absent information on firm-specific input factor prices, we can only calculate the measure called "technical cost efficiency" by Jamasb et al. (2008) in their study on the productivity of US gas transmission companies.[19] To ensure a homoscedastic distribution of inefficiencies, the costs and explanatory variables are introduced in logarithms according to the Cobb-Douglas functional form. The inefficiency component is separated from the stochastic error term by applying the Jondrow et al. (1982) estimator.

Generally, cost functions in efficiency analysis of the local public transport sector are estimated with firm-level data assuming a cost-minimizing behavior (see, e.g., Farsi et al. 2006). In our approach, we look at the efficiency of winning offerings in public tenderings chosen from a set of competing offerings, which can amplify the cost-minimizing provision and easily reveal the appearance of over-compensation in the inefficiency component. We assume that FP_i represents the total costs of the transport firm for providing the tendered services p.a., acknowledging that these services may only represent a portion of the firm's business plus an adequate profit. We observe that firms winning more than one lot can appear more than once in our dataset. However, each lot has to be calculated as its own imaginary subsidiary, because contractual lengths can differ and the potential economies of scale are hence uncertain. This is particularly valid for the newcomers that win 73% of all lots in our database.

9.4.2 SFA-Results and Interpretation

Table 9.3 presents the coefficients and significance levels of our SFA-Model. It confirms the results for several variables already presented in the SUR-Analysis,

[19] A similar approach was taken by Agrell et al. (2008a, b) on the incentive regulation of German gas and electricity distribution companies.

Table 9.3 SFA results (Altogether we tested 45 efficiency models, while Table 9.3 shows the results for the model with the best fit with respect to e.g., significance levels, number of significant variables, pairwise Pearson correlation between the independent variables identified and sigma *u*. The program code is shown in the Appendix Sect. A.2.4)

Dependent variable	$\ln(FP_i)$
ln(*vkmpa*)	0.9674***(0.0163)
ln(*kmpervehcl*)	–0.2561***(0.0331)
declwage	0.0400*(0.0218)
ln(*lengthbus*)	0.5545***(0.1309)
renewal	–0.0413(0.0356)
revrisk	0.1064*(0.0592)
ln(*submdays*)	0.0932*(0.0545)
spatial	–0.0748***(0.0151)
Constant	15.3464***(0.5779)
Observations	157

Significant levels: *** 99%, * 90%, Standard errors in parentheses, *ln* logarithm natural

but on a significant level for the full dataset. Such significance can be detected for economies of scale, measured by vkm p.a., and the variable service, as a measure for population density. Unlike the SUR-Analysis, the impact of *vkmpa* is confirmed on a very high significance level for the full dataset; increasing the vkm p.a. volume per lot by 1% shows a sub-proportional increase of the full price p.a. by 0.97%. This confirms the existence of economies of scale. Increasing the productivity per vehicle per lot, measured by *kmpervehcl*, confirms the decrease in the full price to be paid p.a. on a high significance level. We also identify the influence for the variable *declwage*, which shows that tendering conditions that require operators to use any or even a specific labor agreement have a significant price-increasing effect. Nevertheless, preventing the use of dumping-wages by PTAs for social reasons may justify this instrument in the view of employees. To secure fair conditions on the labor market the results of our interviews show that even operators demand PTAs to use such standards.

Matters of risk are confirmed to have a price-increasing effect. As presented in Sect. 9.3.2, the variable *lengthbus* as a measure for the relative investment risk per bus again has a highly significant price-increasing effect. Surprisingly, tendering conditions that make it necessary for operators to renew the fleet during the contract, for example, due to a maximum age of vehicles permitted that is below the contract term, show no significant influence. It is likely that the amount of maintaining costs has a high influence, and balances out the risk of realizing a selling price that is below the book value of the vehicle at the point of renewal.

A further aspect that demands operators to increase the risk premium to be calculated is the revenue risk, confirmed by the variable *revrisk* on a significant level. As expected, calculating passenger figures, compensatory payments for fare reductions, as well as tariff structures and liquidity management in the German transport associations and/or tariff cooperation's (Verkehrsverbünde), which in

Table 9.4 Efficiency comparisons and Kruskal-Wallis tests

Non-Hesse vs. *Hesse*	
Mean efficiency for *Non Hesse* (n = 85)	89.15%
Mean efficiency for *Hesse* (n = 72)	88.90%
χ_1^2-value	2.883
Probability	91.05%
expr < 6 vs. *expr* > 6	
Mean efficiency for *expr* < 6 (n = 45)	88.38%
Mean efficiency for *expr* > 6 (n = 112)	89.30%
χ_1^2-value	4.443
Probability	96.50%

n number of observations per group

Germany is often based on an insufficient database (see Sect. 7.4.2), seems to increases the price.

Surprisingly, and unlike Sect. 9.2.3, the variable *submdays* shows a price-increasing influence. Increasing the period between the date of the public call for tenders and the date to submit bids tends to increase the full price to be paid by the PTA p.a. It appears as though operators calculate more aggressively when there is a short period for submission and perform more sophisticated calculations when there is a longer period; obviously more time could enable them to identify more uncertainties where a risk premium appears necessary, thus preventing the occurrence of a winner's curse. Furthermore, a short submission period introduces the possibility of miscalculation by the bidders. Both cases may be problematical for PTAs should operators go bankrupt and services are interrupted.

When comparing the efficiency levels, the Kruskal-Wallis tests confirm on a 91.05% significance level that lots tendered out in the federal state of *Hesse* (including FFM and the VRN area) show 0.25% less efficiency, on average, than procedures conducted elsewhere (see Table 9.4).

Comparing the mean prices of the different regions shown in Fig. 9.3 reveals that prices in *Hesse* are somewhat lower. We conclude that PTAs in *Hesse* probably tender out lots that enable lower prices than elsewhere (*Non-Hesse*) due to a low level of risk (for example, usually gross-cost contracts) and good productivity parameters with respect to *kmpervehcl* or *vkmpa*.

The values in Fig. 9.3 also show that on average the lowest prices are realized in the *Munich area*, which differs slightly from *Hesse*. Nevertheless, the result shows that producing services in *Hesse* is slightly less efficient than elsewhere due to factors not included in SFA. One explanation could be the lack of competition due to diminishing bidders per procedure and the trend to market consolidation observed in recent years in *Hesse* (see Sect. 8.4.2). A lack of competition due to oligopoly structures may then be a reason for over-compensating the winning bidder. With respect to the price-increasing effect over time shown for *HesseX* discussed in Sect. 9.3.2 we suggest examining whether the weak difference in the efficiency levels observed will become more distinctive in the near future.

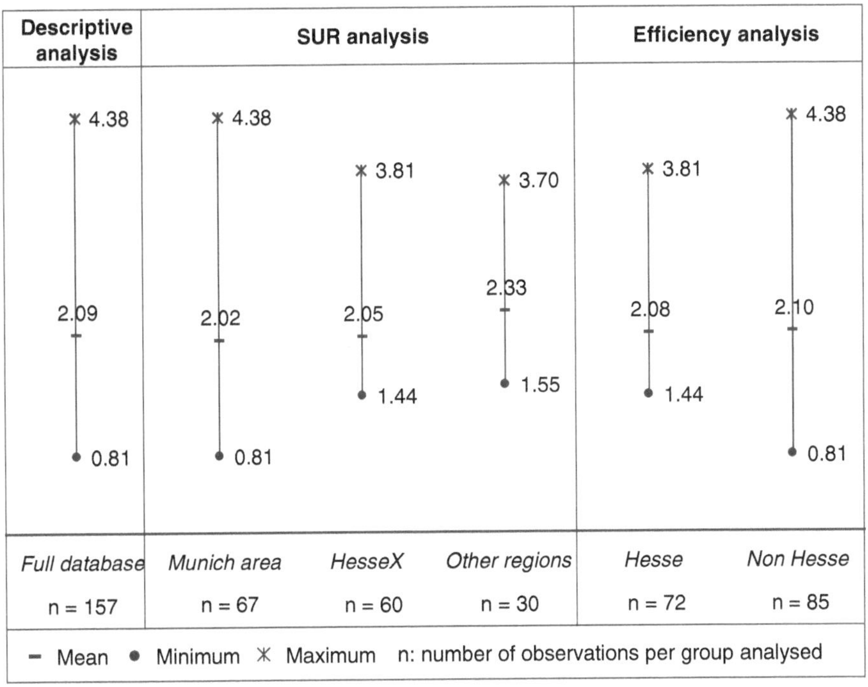

Fig. 9.3 Distribution of prices per vkm in € for the regional groups

Regarding the experience level as measured by *expr*, SFA reveals that PTAs' experience has an efficiency-increasing impact. The Kruskal-Wallis test confirms on a 96.50% significance level a 0.93% increase in the efficiency scale for procedures where PTAs have already conducted at least six tenders. The results show that an experience level higher than six tenders enables PTAs to set tendering conditions such that operators are able to deliver more efficient services. In testing other variables like *revrisk*, *deposit*, *bidders* and *startoyear*, none showed significant differences in the mean efficiency levels.[20,21]

[20] We only see with a low probability of 82.30% that services won by SMEs show a 0.35% higher efficiency scale than services won by other operators, and that cases with a change of the operator show a 0.44% higher efficiency scale than other services with a low probability of 81.90%, an indication that further research is needed.

[21] We attempted to include the variables turning out to be significant efficiency separators in the Kruskal-Wallis tests as heteroscedastic variables in the inefficiency function. However, this did not lead to significant coefficients.

9.5 Conclusions

Based on a comprehensive data set of 157 observations and a detailed adjustment of price data with respect to the price differences between states due to peculiarities beyond the influence of PTAs, we identified three groups of impact factors on tender prices: the contract conditions set by the PTAs with direct influence on operator productivity; the contract conditions set by PTAs with direct influence on the risk level for operators; and exogenous aspects beyond the influence of PTAs. Using SUR analysis and SFA analysis we identified numerous impact factors that partially differed among the regions due to specifics such as the level of experience and the tendering philosophy.

Based on our results, we conclude that properly setting the contract conditions for a given lot allows PTAs to realize added efficiency improvements. Directly, the improvements occur by contract conditions increasing productivity per lot and limiting the risk level assumed by the operator. Indirectly, the improvements occur by conditions that increae the level of competition. For example, optimization of bus utilization has a cost-decreasing impact, confirming that PTAs are able to reduce prices with adequate transport and (line) network planning. Generally, we suggest that PTAs should determine contract conditions in a manner that enables operators to improve productivity and minimize their risk premia.

Moreover, the result that an increasing level of experience has a price-decreasing impact may enable further efficiency gains by assigning the tendering process to one or more over-arching authorities per region vested with the expertise required. This authority, which might also function as a competence pool for tendering procedures, may be able to utilize the effects resulting from a faster learning curve.

Nevertheless, actions by the PTAs are limited by exogenous factors that are outside their sphere of influence of PTAs, such as population density, or political objectives, such as the aim to prevent dumping-wages for fair market conditions and social reasons. Furthermore, there are trade-offs, e.g., net-cost contracts entail a higher risk level, but are generally preferable to gross-cost contracts with respect to incentives.

The different results for price developments over time for Hesse and the Munich area suggest the need for further research on whether strategic prices or even a market consolidation might have influence. This holds especially for the efficiency level, which shows slightly less efficient prices in Hesse, although it also requires confirmation by future analysis. Finally, the results show that differing contract conditions in the regions may lead to differing results, and confirms that analysis must always include region-specific aspects, especially with respect to the adjustment of the data for tender prices.

Part IV
Competition for Commercial Services

Chapter 10
Market Entry Barriers for Commercial Services

10.1 Introduction

After decades of stagnation, the market for commercial public bus transport services in Germany is heating up, with observable competition on the rise. As explained in Sect. 4.4.3, the competitive market for commercial services is based on market initiative by operators and is distinguished from the competitive market for non-commercial services and from the market segment in which contracts are awarded, without tendering. The essay presented in this Chap. 10 asks whether the current level of competition is satisfactory and provides evidence of a thriving competitive environment, or whether it indicates the existence of barriers to market entry. If entry barriers are impeding more dynamic market development, the question arises where they can be identified.

Chapter 4 found that the existing federal institutional framework plays a central role in defining and in some cases constraining market participants' opportunities to act. The essay presented will also probe the extent of the framework's effectiveness in promoting competitive development in the market for commercial services.[1]

Analyzing the competitive market for commercial public transport services by bus in Germany is a difficult task, primarily due to the lack of economic research on this subject and a system of market organization that differs fundamentally from competitive markets such as those in the UK and Scandinavia. While this issue has received increased attention from German legal scholars (a.o., Landsberg 2003; Werner 2004; Klinger 2006 and Recker 2007), economic papers on commercial services as well as on entry barriers to the German market for public bus transport are rare. Major German studies have focused on competitively awarded non-commercial services (e.g., Achenbach 2006; Augustin and Walter 2009 and Beck and Wanner 2008). Only a limited number of German papers, however, have

[1] The examination is based on Beck (2009d, f) and Beck (2010b), a study completed in 2009.

A. Beck, *Competition for Public Transport Services*, Contributions to Economics,
DOI 10.1007/978-3-7908-2802-3_10, © Springer-Verlag Berlin Heidelberg 2012

considered competition for commercial services from an economic perspective (see Beck 2007; Beck and Schnell 2008; Beck and Wille 2009 and Walter et al. 2009).

Internationally, several articles published in recent years analyze the competition for public bus transport services (e.g., Alexandersson and Pyddoke 2003; Amaral et al. 2006; Hensher and Wallis 2005, and Mathisen and Solvoll 2008). Several look at the level of competition, but to my knowledge, no one has yet focused on market entry barriers for commercial services and the specific effects of the regulatory framework on competition. By examining current developments in the competitive market for commercial services in Germany, I aim to provide a comprehensive economic analysis of entry barriers and the regulatory framework in this embryonic market. The results provide an in-depth understanding of the real developments on this market and of the main factors that may promote more intense competition.

To help explain the institutional framework in Germany, Sect. 10.2 describes the basic structure of the awarding procedure for licenses to operate commercial services and classifies the types of competitive procedures. It also discusses entry barriers for this market segment. Section 10.3 presents database III and describes the important market developments of recent years. The results of the empirical analysis of market entry barriers are presented. Section 10.4 discusses the results regarding the regulatory framework and their implications for newcomers and policy-makers. Section 10.5 presents key findings and conclusions. The List of Abbreviations, List of Symbols, Glossary and List of the Acts of Law in this book are intended to ease understanding of specific terms for readers not familiar with the regulatory framework of German public transport by bus.

10.2 Surrounding Conditions

10.2.1 Basic Structure for Awarding Licenses for Commercial Services

There are three main stages of the awarding schedule for commercial operating licenses: the preparation phase, the approval phase, and the license term (see Fig. 10.1).[2]

In the *preparation phase*, competitors gather information about commercial operating licenses that are nearing expiration. Public transport authorities (PTAs) establish (or adjust) their (local) public transport plan (PTP), and licensing authorities (LAs) determine minimum criteria. PTAs are permitted to promote

[2] This explanation is based on the framework presented in Sect. 4.3; the awarding schedule follows the illustration in Fig. 7.1 presented in Sect. 7.1.

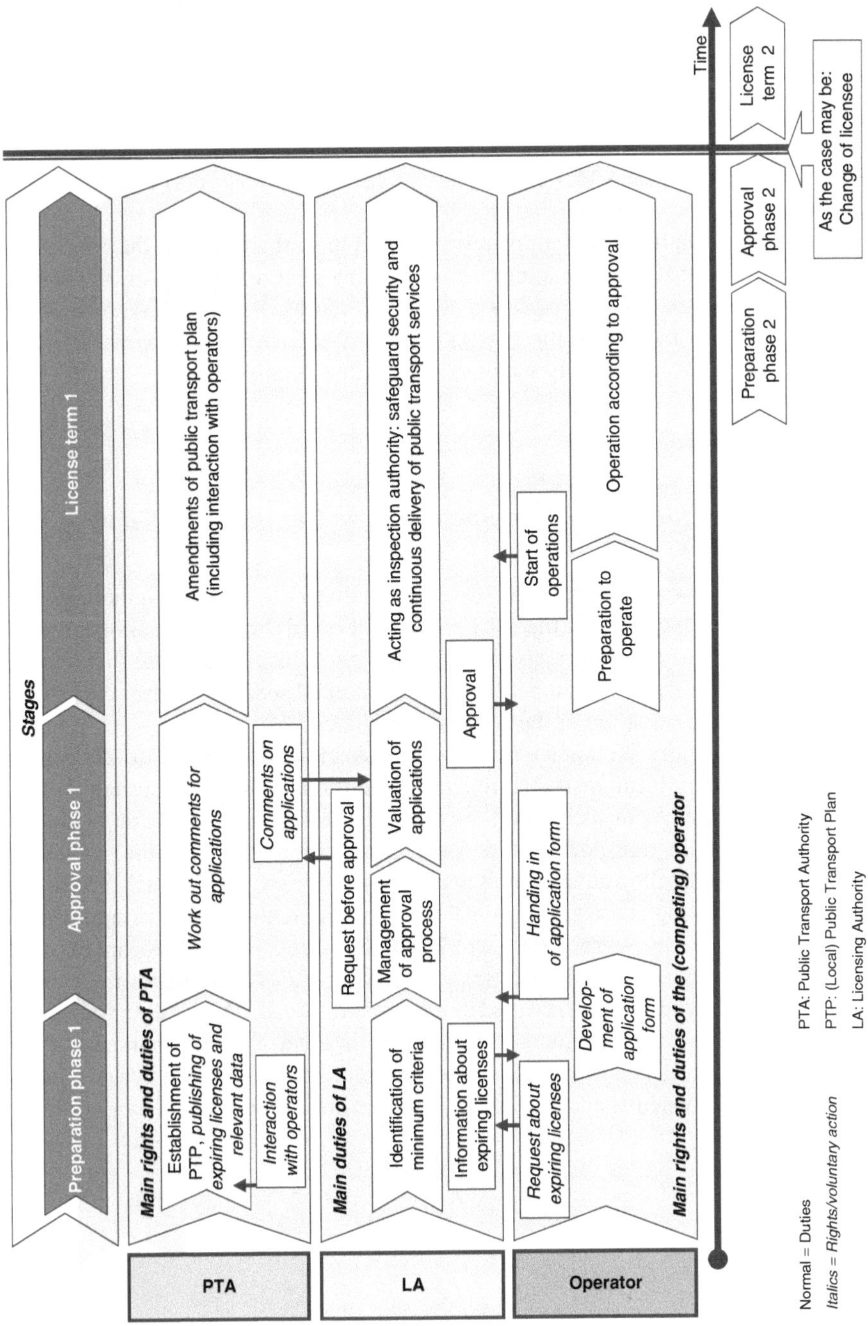

Fig. 10.1 Award schedule for commercial services

competition by announcing licenses that are due to expire, thus signaling their support for competition in their local market.

Since LAs usually did not set time limits in the past, the *approval phase* starts with the submission of the first application. The LA manages the process that follows, asking the PTA (and other major market participants) for recommendations (see § 14 PBefG), validating the application(s) and approving the best offer.

Upon approval, the winning operator prepares to start and begins the operations stated in the approved application. This determines the beginning of the *license term*. The LA acts as an inspection authority during the term (Werner 2001, pp. 131–134). At the end of the license term of usually 8 years maximum, a new procedure is initiated, possibly with a change of the licensee.

10.2.2 Classification of Competition for Commercial Services

Based on interviews conducted with 54 representatives of operators, authorities and related experts, I classified the CCL-cases, followed by a re-assessment with selected experts to establish a clear and unambiguous categorization. Figure 10.2 illustrates the four types of competition for commercial services. These types differ primarily in the motivation of the respective initiator.

The first category is characterized by the fact that PTAs want to encourage efficiency in their local market through competition (which they usually do in consultation with LAs in such cases). From a strictly legal view, the right to initiate commercial public transport services and competition lies with the operators. Operators are only allowed to submit applications for new commercial services or to submit competing applications in the run-up to the renewal of existing licenses (market initiative, see Werner 2001, pp. 73–74, and Sect. 4.4.3). PTAs are allowed to actively promote CCL only. Consequently, when a PTA announces the expiration of an authorization, it is classified as *authority initiated*.[3] A good example is the Wittenberg case, in which the authorities published a call for applications for commercial services and provided all relevant information, e.g., passenger figures, compensatory payments, and minimum service criteria (for a detailed description, see Sect. 5.4.2).

[3] This holds even if competition does not actually arise due to the existence of only one bidder. Note that authority initiated CCL procedures with zero bidders, where delivering commercial services is not profitable from an operator point of view, are not included in the database III analyzed in this section.

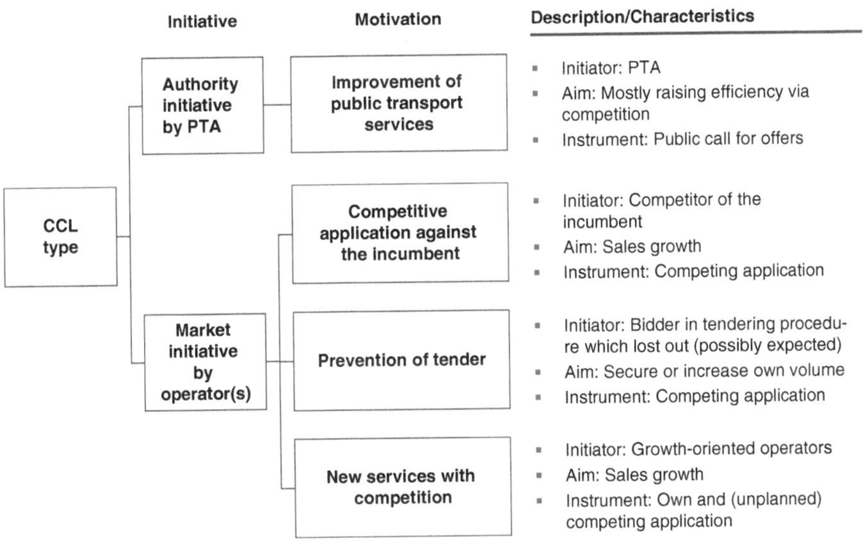

Fig. 10.2 Classification of competition for commercial services

All other cases are classified as *operator initiated* (market initiative), where operators handed in a competing application without any efforts by PTAs to encourage competition (*really operator initiated*). These cases include applications submitted by newcomers competing against incumbents. A recent example of such a *competitive application* is the Gifhorn case. Here a public operator in a rural district was successfully challenged by a competitive application submitted by a former subcontractor which was a medium-sized private operator (see Sect. 5.4.2 for a detailed explanation).

Another type of operator initiated CCL is an application for commercial services submitted to counter or *prevent a tendering procedure* for non-commercial services. An example is the suburban area of Hamburg, in which the incumbent VHH, a public operator, applied to operate commercial bus services on a route for which a tendering procedure for non-commercial services was already underway (see Sect. 5.3.2). It may also be equivalent to what is called a "nil tender" in the UK, where an authority specifies a service to be provided and issues a call for tenders, but an operator – either the incumbent or a newcomer – is willing to register the service commercially (whereas, in contrast to the UK, a license in Germany usually provides exclusivity to the operator for the specific service). The problem of an incorrect classification of the underlying services as non-commercial by the responsible PTA, although they are commercially feasible, is also discussed in Sect. 4.6.3.

Applications for *new commercial services* not currently provided can also be countered by competing operators which attempt to jump on the idea developed. Summing up, the main motivations of operators entering CCL procedures are to achieve economic growth, or to oppose tendering processes that they cannot be expected to win (e.g., as incumbents).

10.2.3 Barriers to Entry for Newcomers

When analyzing competition for commercial services, a recapitulation of the main aspects on market entry barriers and risk presented in Chap. 7 and an adoption to our object of investigation is needed. The economic literature defines market entry barriers in a wide variety of ways. Initial research on market entry barriers was done by Bain, who established the following definition (see Bain 1956, p. 3): "A barrier to entry is an advantage of established sellers in an industry over potential entrant sellers, which is reflected in the extent to which established sellers can persistently raise their prices above competitive levels without attracting new firms to enter the industry." Applied to CCL procedures in Germany, this means that if an incumbent can provide a level of service quality (e.g. with respect to frequency of service provision) below competitive levels without attracting competing applications, then market entry barriers are assumed to exist. In these cases, the incumbent will reduce its quality to a level slightly above the level where competing applications are expected, with the goal of maximizing its own profits. If no competing applications are expected, the resulting market equilibrium of this monopoly ensures that passengers are provided a quality level significantly below that expected from a CCL procedure (see Sect. 4.6.1 for a detailed explanation of this specific issue).

An efficient awarding procedure therefore focuses on reducing market entry barriers wherever possible and ensuring a high level of competition to:

- Obtain the best possible offers with respect to quality offered (fulfilling the participation constraint for a high number of operators)[4]
- Prevent the incumbent from anticipating a safe renewal of its licenses (which entails reduced efforts to provide the best service possible)[5]

According to McAfee et al. (2004, p. 465), market entry barriers are disadvantages for newcomers compared to the incumbent. McAfee et al. stress the issue of "uncertainty about market conditions" when there are sunk costs in the market and that even a group of smaller barriers "may constitute a significant entry barrier." If the level of uncertainty from a newcomer's point of view is considerably higher than the respective level for the incumbent, thus forcing the newcomer to reckon with higher risk costs than the incumbent, this might also be classified a "disadvantage" (McAfee et al. 2004, p. 465). Newcomers can reduce the level of uncertainty by closely analyzing the market. Obviously, this will result in research costs which have to be classified as sunk costs and, according to Bain and McAfee, also represent an entry barrier. For bus service operators, one of the main economic advantage incumbents have over newcomers is that investments with sunk costs

[4] An optimized structure of incentives to ensure that quality will be delivered as promised in the license term (fulfilling the incentive compatibility constraint for the licensee) is not part of this analysis.

[5] The higher the number of bidders the higher the efforts of the winning bidder (see Laffont and Tirole 1993, pp. 309–318).

have already been made (e.g., building a depot) and have been depreciated for at least the period of the existing license term. Furthermore, the incumbent is familiar with the regional market and is typically better at analyzing customer reactions to a shift in the level of quality offered.

10.3 The Market for Commercial Services and its Challenges

For a clear quantitative analysis of the market for commercial services, my investigation covers three sections: Section 10.3.1 describes the database used; Sect. 10.3.2 provides a descriptive analysis; and Sect. 10.3.3 shows the results of the empirical analysis.

10.3.1 Database III

There are constraints to data availability on commercial services. Unlike tendering for non-commercial services, where the responsible PTAs are obliged to release at least a minimum amount of information to bidders (see Official Contracting Terms for Awarding Service Performance Contracts, Part A – Verdingungsordnung für Leistungen, Teil A [VOL/A]), information on competition for commercial lines or services is difficult to obtain. The reason that official statistical data on this subject is not available may be that CCL is based on market initiative.

Therefore, I developed a database, I termed database III, derived from publicly available information, document analysis[6] and expert interviews with market participants involved in the respective cases. For this purpose, open interviews were conducted with 54 representatives of operators and authorities and related experts. Before entering the data gained from these sources into the database, its reliability was validated (usually by double-checking with other sources); incomplete or questionable information was identified and checked against other published information and/or additional results from expert interviews. Only publicly announced and/or confirmed CCL procedures were classified as reliable information and entered in the database.

Database III contains n = 117 German CCL-cases with start of operations in 2003–2008, mostly in rural or suburban areas. The database may not contain all CCL procedures that have taken place, since not all were made public; however, the 54 experts interviewed were not able to identify others. I thus conclude that almost all CCL-cases are included in the database III.

[6] These included the *Official Journal of the European Union* and well-known information systems that specialize in public transport in Germany, i.e. Newstix, convia, and the Gesellschaft zur Information des Verkehrsgewerbes.

The data is based on CCL cases observed. I define "case" as a CCL procedure with a start date of operations, an incumbent (including consortia), and a winner (including consortia), comparable to lots in tendering processes.[7] Data collected includes location (e.g., federal state), the responsible PTA, the responsible LA, classification of the incumbent and the (first) competitor/newcomer, number of bidders, and the volume of the case with respect to the number of lines and vehicle kilometers p.a. (see Table A.7 in Appendix A.3.1). On average the cases observed show 6.7 lines per case (117 observations) and a volume of 600,728 vehicle kilometers p.a. (data available for 46 observations only; see also descriptive statistics in Table A.9 in Appendix A.3.1). The mean number of bidders per case is 1.82. For a quantitative analysis, a numerical database is necessary. Therefore all qualitative information collected is classified and operationalized according to a catalog of definitions (for those criteria where analysis seems appropriate).

10.3.2 Descriptive Analysis of a Market in Motion

In recent decades, licenses for commercial services are usually granted to applicants without a single competing application (Werner 2004, p. 91).[8] The chief entry barrier has probably been the practice, common since 1978, of not publishing the expiration date of existing licenses to any operator other than the incumbent (see Landsberg 2003, p. 411). Absent this information, it is virtually impossible to enter the market by the application process.

On July 2, 2003, the German administrative court ruled that LAs are obliged to inform operators about expiring licenses upon request (see BVerwG 3 C 46.02). Since then, the number of CCL procedures has increased; annual growth rates vary between 19% and 100% in recent years (see Fig. 10.3). Experts interviewed could cite only a limited number of cases prior to 2003. For this reason, my assessment of competition for commercial services uses 2003 as the starting point. The analysis shows that operators initiate almost two-thirds of the cases (real market initiatives, altogether 70 cases, or 60% of all n = 117 cases). The other 40% are authority initiated (PTAs encouraged submission of bids for commercial services by public request for offers).

Altogether, 61% (43 cases) of the 70 initiatives by operators are CCL procedures with at least one competing application against an incumbent. Prevention of tendering (operators apply for commercial services in a tendering procedure organized by the PTA) is observed for 31% (22 cases) of the initiatives by operators. New services with competition account for 7% (5 cases). As shown in Fig. 10.4, CCL procedures occur in most regions.

[7] Sometimes a subdivision is necessary to define clear cases for further analysis.

[8] Being a renewal of licenses, see Sect. 4.3.4 for a more detailed explanation.

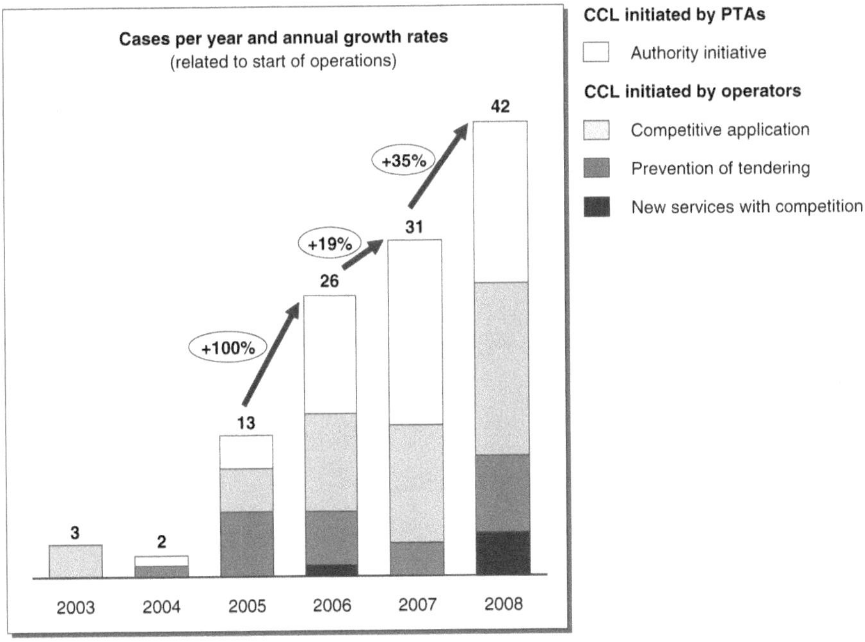

Fig. 10.3 Market development of competition for commercial services

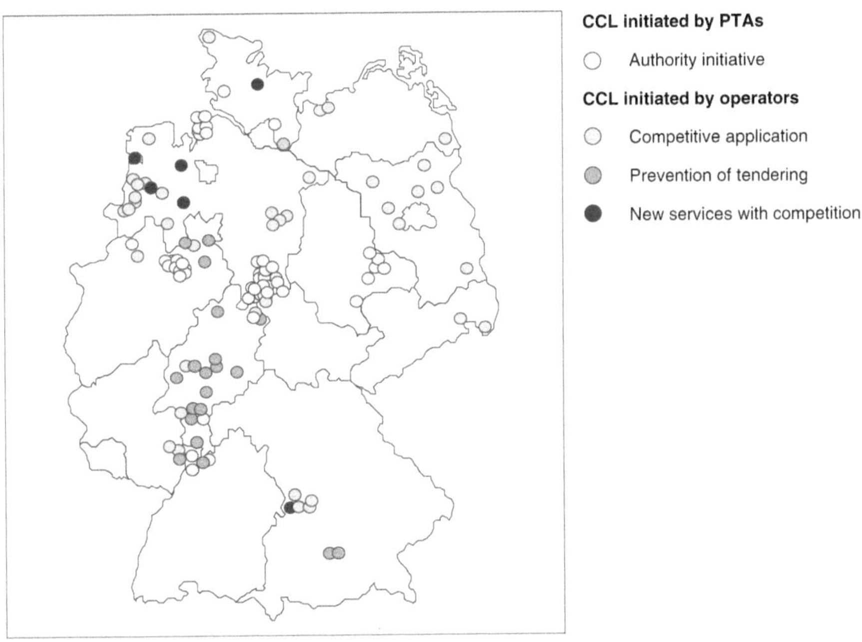

Fig. 10.4 Regional distribution of competition for commercial services

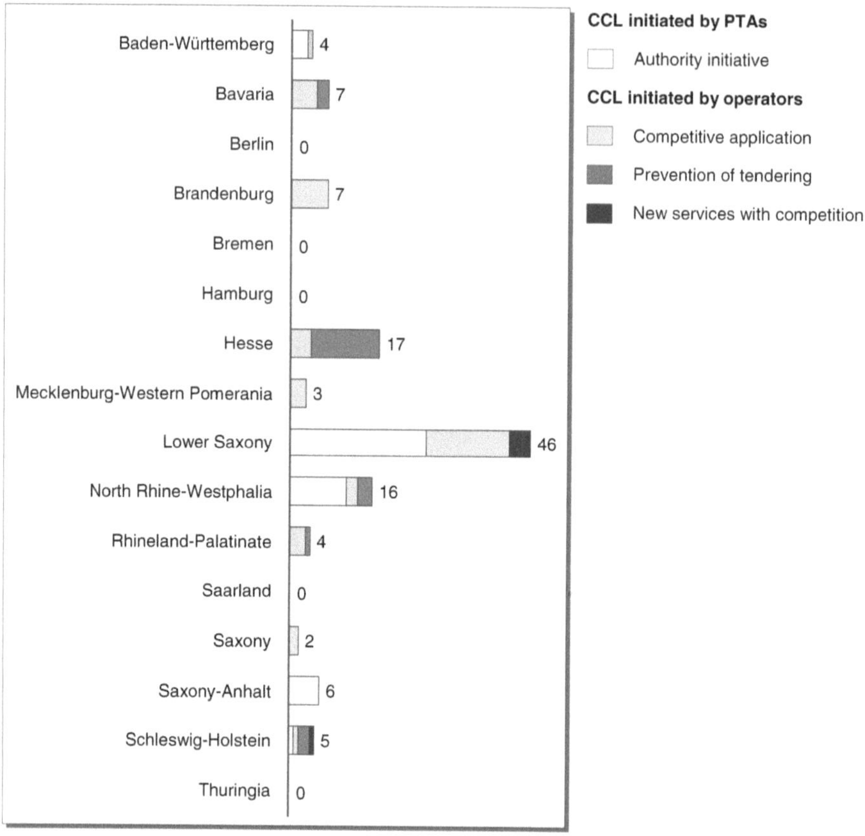

Fig. 10.5 Competition for commercial services: number of cases per state

Although the competitive market for commercial services shows extraordinary growth rates in recent years, the number of cases observed is still small compared to the total market volume. For example, according to Rainer Peters, head of the LA for Lower Saxony, only 130 (6%) of a total of 2,200 bus lines had at least one application to operate competitively between 2003 and 2008 via either authority initiated or market initiated procedures, although almost all of the lines were classified as commercial services according to § 13 PBefG.[9] Lower Saxony has the highest concentration, accounting for 39% of all CCL procedures in the database.

Figure 10.5 shows the other federal states with a high number of procedures, i.e. Hesse (15%, with a concentration of cases in which prevention of tendering is the

[9] The LA of Lower Saxony granted the license to the incumbent in 75% of all CCL procedures where there was an existing operator and more than one bidder. Note that the number of CCL procedures in database III differs because it includes authority initiated CCL procedures where only one bidder was observed.

motivation) and North Rhine-Westphalia (14%, with a concentration of authority initiated procedures).

A comparison of the market development for commercial and non-commercial services shows that the competitive market for commercial services is growing. Since 2003, when the German administrative court obliged LAs to inform new operators about expiring licenses, the number of cases has taken a sharp upswing. Nevertheless, the number of cases remains small (see also Sect. 4.3.4). Only in a few instances have operators tried to expand their business via CCL procedures to date. Compared to the increasing number of CCL procedures, the competitive market for non-commercial services remained more or less at the same level in the period 2003–2008 (see Schnell 2009, p. 25), without such a clear upwards trend as observed for the competitive market for commercial services.

This comparatively slow market development continues, although tendering procedures, the only relevant alternative to CCL procedures with respect to volume, stagnated. Until 2008 only six global players entered the market (Veolia, Arriva, First, Transdev, Keolis and the investment fund Babcock Brown via its subsidiary Bene). The global players are only observed as being the (first) competitors/newcomers in seven of the 70 real market initiatives. In reality, SMEs which were the first competitors in 57% (43 cases) of the real market initiatives propelled development. Municipal operators represent 17% (12 cases) and the national railway operator Deutsche Bahn AG, being one of the main bus operators in Germany, represents 16% (11 cases).

For the most aggressive form of CCL procedures, in which the first newcomer tries to compete against the incumbent directly on its own initiative (without a PTA which i.e. encourages a tendering or CCL procedure), SMEs hold a market share of 63% (see Fig. 10.6) and are thus also the main drivers. Market shares by competitor

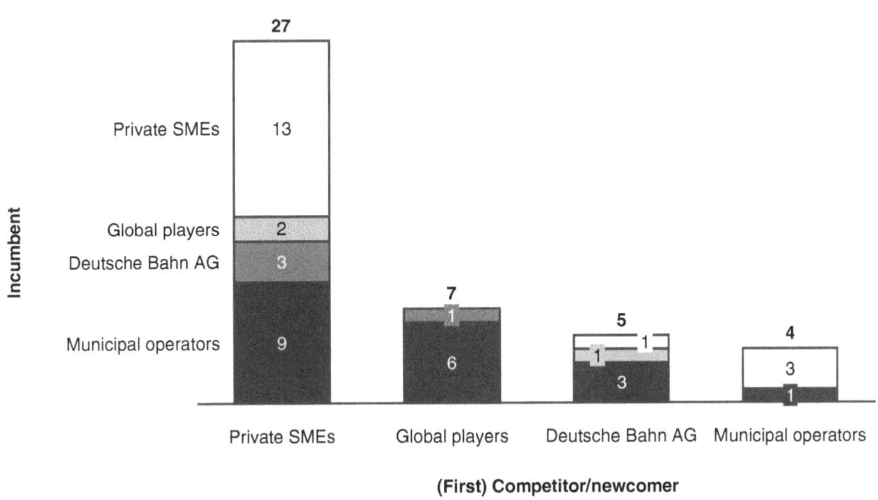

Fig. 10.6 Number of competitive applications 2003–2008

are: 16% global players (7 cases), 12% Deutsche Bahn AG (5 cases), 9% municipal operators (4 cases). The incumbent market shares are: 44% municipal operators (19 cases), 40% SMEs (17 cases), 9% Deutsche Bahn AG (4 cases), 7% global players (3 cases). Note that this is significantly different to the development of the structure of operators within the market for non-commercial services presented in Sect. 8.4.2, where currently global players are the main actors.

All in all, when analyzing the CCL market, the question arises whether a stronger increase is being prevented by market entry barriers. Within the following section the empirical analysis therefore aims to evaluate whether entry barriers for commercial services exist.[10]

10.3.3 Empirical Analysis

10.3.3.1 The Existence of Entry Barriers for Commercial Services

For operators aiming to grow tendering is the only realistic alternative to CCL procedures. Therefore, I compare the level of competition between tendering and CCL. To verify whether barriers to entry exist for CCL procedures, I hypothesize:

Hypothesis IV.1: The number of bidders per case is lower in CCL procedures than in tendering procedures

In a first step, I measure the levels of competition by the average number of bidders per procedure as given by the CCL-database (database III) compared to the level of competition in tendering procedures as published in well-known empirical studies on tendering procedures in German public bus transport services. In a second step, I present the results of the empirical comparison. This analysis is based on database I (113 lots tendered in the period 2003–2008 described in Chap. 8) and database III (117 CCL procedures with start of operations in the period 2003–2008).[11] Figure 10.7 shows that the number of bidders for CCL procedures is low compared to tendering procedures. While an average of 1.8 bidders is observed in the CCL procedures in database III (procedures mainly in rural and in suburban areas), the study by Beck and Wanner (2007, p. 27) shows an average of 7 bidders per case, for 81 lots for gross-cost contracts tendered out in the period 1996–2006 in the rural and suburban areas of Hamburg, Frankfurt am Main and Munich. The high level of

[10] The lack of detailed data available makes difficult any in-depth analysis of the experiences of CCL similar to Chap. 8 (e.g., with respect to the development of the level of quality, impacts for employees, . . .).

[11] I chose tendering-database I instead of tendering-database II because only database I covers the same period (2003–2008) as database III, whereas tendering-database II includes data for 2009.

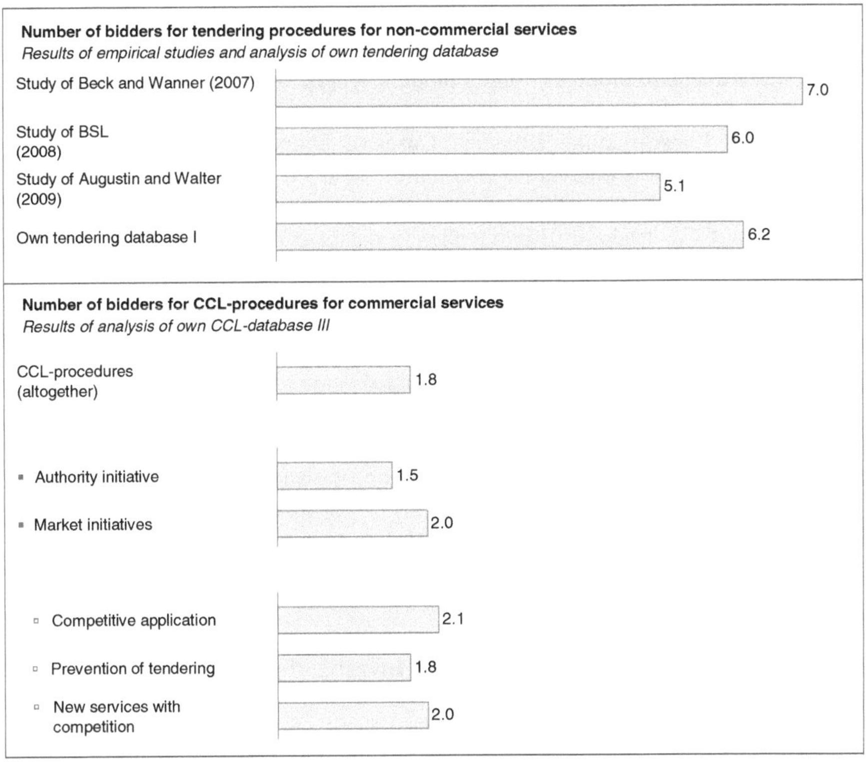

Fig. 10.7 Number of bidders

competition in the competitive market for non-commercial services is confirmed by a study by BSL (2008, p. 15) that shows 6 bidders per case for 60 lots for gross-cost contracts in the period 2003–2007 mainly located in the rural and suburban areas of Frankfurt am Main. The most recent work is Augustin and Walter (2009, p. 9) who show 5.1 bidders per case on average for 196 lots tendered in 1997–2009 in rural, suburban, and urban areas. Database I show 6.2 bidders on average. In summary, these empirical studies indicate that the number of bidders is significantly lower for CCL procedures than for tendering procedures.[12]

Database III shows the heterogeneity of competition in the different classifications of CCL procedures. Authority initiatives account for just 1.5 bidders per CCL procedure. More than 2 bidders per case are observed for only three procedures conducted by the public transport association Verkehrsverbund Rhein-Neckar GmbH (VRN) in the rural and suburban Mannheim area (8, 4, and 3 bidders per case) and for the procedures conducted by the PTA rural district Wittenberg

[12] Interestingly, numerous cases in the Frankfurt am Main area and some in the Munich area show this difference in the same region.

(3 bidders per case).[13] Among the market initiated applications, cases of competing applications against an incumbent have 2.1 bidders on average, with just two cases having more than two bidders (7 and 3 bidders, respectively). Cases of commercial applications to counter a non-commercial tendering procedure have 1.8 bidders on average, with 4 cases having 3 bidders. Cases of competing applications for new services have 2 bidders on average. For a more detailed description see Table 10.1 below and Table A.9 in the Appendix A.3.1.

Integrating CCL-database III into tendering-database I and thus forming database IV, leads to the question whether a simple empirical investigation of the Model 10.1:

$$(10.1)\ \textit{number of bidders per case} = \alpha + \beta_1\ (\textit{CCL procedure}) + \upsilon$$

would confirm the results as indicated in Fig. 10.7 above. The empirical analysis of an integrated database IV of all 230 cases conducted using ordinary least squares (OLS) regression shows a clear negative correlation between the dependent variable *number of bidders per case* and the independent (dummy) variable *CCL procedure*, which is highly significant at 99.99%.,[14 15] Summing up, the analysis confirms Hypothesis 10.1: the level of competition is significantly lower in the competitive market for commercial services than in the competitive market for non-commercial services.

10.3.3.2 Other Results of the Empirical Investigation

When looking at the results above, indicating market entry barriers for CCL procedures, the question arises: What factors prevent more newcomers from entering the market for commercial services? What entry barriers prevent more bidders from applying to operate commercial services despite the significantly higher statistical probability of winning a CCL procedure compared to a normal tendering procedure?

To identify the factors that prevent market entry, I undertake a second empirical analysis using OLS-regression and the likelihood ratio test.[16] Based on the interviews with experts, I selected criteria as independent variables to examine whether a significant correlation could be identified with the dependent variable *number of bidders per CCL procedure*. Table A.11 in Appendix A.3.1 shows that a clear correlation cannot be identified. The same applies to a sub-analysis based on the data samples per classification of CCL procedures as presented in Table 10.1 above, where a sufficient database with a minimum of 30 cases is only available for *authority initiatives*, *real market initiatives* and *competitive applications*. Other than for the

---

[13] These authority initiated CCL procedures are described in Table A.8 in Appendix A.3.1.

[14] The empirical analysis is conducted using Stata for Windows 9.1. The 230 cases analyzed are the sum of n = 113 tendering procedures (database I) and n = 117 CCL procedures (database II).

[15] Further results are in Table 10.2 below; descriptive statistics and the correlation matrix are in Tables A.12 and A.13 in Appendix A.3.2.

[16] For a more detailed description of database III and a pairwise Pearson correlation matrix, see Table A.9 and Table A.10 in Appendix A.3.1.

Table 10.1 Descriptive statistics for number of bidders and volume per case for database III

	Observations	Mean	Maximum	Minimum	Standard deviation
All CCL procedures	117				
Number of bidders	117	1.82	8	1	1.01
Number of lines	117	6.7	50	1	8.90
Vkm p.a.	46	600,728	3,400,000	20,000	625,229
Authority initiatives by PTA	47				
Number of bidders	47	1.53	8	1	1.25
Number of lines	47	6.36	50	1	8.52
Vehicle kilometers p.a.	25	545400	25,000	3,400,000	661,600
Real market initiatives	70				
Number of bidders	70	2.01	7	1	0.7517
Number of lines	70	7.04	40	1	9.3273
Vkm p.a.	21	666,595.2	2,513,000	20,000	588,143
Competitive application	43				
Number of bidders	43	2.14	7	2	0.77
Number of lines	43	8.74	40	1	11.41
Vkm p.a.	4	863,750	2,513,000	100,000	1,113,692
Prevention of tendering	22				
Number of bidders	22	1.77	3	1	0.75
Number of lines	22	5.09	13	1	2.53
Vkm p.a.	15	699,033	180,000	1,330,000	397,567
New services with competition	5				
Number of bidders	5	2.00	2	2	0.00
Number of lines	5	1.00	1	1	0.00
Vkm p.a.	2	29,000	20,000	38,000	12,727.92

criteria in Table A.11, the independent (dummy) variables, *competitive application* and *authority initiative by PTA*, show a correlation on a significant level when using simple OLS-regression.

The analysis shows a positive correlation for Model 10.2.1:

(10.2.1) *number of bidders per CCL* $= \alpha + \beta_2$ *(competitive application)* $+ \upsilon$

with a significance level of 99.2% (see Table 10.2 below), while a distortion cannot be excluded for the only 2 cases with more than 2 bidders (see explanations above). Note that in addition to the positive correlation for *competitive application*, authority initiated CCL procedures show a negative correlation for Model 10.2.2:

(10.2.2) *number of bidders per CCL* $= \alpha + \beta_3$ *(authority initiative by PTA)* $+ \upsilon$

with a significance level of 99%, while a distortion cannot be excluded for the only two PTAs with more than two bidders (see explanations above and further results in Table A.8 in the Appendix A.3.1).

As shown in Fig. 10.7 above, the empirical analysis confirms that authority initiated procedures attract fewer applicants than market initiated procedures with competitive application processes. Furthermore, the analysis of authority initiated

Table 10.2 Results for simple OLS-regression for Models 10.1, 10.2.1 and 10.2.2

Model Explanatory Variables	(10.1) Number of bidders per case	(10.2.1) Number of bidders per CCL	(10.2.2) Number of bidders per CCL
CCL procedure ∈ {0;1}	−4.4096*** (0.29509)		
Competitive application ∈ {0;1}		0.5044*** (0.1878)	
Authority initiative by PTA ∈ {0;1}			-0.4824*** (0.1850)
Constant	6.2301*** (0.2105)	1.6351*** (0.1139)	2.0143*** (0.1137)
Observations	230	117	117
F-value	223.30	7.21	6.80
Prob > F	0.0000	0.0083	0.0103
R^2	0.4948	0.0590	0.0558

Standard errors in parentheses
Significance *** 99%

CCL procedures presented in Table A.8 in the Appendix indicates that providing sufficient passenger-related data promotes a higher number of applicants per procedure. However, due to the low number of cases with sufficient passenger-related data, a significant correlation cannot be confirmed by the empirical analysis of database III.[17]

10.3.4 *Intermediate Results*

The results presented so far show that public transport bus services in Germany are characterized by a high level of freedom for operators to design the service in the market for commercial services compared to the level in tendering procedures, where PTAs award public service contracts usually with detailed conditions (see Sect. 4.4.2 and Sect. 5.5). Operators should therefore be interested in (and able to)

[17] Other than for CCL procedures, as shown by the empirical analysis of CCL database III, the empirical investigation of tendering-database I presented in Sect. 8.4.3 indicates that market entry barriers within tendering procedures exist for several parameters on a significant level. An empirical analysis of integrated database IV might identify additional impact factors on the level of competition. Since this latter analysis would presumably contain a bias with respect to (1) an awarding procedure and a market organization that differs substantially between CCL procedures and tendering procedures and (2) totally different empirical results (no relevant correlations identified for the CCL database, several such correlations identified for the tendering database), it will not be discussed further. Note that the assessment of a bias was affirmed by the results of an analysis in which a significant correlation with the dependent variable number of bidders per case was indicated for several parameters (e.g., negative correlation to federal states where only CCL procedures had been observed [especially Lower Saxony and North Rhine-Westphalia], positive correlation to the federal state Hesse, where most of the tendering procedures were conducted [63% of all n = 113 tendering procedures in database I]).

initiate a more intensely competitive environment by handing in competing applications for commercial lines or services without any efforts of PTAs to encourage competition. However, Sect. 10.3.3 shows that the level of competition in CCL procedures compared to tendering procedures is lower, so that market entry barriers have to be assumed. The empirical analysis of database III shows no evidence of a correlation for most of the influence factors assumed, and that the two correlations identified are in opposition and are only relevant for two of the four classifications of CCL procedures. The issue then becomes identifying other factors that might hinder more intense competition for commercial services with a higher number of bidders per case and possibly more CCL procedures.

10.4 Uncertainty as a Structural Problem

10.4.1 Uncertainty: An Entry Barrier for Commercial Services?

Section 4.6 shows the existing federal institutional framework has a major impact on market participants' opportunities for action. This raises the question whether this regulatory framework is adequate to promote a competitive environment in the market for commercial services, or is a hindrance. Given numerous critical discussion papers on this subject (a.o. BLFA 2006; Recker 2007 and VDV 2008), one can hypothesize that the existing framework for commercial services does not foster a competitive market but rather impedes a greater number of competitive applications by operators. Thus, I analyze this framework in more detail in the following.

As already presented, McAfee et al. (2004, p. 465) stress that market entry barriers are all disadvantages to newcomers compared to incumbents, including "uncertainty about market conditions". They find that even a group of smaller barriers together may form a relevant entry barrier. If the level of uncertainty from a newcomer's view is (significantly) higher than the level for the incumbent, thus forcing the newcomer to reckon with higher risk costs than the incumbent, it may also be classified as a disadvantage. I therefore test the following hypothesis:

Hypothesis IV.2: The level of uncertainty for a typical CCL procedure is significantly higher than for usual tendering procedures

As questions arise whether the framework is adequate, I will explore whether this regulatory system creates a high level of uncertainty that negatively influences the competitive market for commercial services as compared to tendering for non-commercial services. The investigation of entry barriers begins in Sect. 10.4.2 with an overview of general aspects such as market organization and organization of public funding. Section 10.4.3 analyzes the procedural setting. Finally, the market development is assessed on a state level in Sect. 10.4.4. All analysis is based on the framework relevant for the CCL database III for the period 2003–2008 which corresponds to the framework described in Chap. 4.

10.4.2 Uncertainty About General Aspects

Uncertainty on the part of operators can prevent newcomers from entering the market, thereby resulting in a lower level of competition per case and a lower number of CCL procedures overall. Proper market organization and public funding are crucial for newcomers when assessing the overall risk level. The German market for public bus transport services is characterized by a market organization in which commercial and non-commercial services exist side by side. The theoretical examination in Sect. 4.6 raises doubts about the feasibility and user-friendliness of this system for operators and authorities alike. These doubts arise especially at the threshold between commercial and non-commercial, and they relate especially to the current system of market organization and an awarding procedure that fundamentally differs across service types. The potential for uncertainty about the classification of services as commercial or non-commercial is one of the main pitfalls of this system. Nevertheless, since this aspect of uncertainty will generally affect commercial as well as non-commercial services, its influence on the level of competition for commercial services remains unclear (although undeniable).

The financing structure for public funding of bus transport services is also troublesome. As previously noted in Sect. 4.3.1, even describing the main aspects of the financing structure in Germany is a daunting task. The differences between the states, and often at the regional and/or local levels, with no clear obligation on the part of authorities to publish all information on public funding is even more troublesome.[18] In response the states Brandenburg, Saxony-Anhalt and Schleswig-Holstein have adjusted compensation payments to operators for reduced fares for pupils and the disabled (now being a simple lump-sum payment). Other states are discussing such a reform, too. Figure 10.8 provides an overview of the reforms of public co-funding by states. Note that these compensation payments are one of the main sources of public funding for operators of short-distance services.[19]

Indeed, incumbent operators which have delivered services over years or decades should be able to calculate all public funds they can expect to receive for a specific service. For newcomers to the market, the multitude of financing

[18] See Sterzenbach (2008, pp. 97 and 101) for examples on state and local levels and Sect. 5.4 as well as Hickmann et al. (2008) for an example of states that have revised their financing structure in recent years.

[19] See Sect. 4.3.1 for more details on these compensatory payments.

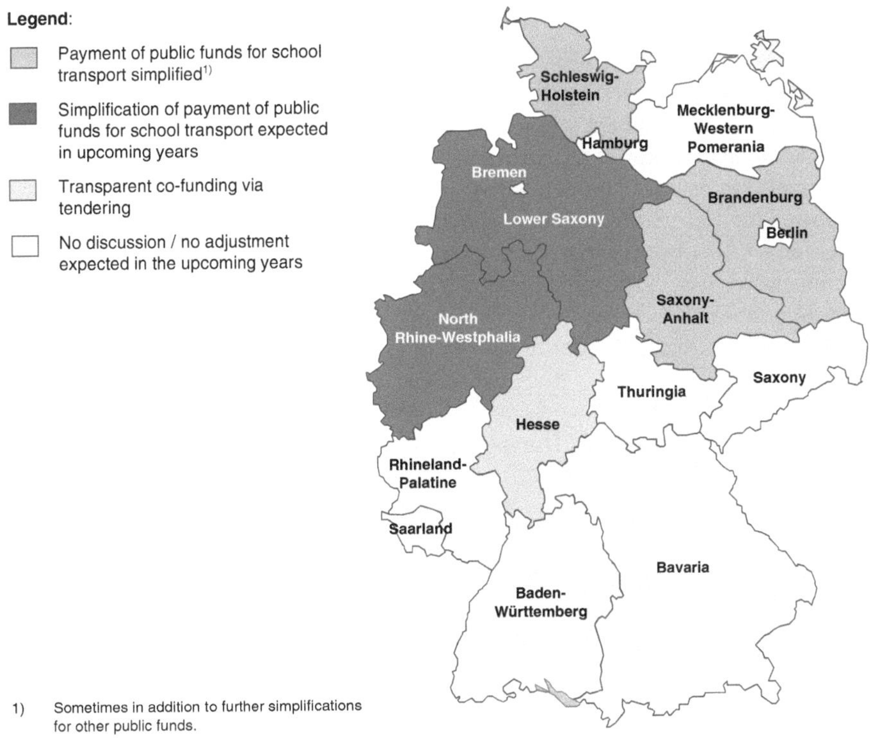

Fig. 10.8 Public funding within the states: lump sum payment of § 45a funds

instruments available makes it difficult to assess the expected subsidies. As described in Sect. 4.3.1 Sterzenbach (2008, p. 105) classifies the German financing structure for public transport with its numerous financing sources and streams as "non-transparent." This was confirmed by the Academic Advisory Council at the Federal Ministry of Transport, which describes the financing structure as "historically developed, complicated, and widely in transparent" (see Wissenschaftsrat of the BMVBS 2008, p. 82). Since public service contracts for non-commercial services provide operators with a clear funding scheme usually based on the amount of vehicle kilometers ordered and more or less fixed for the term of a contract, the level of uncertainty remains low for tendered services.[20] In contrast to this calculable public funding for non-commercial services, assessing public funding for commercial services is extremely difficult for newcomers.

[20] See gross-cost contracts of RMV (2005) and MVV (2009).

10.4.3 *Analysis of Uncertainty Within the Procedural Setting*

As explained above, a setting that minimizes market entry barriers is characterized by limiting the incumbent's potential to discriminate and reducing newcomers' uncertainty and risk costs. Authorities may also undertake active efforts to promote a competitive market through other independent measures. This Sect. 10.4.3 compares the typical regulations for tendering procedures for gross-cost contracts based on VOL/A to the typical regulations for CCL procedures based on German administrative law.[21] The structure of the assessment follows the three stages of the awarding schedule (see Sect. 10.2.1): preparation, approval, and the license term.[22]

10.4.3.1 Possible Barriers During the Preparation Phase

Role of the Incumbent

In the preparation phase, there are several possible barriers to entry. A minor one is the potential for discrimination by the incumbent resulting from the requirement of the Passenger Transport Act (§ 8 [3] PBefG) requiring PTAs to include existing operators in developing the local public transport plan (PTP). Since the PTP is the LA's basis for determining the level of minimum quality to be delivered by applicants, setting its own standards in the developmental process might benefit the incumbent. Moreover, the PTP must respect "existing structures of public transport."[23] Although the same paragraph obliges PTAs to avoid discrimination against operators, it is questionable whether this obligation is sufficient to limit the influence of the incumbent (e.g., by optimizing network aspects with respect to the location of its own bus depot).[24]

[21] See Sects. 4.3, 7.1 and 10.2.1 for a detailed explanation of these procedures.

[22] The institutional problem of overlapping responsibilities and areas of authority between LA and PTA in the three stages (see Werner 2001, pp. 161–165 among others) is not analyzed in detail here.

[23] The PBefG states that "the formation of the PTP, decided on by the PTA, is mandatory. Further, in this plan existing transport structures have to be taken into account. In addition the formation of the plan has to involve existing companies and should not lead to unequal treatment of operators." Barth (2001, pp. 63–64) favors the involvement of operators, since PTAs usually lack data about passenger figures, revenues and linkages in local public transport.

[24] See Barth (2001, pp. 64–67) for a description of the unclear legal framework on this matter; according to Graetz et al. (2007, p. 14), at least 3% of the 150 PTAs in their database confirmed that their PTP was developed entirely by the incumbent operator.

Revenue Risks

Another aspect that plays a role for the operator is his assessment of the revenue risk. Since operators of commercial services must assume revenue risks, the services tend to be comparable to net-cost contracts with respect to the risk level. Section 7.3.2 explained that operators usually assume a higher level of risk in net-cost contracts than in gross-cost contracts. Gross-cost contracts are used for most of the non-commercial services tendered in Germany (~ 75% according to experts). Databases compiled by Beck and Wanner (2007) and BSL (2008) are exclusively based on gross-cost contracts, with an average number of 7.0 and 6.0 bidders, respectively. The database of Augustin and Walter (2009) and my tendering-databases I and II are based on a set that includes only a very limited share of net-cost contracts, and show 5.1, 6.2 and 5.4 bidders on average, respectively. The results of these studies also indicate a negative correlation on a significant level for the independent dummy variable *net-cost contract*. A rough analysis of the small number of ten net-cost contracts tendered by the VRN in 2006–2008 shows 3.5 bidders on average, well below the overall average for gross-cost contracts of 5–7 bidders.[25] This again confirms the assessment in Sect. 7.4 and the results in Sect. 8.4.3 that revenue risks influence the level of competition. Nevertheless, net-cost contracts are generally favorable to gross-cost contracts with respect to incentives (see Beck 2009a, pp. 64 and 118–120), although the risk trade-offs should always be borne in mind (see also Sects. 7.3.2 and 7.5).

Collecting sufficient market intelligence is a basic requirement for operators in a functioning competitive market. However, no specific legal obligation exists for LAs, PTAs and incumbents to provide at least a minimum level of relevant revenue information in a non-discriminatory manner. Nevertheless, since significant information costs and/or risk costs only arise for newcomers, PTAs should encourage and facilitate competing market initiatives for commercial services through timely, transparent, and complete publication of the data. Doing so decreases the risk of winner's curse, a common experience that also prevents newcomers from entering the market for commercial services.

Legal Security

Another aspect that might induce uncertainty for an operator in the preparation phase is that the likelihood, duration, and cost of legal proceedings following an LA's approval are uncertainties in CCL procedures. CCL-database III shows that 49 CCL approvals by LAs (42% of all procedures) resulted in litigation

[25] Own calculation based on VRN's publications in the Supplement of the *Official Journal of the European Union* up to December 31, 2008, verified with Michael Winnes, legal advisor to the VRN. To date, VRN is the only German PTA that has conducted numerous tendering procedures with net-cost contracts.

(17 reversals, 25 administrative court procedures, and 7 higher administrative court procedures).[26] Since the CCL procedures are based on German administrative law, rather than German public procurement law,[27] court procedures for CCL are frequently lengthy. The average duration in CCL-database III terminated by the end of 2008 (22 of all proceedings) is 10 months; 27 other proceedings that had not terminated by the end of 2008 had already lasted for 19 months on average from the planned start of operations (and renewal of the respective license). In fact, one proceeding dragged on for 56 months.

The experts interviewed stated that due to lack of time limits especially in market initiated procedures, the first application is usually submitted in a few months, and sometimes a few weeks, before the start of operations. Thus, legal procedures usually are not concluded before the termination of the old license. In these cases, the LA is required to grant a provisional approval (§ 20 PBefG) to secure continuous delivery of services (see Werner 2001, pp. 147–148). Here, the preliminary licensee never knows whether the final legal decision will confirm the LA's provisional approval, or whether a successful settlement or agreement between the competitors will be reached.

In contrast, the usual duration of legal proceedings following tendering in accordance with VOL/A is shorter. According to the lawyers interviewed, the legal proceedings for straightforward non-commercial services usually takes just 3 (for decisions in awarding chamber) to 6 months (for decisions in regional appeals court) to conclude following a tendering procedure. This reduces the financial risk substantially. Moreover, PTAs tend to allow enough time for potential legal proceedings in the tendering schedule (see the recommendations in the annex of VDV 2007). Again, the conclusion must be that the existing legal framework is inadequate for a competitive market for commercial services.

10.4.3.2 Possible Barriers in the Approval Phase

Incumbent Privilege

If the incumbent has provided adequate services in the past, the LA must consider this in the validation procedure (privilege of the incumbent, see § 13 Art. 3 PBefG and Werner 2001, pp. 104–106). This regulation aims to ensure well-established local structures, to award contracts to operators who have provided reliable services in the past, and to secure the long-term investments of the incumbent. However, if the extent of preferential treatment in the LA's validation procedure is unclear, it

[26] Since the court decision has not been released for the other 68 CCL procedures of the n = 117 CCL in database III, the total number of litigations may be greater than 49.

[27] In particular, the Official German Contracting Terms for Award of Service Performance Contracts, Part A (Verdingungsordnung für Leistungen, Teil A – VOL/A).

poses another source of uncertainty for newcomers. There are no such obligations favoring the incumbent in tendering procedures or in any other market.

Validation Procedure

By validating the fulfillment of minimum standards in the first step as explained in Sect. 4.3.2, the authority aims to prevent or reduce any hidden characteristics arising from informational asymmetry in this principal-agent-relationship to the operator. The authority (the principal) usually has little knowledge of the capabilities of the applicant (agent) compared to the operator and desires to avoid a so-called negative selection, whereby it awards an incapable operator. The authorities are therefore in a position to utilize their first-mover advantage by determining procedural conditions. If utilized properly, this advantage may influence market results significantly. The validation conditions set by the LA thus are a key condition for the success of a CCL.

Section 4.3.2 also shows that although the PTP is usually the instrument by which PTAs establish a minimum quality, the LAs have no clear legal obligation to take the PTP fully into account. This again may lead to uncertainty for operators. Additionally, the main problem is probably the validation procedure itself. While it may be relatively easy for the LAs to determine whether an application fulfils the minimum requirements, e.g., security aspects, economic capability, reputation, delivery of appropriate services according to the PTP, it is more difficult to select the best bid regarding quality levels. Again, there is no legal regulation on how to make such decisions (see Beck 2007, p. 425). This important aspect will therefore be discussed in the following.[28]

Tendering procedures in Germany as well as in other European countries like Britain, Denmark and Sweden usually use price competition whereby the PTA mainly defines the quality level (see Beck 2007, RMV 2005; MVV 2009; Amaral et al. 2006 and Alexandersson and Pyddoke 2003). Without direct subsidies, however, this quality level is usually not commercially feasible for operators. The PTAs judge bids largely or entirely based on the single-dimension level of subsidies/price to be paid in Euros. This promotes a transparent and easy-to-handle validation procedure for authorities and provides a calculable procedure for newcomers.

In contrast, CCL procedures are characterized by competition over quality levels above the minimum level of the PTP. This is a quality competition with a multi-dimensional validation procedure. For a clear, single-dimension based ranking, LAs should be able to provide operators with a transparent catalog to validate the multitude of ideas, applications and proposals received. Due to the fact that a monetarily based transformation system, a system rooted in welfare theory, was

[28] On this issue see Werner (2001, pp. 102–103) and Sect. 4.3.2.

not observed, it may be that it is impossible to develop such a catalog due to the complexity of such methods.[29] The quality index developed by the LA in the Wittenberg case still remains one of the most detailed ones published in Germany to date.[30] The LA assigned a value to each quality criterion according to a specified grading system, and weighted each aspect by importance; the quality index represents the sum of all marks. I note, however, that even this index cannot prevent different validation results from different assessors, making these decisions susceptible to appeals by the losing party and creating more uncertainty for newcomers.[31]

There is no legal obligation for LAs to publish or even develop an internal assessment catalog prior to the approval phase. In a sense, this increases flexibility for the LAs during the approval phase. It also gives a great deal of freedom to the operators since they are free to engage in a process in which their innovative activities are not measured by a rigid assessment system (also called beauty contest). While it can be argued that the risk of wrong expectations about the focus of the assessment system is a common business risk, such frameworks can increase uncertainty for newcomers unfamiliar with LAs' decisions and preferences. Lack of transparency also gives rise to a biased validation of offers, unlike tendering procedures (according to VOL/A) that oblige PTAs to publish selection criteria for the selection of the winner before undertaking the approval phase.[32]

10.4.3.3 Possible Barriers During the License Term

During the license term, the most critical aspect from an operator's view is how potential cost risks develop (cost risks for input factors). Operators can underestimate the increase in costs for input factors, such as the price of fuel and personnel or other external effects, over the entire license term.[33] According to the experts interviewed, LAs which, according to § 39 PBefG, are responsible for keeping track of fare adjustments usually approve operators' applications for fare increases and ensure that these increases are high enough to refinance the expected rise in

[29] See Borrmann (2003, pp. 108–128) for this method in the public transport industry and Beck (2007, p. 429) for problems of multi-dimensional validation for CCL procedures. For more details on multidimensional auctions, see e.g., Branco (1997) and Che (1993).

[30] See Borrmann (2003, pp. 129–140) for quality index in public transport services and Sect. 5.4.2 for a detailed explanation of the Wittenberg case.

[31] This is one reason why this aspect is still in litigation as of the end of 2008, for the first Wittenberg case, where the LA first approved the best application form in October 2006 (according to Holger Zubke, Wittenberg district council).

[32] The importance of a transparent validation procedure for awarding procedures in public transport to prevent uncertainty and encourage bidders to participate is confirmed by Amaral et al. (2008).

[33] § 16 (2) PBefG permits a maximum of 8 years, the usual term for commercial services according to the experts interviewed.

costs for input factors. Upon an operator's request, LAs can approve a partial reduction of services to ensure the operator's commercial stability either temporarily or permanently (see § 21 [4] PBefG and Werner 2001, pp. 142–144).

Nevertheless, there is no guarantee that the LA will approve the above measures requested by each operator. Moreover, the licensee is obliged to continue the full delivery of services until the requested change of services is approved and taken effect. In tendering procedures, indexation or other PTA regulations can lower the risk of increasing prices for the major input factors, such as fuel and personnel, and the major external effects for operators.[34] It can be argued that rises in input factors and time lags in decision-making of authorities are common risk factors. Yet, compared to non-commercial services where such aspects are regulated in public service contracts, the risk level for commercial services is slightly higher due to uncertainty about the extent (full or partial approval of applications to amend the license by LA) and the timing of approval by the LA.

10.4.3.4 Overview of Uncertainties

The analysis of the procedural setting provided insight into numerous aspects of uncertainty from a newcomer perspective in the market for commercial services. Summing up, Table 10.3 shows that the overall level of uncertainty for operators in the procedural setting for usual CCL procedures is higher than in the setting for usual tendering procedures analyzed by e.g., Beck and Wanner (2007) and BSL (2008). The complex financing structure of public funding explained in Sect. 10.4.2 further increases the level of uncertainty for commercial services from a newcomer's perspective.

The total level of uncertainty helps to explain the low number of bidders observed for CCL procedures compared to tendering procedures and therefore confirms Hypothesis 10.2. Thus, this overview indicates that uncertainty is a main entry barrier within the competitive market for commercial services.

10.4.4 Different Developments in the Federal States

10.4.4.1 Opportunities to Encourage Competition at the State Level

Although entry barriers obviously exist in the current institutional framework on the national level, federal states and/or their authorities are free to encourage competition in their sphere of responsibility. The next sections thus analyze the activities of (1) federal states, (2) their licensing authorities, and (3) public

[34] See RMV (2005) and MVV (2009).

Table 10.3 Assessment of possible barriers to entry with respect to uncertainty

	Aspect	Usual regulation within (German) tendering procedures for gross-cost contracts based on VOL/A	Usual regulation within (German) CCL-procedures based on German adminstrative law	Supposed level of uncertainty for tendering compared to CCL
Preparation phase	Contribution of existing operators to PTP	PTA defines q with awarding conditions based on q_m out of PTP	Operator determines q with application form based on q_m out of PTP	→
	Revenue risk to be borne by operator	No revenue risk for ~75% of procedures tendered so far	Full revenue risk	↓
	Risk form legal proceeding following approval/awarding (costs for proceeding, legal security at start of operations)	Legal proceedings based on German public procurement law	Legal proceedings based on German administrative law	↓
Approval phase	Privilege of the incumbent	No privilege usual	Privilege within approval if services were delivered appropriately so far	↓
	Validation procedure in a clear manner (leaving no question mark)	Usually price competition, validation (almost) totally with respect to price offered (single dimension)	Quality competition only (multi-dimension), no regulation on establishment of assessment catalogue	↓
	Transparency about validation procedure in preparation phase	Obligation to publish the validation criteria	No obligation to publish assessment catalog or validation criteria for quality competition	↓
LT	Risk from increasing prices for main input factors	Assumed via indexation or other regulations by the PTA	Adjustment upon application of license	→

↑ higher risk level assumed, → similar risk level, ↓ lower risk level assumed
LT License term, q quality offered/delivered by operator, q_m minimum quality level as defined by the PTA in its PTP

authorities to promote or support competition for commercial lines or services by the end of 2008 based on the research presented in Table 10.4.

10.4.4.2 Initiatives by the Ministries of Transports

As can be seen in Table 10.4, only a limited number of federal states engaged themselves in restructuring CCL procedures in their area of responsibility, namely the ministries of transport in Brandenburg, Hesse, Lower Saxony, North Rhine-Westphalia, and Saxony-Anhalt. In Brandenburg the ministry of transport obliged the LA to publish lists of license expiration dates in the summer of 2007 and improved clarity about the procedural setting via official recommendations about conducting CCL procedures. As discussed in Sect. 5.4.1, Hesse reformed the awarding of public transport services and obliged PTAs to tender services to a large extent and published recommendations on how to award services. The LA of Lower Saxony, supported by the ministry of transport, was one of the first to structure the CCL procedures with respect to time limits (2002). In 2007 it restructured procedures based on first experiences. In North Rhine-Westphalia the ministry of transport published official recommendations to the LAs on how to conduct CCL procedures, including publication of license expiration dates 12 months in advance, fair and non-discriminatory procedures, and time limits for filing applications. Saxony-Anhalt is the only state that has made a clear decision to solely promote CCL procedures. It has also published recommendations on how to award licenses for commercial services (see Sect. 5.4.2).

10.4.4.3 Initiatives by Licensing Authorities

Most LAs failed to structure their approval procedures in a transparent manner.[35] For example, time limits on applications were not published in most of the cases observed, which, according to Werner (2001, pp. 40–41, 56–58, and 165), resulted in operators applying at strategic points in time. In recent years, a few states (see Table 10.4) and/or their LAs, in addition to some PTAs, have chosen to structure the preparation and approval phases, publish transparent information about license expiration dates and/or promote competition for public bus transport services.

---

[35] Procedural regulations for tendering are strongly and clearly regulated by national procurement law (see VOL/A as well as Klinger 2006, a.o.) and their execution is based on a history of best practices by several important PTAs (e.g., the awarding conditions of MVV 2009, based on awarding experience for more than 70 networks in the period 1996–2009; the awarding conditions of RMV 2005, based on awarding experience for 20 networks in the period 2003–2005; and VDV 2007).

Table 10.4 Analysis of regulatory adjustments in order to clarify the framework (See a.o. Bezirksregierung Arnsberg (2008) and Bezirksregierung Detmold (2008))

State	Regulatory adjustments
Bavaria	
At state level	No relevant activities observed
Licensing authority	No relevant activities observed
Public transport authorities	Especially since 1999, suburban districts of Munich have used tendering for non-commercial services with a clear commitment to introduce competition
Brandenburg	
At state level	Online publication of license expiration dates since summer 2007, initiated by the ministry of transport of the state of Brandenburg (see Landesamt für Bauen und Verkehr Brandenburg 2008), as well as official recommendations from the Brandenburg Ministry of Transport to the Brandenburg LA on how to conduct CCL procedures (see MIR 2007). With only one exception, all CCL procedures in the database located in Brandenburg occurred after summer 2007
Licensing authority	Licensing authority acts under the direct order of the ministry of transport
Public transport authorities	No relevant activities observed
Hesse	
At state level	Awarding policy of the state and most PTAs reformed since 2002, caused by a re-classification of the public transport services as non-commercial. Since then bus transport services not operated by municipal operators are in most cases tendered by PTAs at time of renewal of the license (see Sect. 5.4.1 for the awarding policy of Hesse). Some services operated by municipal operators are also tendered out (e.g., Frankfurt am Main). Recommendations for LAs are published by the Hesse Ministry of Transport
Licensing authorities	LAs act according to the recommendations of the ministry of transport
Public transport Authorities	See above
Lower Saxony	
At state level	Ministry of transport supports activities of the LA described below
Licensing authorities	According to Rainer Peters, chief officer of the LA for Lower Saxony, the first decisions to structure the procedures with respect to time limits dates to 2002 (e.g., first applications only possible from 21 months before start of operations). A complete internal procedure was developed for the first time, including regulations for full transparency, in 2005, revised in 2007 as a result of debates with local associations and published at the beginning of 2008 (see LNVG 2008)
Public transport Authorities	Only two PTAs (ZVSN and rural district Cuxhaven) initiate CCL procedures on their own
North Rhine-Westphalia	
At state level	Official recommendations from the state ministry of transport to the licensing authorities on how to conduct CCL procedures, including publication of expiration dates for licenses 12 months in advance, fair and non-discriminatory procedures, time limits for filing applications (see MBV NW 2008)

(continued)

Table 10.4 (continued)

State	Regulatory adjustments
Licensing authorities	According to Friedrich Drewes of the LA Detmold, online publication of license expiration dates since mid-2007 (LAs Düsseldorf, Cologne, Arnsberg), and by the end of 2008 (LA Detmold)
Public transport authorities	Promotion of competition for commercial services through 11 invitations for bids since 2005 for Detmold/Bielefeld/Gütersloh area by VVOWL
Saxony	
At state level	No relevant decisions published until the end of 2008
Licensing authorities	Online publication of license expiration dates since December 15, 2008 (see, as an example, Landesdirektion Dresden 2008), only two CCL procedures prior to 2008
Public transport authorities	No activities observed
Saxony-Anhalt	
At state level	New regulatory framework in 2005 promotes competition for commercial services (see Sect. 5.4.2 for a detailed explanation of the new warding policy), all CCL procedures in the database from that federal state occurred after 2005
Licensing authorities	See below
Public transport authorities	In rural areas several PTAs and LAs co-initiate CCL procedures
Other nine states	No significant adjustments observed

By the end of 2008 a few LAs (Bezirksregierung Detmold and Bezirksregierung Arnsberg in North Rhine-Westphalia, Landesdirektion Dresden in Saxony, Landesamt für Verkehr Brandenburg in Brandenburg) began publishing license expirations online. However, LAs have only been obligated to inform operators upon direct request since the ruling of the BVerwG (see Sect. 10.3.2). Again, there is no legal obligation to publish this information. This existing legal framework might be sufficient where there is low interest from operators in a market. However, it does not confirm active promotion of competition by most LAs.

10.4.4.4 Initiatives by Public Transport Authorities

A reliable way to encourage competition is to issue an invitation for bids by PTAs (authority initiative for CCL procedures). Forty-seven such cases observed in the period 2003–2008 represent a marginal number of cases compared to total market volume. For example, the state with the highest number of authority initiatives for CCL, Lower Saxony, experienced 26 such cases by only two PTAs, the Zweckverband Verkehrsverbund Südniedersachsen – ZVSN (PTA association for the area around the city of Göttingen), and the rural district Cuxhaven. Both PTAs conducted authority initiated CCL procedures for 162 lines, only 7.4% of all 2,200 lines approved by the LA in Lower Saxony. Saxony-Anhalt, with its clear decision to promote competition for commercial services at the state level, had six cases of authority initiatives where operations had started by the end of 2008 and eight cases where operations started in 2009 (cases for 2009 are not included in CCL-database III or in the figures presented here).[36] Some PTAs decided to individually initiate authority-based competitive procedures for commercial and non-commercial services in addition to the decisions by states and their LAs to structure the procedures and promote competition. These decisions further encouraged the development of a market for commercial services with more competition among operators than in other regions/states.

10.4.4.5 Success of Reduced Uncertainty at the State Level

Illustrated in Fig. 10.5 and described in Sect. 10.3.2, a greater number of market initiatives occur where initiatives to structure or to promote CCL procedures exist on the state level, e.g., transport ministries, by LAs and/or PTAs than in states without such initiatives. This higher number appears especially for Bavaria, Brandenburg, Hesse, Lower Saxony, North Rhine-Westphalia, and Saxony-Anhalt. The results show again that a reduction of uncertainty from a newcomer's view propels this development. I conclude that authorities will further competition by publishing license expiration dates online, structuring CCL procedures and actively supporting competition.

10.5 Conclusions

The market for commercial public transport services by bus has undergone a fundamental transformation, mainly due to a ruling by the Federal Administrative Court in 2003 that obliges licensing authorities to inform operators of license expiration dates upon request. Furthermore, an increasing number of public transport authorities in recent years have promoted competition for commercial services in their area of responsibility.

Significant growth in competitive procedures has been observed since 2003, yet the actual number of cases where competition for commercial services was observed remains small compared to total market volume. The analysis of the level of competition confirms the supposition that market entry barriers exist, since the average number of bidders per competitive procedure is far lower for commercial services than for tenders of non-commercial services.

An empirical assessment of possible influence factors was unable to identify a clear correlation between the number of bidders and major criteria, such as volume

[36] See the case study on Saxony-Anhalt in Sect. 5.4.2 above. Despite these procedures, authority initiatives with start of operations in 2009 were identified for Brandenburg (1) and Lower Saxony (1) by the end of 2008.

per case, time, classification of incumbent, etc., for commercial services. The analysis demonstrates instead that the regulatory framework or lack thereof creates uncertainty, especially for newcomers, regarding both public funding and procedural settings. Several of the discriminatory pitfalls and sources of risk identified occur in the preparation phase, the approval phase, and during the license term. The reality that 42% of all competitive procedures for commercial services went into costly litigation lasting 10–19 months on average should raise doubts as to whether the existing institutional framework is yet sufficient to support a truly competitive market.

The aggregated analysis of the procedural setting indicates that the overall level of uncertainty about competitive procedures for commercial services is higher than in normal tendering procedures. Analysis of market development by federal state confirms that uncertainty remains the major entry barrier for newcomers compared to incumbents. States where authorities take the initiative to limit uncertainty by improving the regulatory framework generally experience more intense competition. Germany's existing institutional framework, a patchwork system that curbs competition for commercial services, underscores the crucial importance of developing an effective, transparent, one-size-fits-all legal framework if encouraging competition is the aim of policymakers.

Future research that verifies the entry barriers identified in this Chap. 10 after a new federal legal framework comes into force should include the analysis of expected new proposals and/or revised legal frameworks. Since monopolistic profits cannot be excluded in today's markets, I suggest that future research must also compare the quality offered to passengers and/or profits by incumbents and successful newcomers.

Part V
Conclusions and Outlook

Chapter 11
Conclusions

Introducing competition in the German market for regional and local public bus transport services has brought successes, but also some notable failures. Following the international trend towards liberalization in the mid-1990s, German legislators introduced a framework for awarding contracts that is structured around two different license types, non-commercial licenses and commercial licenses, both of which provide exclusivity for the licensee within a specified market. The resulting complexity is generally considered a reason why researchers as well as global players entering the German public transport market often describe the regulatory framework as initially incomprehensible.

The analysis provided in this dissertation reveals that this dichotomous system provides numerous opportunities, but also contains pitfalls. Contrary to the apparent view of many legislators, the examination emphasizes that the distinction between commercial and non-commercial services is not itself inherent in the "nature" of services. Apart from the local characteristics of the specific service (e.g., population density), Chap. 4 shows that the classification of services as commercial or non-commercial is determined in large part by the public transport authorities that set the minimum quality standards to be provided by operators. In reality, the authorities awarding the contracts can affect market organization significantly depending on how they make use of their power. Since market organization differs substantially between commercial and non-commercial services in terms of both awarding structure and contractual relationships, this situation creates challenges for operators and authorities alike. The potential for uncertainty identified at the threshold is thus one of the main pitfalls. Understanding the possible courses of action could help authorities to identify the form of market organization that best fits their aims, and could help operators to select the business opportunities that match their corporate philosophies.

This dichotomic regulatory framework then has been the basis for different institutional models that have been established in practice. Based on an intensive discussion within the market in the past decade about introducing competition in the bus sector and the forms of competition with the potential to enhance quality and efficiency, two major cases of adjusting the framework on a federal state level

A. Beck, *Competition for Public Transport Services*, Contributions to Economics, DOI 10.1007/978-3-7908-2802-3_11, © Springer-Verlag Berlin Heidelberg 2012

are central to the debate: Hesse and Saxony-Anhalt. Evaluating their successes and failures (Chap. 5) shows several ways to introduce competition, through tendering of non-commercial services or through competition for commercial services, either authority initiated or market initiated. The array of possibilities for the German market allows both public transport authorities and operators numerous opportunities to take action. While most EU Member States have implemented a market model (authority initiated competition in Sweden and Denmark; market initiated competition in Britain outside of London), Germany has introduced a parallel structure of authority initiated and market initiated competition, both of which are remarkably successful in enhancing the level of quality and efficiency. Nevertheless, both also showing remarkable failures and pitfalls in some areas and a limited market share as the majority of services is still awarded directly to incumbent operators.

When evaluating the international attempts to introduce competition to the public transport services market, it quickly becomes obvious that numerous models have been developed and introduced. As shown in Chap. 6, most countries and regions contemplating the introduction of competition-based organizational forms failed to perceive the UK's deregulated bus regime as the best way forward. In fact, a rush to competitive tendering was fueled by the European Commission's endeavor to enact legislation promoting competitive tendering of exclusive contracts as the preferred means of organizing local public transport markets. However, in recent years deregulation in various guises has played a growing role in local and regional transport, i.e. in long-distance coach transport and in (international) European railway markets. It has also been discussed for local public transport services. Although some major international models to establish a more market oriented framework have been discussed here, we note that no approach has yet arisen as the model to follow. In fact, issues persist for each proposed model as well as new topics for additional research. Even the attempt to design a new market initiated regime shows that several approaches are conceivable to enhance the engagement of operators. Nevertheless, the wide-ranging debate makes clear that more market initiatives might be possible by implementing an adjusted framework. Such an amendment follows the aim to use this competitive threat to enhance quality, efficiency and innovative activities.

When evaluating the German market for non-commercial services, the evaluation of the structure of tendering procedures presented in Chap. 7 indicates that barriers to entry have to be assumed with respect to uncertainty. A study of 34 public service contracts in Europe shows that when concluding a public service contract, operators must cope with a variety of risks that have different impacts and that can be controlled only to varying degrees. To identify and categorize different types of risks for public transport services, a clear structure was developed. The analysis then shows that revenue risk for Germany's public bus transport services is particularly important because numerous cases of the winner's curse have been reported, while net-cost contracts are assumed to increase the risk premia to be calculated. Here, the incumbent operator's information advantage should also be viewed critically. Since bidders consider the information provided by the public transport authorities as more reliable than other sources, the tendering authority should be required to furnish a comprehensive report on demand potential. Nevertheless, net-cost contracts tend to provide better incentives than gross-cost contracts because the operator's revenue is at least partly connected to the quality of its performance in the passenger market. In principle, therefore, public transport authorities must evaluate whether the risk premium to be calculated by the operator is lower than the positive effects from using such incentives.

Analyzing the general market development in the segment of tendering of non-commercial services from the positions of different market participants in Chap. 8 produces varying results. From the public transport authorities' view, the main effect is the decrease in subsidy payments achieved with relatively low transaction costs to administer the tendering and contract control. The overall level of competition is high, with 5–7 bidders on average, although declining in recent years. Nevertheless, barriers to entry are identified for several parameters, especially for the volume tendered and the revenue risk to be borne by the operator out of net-cost contracts. The group of small and medium-sized transport operators was able to increase market share in the initial phase of tendering, although with diminishing success rates in recent years. Due to the more ambitious requirements in competitive tendering, the quality of public transport delivered to passengers has improved considerably.

The analysis of prices per vehicle kilometer realized in tendering procedures by public transport authorities focuses on the factors that affect these prices. The alternative regression techniques presented in Chap. 9 show that prices have some regionally varying determinants. For example, while prices in most of the state of Hesse have increased over time, prices in the Munich area appear to have decreased. The analysis also shows that optimizing conditions that affect the operational productivity of services have a cost-decreasing impact. The same applies for several conditions limiting or reducing the risk level to be borne by the operator. Moreover, the empirical investigation confirms that better tendering results are produced by those authorities with a high level of experience.

All in all, it becomes obvious that tendering results are affected significantly by the conditions set by public transport authorities. An important factor is the level of uncertainty, which has been identified as a market entry barrier. Factors that influence the price to be paid by public transport authorities are the conditions that influence productivity, such as the efficiency of the schedule to be operated, external factors like spatial conditions, and again, aspects that increase the risks to be borne by operators, such as investment risk and revenue risk. The conditions also have a strong impact on market outcomes with respect to the market share of small and medium-sized transport operators. Considerable effort is needed to design these conditions in a manner that avoids undesired side-effects. Moreover, the conditions should be aligned with regional settings. With respect to the high impact of tendering conditions, the institutional knowledge needed to successfully tender non-commercial services probably requires pooling a greater number of procedures in one area or region under a single over-arching authority. Here, a higher critical mass might reduce the learning curve, which would likely enable further price reductions.

Examining the prospects and constraints of the market for commercial services, Chap. 10 shows that after decades of relative stagnation, the market is finally coming into motion. However, compared to the total market volume, the number of cases where competition is observable is still small. An empirical analysis of the competition within the commercial market segment compared to the non-commercial market segment confirms the existence of entry barriers as evidenced by the lower level of competition. Clearly, such barriers impede competitive developments in an embryonic market that relies on market initiatives by operators. The key entry barrier in the institutional framework is the significantly higher uncertainty regarding competitive procedures for commercial services, and it poses disadvantages primarily for newcomers as opposed to incumbents.

Finding that the regulatory framework has a major influence on the market development for commercial services by curbing competition underscores the importance of designing an effective legal setting, particularly in situations where policy-makers aim at encouraging competition. Promoting competition for public transport services was a major objective in changing the legal framework during the market reforms of the mid-1990s. However, the analysis in this dissertation emphasizes that further changes are necessary if lawmakers still hope to achieve their objective. Moreover, from the view of incumbents, the current legal framework negatively affects planning reliability since it allows competing bids to be submitted for the operation of commercial lines or services and often results in protracted legal disputes with uncertain outcomes. All in all, concerted efforts by both lawmakers and public authorities are necessary to create a well-regulated setting that will promote further improvements in efficiency and quality in the competitive market for Germany's public bus transport services. In order to support this discussion, Chap. 12 below presents a proposal to clarify the German framework.

Although major issues have been addressed in this dissertation, several questions persist and new topics arose for additional research on market regimes. As indicated, more information about the performance of market initiative regimes is needed. Here a comparative analysis of different approaches to implement market initiatives could assist regulators to enhance social welfare and quality for passengers. Additionally a comparative analysis of successes, failures and transaction costs in both authority and market initiated regimes would be useful in achieving successful economic deregulation.

From a policy and theoretical perspective, an interesting topic is whether the coexistence between commercial and non-commercial services with different forms of market entrance and market organization actually favors a market whereby the licenses for commercial services are awarded after paying a franchise fee. A useful comparison would include truly free market regimes, where the establishment of services is initiated only by operators, as well as the markets where only services are tendered.

Future research should also focus on the barriers that prevent public transport authorities from implementing competitive tendering. Given the successes identified with respect to quality and subsidy payments, and keeping in mind the enhanced level of control via a direct contractual relationship, the question arises whether other factors of influence have to be assumed. The negative results for some groups of operators and, to some extent for employees, probably impede the use of tendering. The absence of a clear legal obligation to introduce competition presumably contributes to the ongoing renewal of existing relationships.

For regions with competition, further research should be undertaken on the development of unit costs and the level of competition in future years. The factors influencing the tender price and the number of bidders per tender require more analysis, especially with respect to a diminishing level of competition and the upcoming new legal framework. The different results for tender prices in Hesse and the Munich area require further examination concerning the potential influence of strategic prices and market consolidation. Finally, an analysis of the effects of introducing competition on company structures and the level of competition in the long run could help to avoid re-oligopolization or re-monopolization.

Chapter 12
A Proposal to Improve the Current Awarding System in Germany

12.1 Introduction

For the German market Chap. 10 presented above indicated that the level of competition for commercial (market initiated) services is impeded to a large extent by the existing regulatory framework. Although legally possible, market initiatives for commercial services are still rare and the level of competition for these services is much lower than for competitive tendering.

Moreover, the complexity of a dichotomic institutional framework characterized by a parallel structure of commercial and non-commercial licenses within a single market is a reason why many researchers, as well as global players trying to enter the public transport market, often describe the regulatory framework as initially incomprehensible. The many different failures and pitfalls of the specific German model presented in Chaps. 4, 5, 7, 8 and 10 raise doubts about the feasibility and user friendliness of this system. Nevertheless the great variety of opportunities for action for authorities and operators remains a major advantage.

An evaluation of international efforts to introduce competition to public transport service markets (see Chap. 6) shows numerous different models and attempts to regulate the functioning of these markets. In Europe, a change of mind, or a possible trend, towards more market based regimes can be observed in recent years. There will also be some effect of the new legislation at the EU level, the European regulation (EC) No 1370/2007 on the awarding of public service contracts for public transport services that took effect on December 3, 2009.

The issue for Germany now is whether a viable alternative to the current model of contract awarding could enhance the regulatory framework. Considering current discussion about the amendment of the German Passenger Transport Act (Novelle des Personenbeförderungsgesetzes – PBefG), the aim of this Chap. 12 is to present an attempt to clarify the regulatory framework for short-distance public transport services in Germany. Based on the main options possible according to (EC) No 1370/2007, the model incorporates the insights presented in the essays above, which examine the market for commercial and non-commercial services.

A. Beck, *Competition for Public Transport Services*, Contributions to Economics,
DOI 10.1007/978-3-7908-2802-3_12,

Moreover, the model is based on discussions with many transport experts, notably my former colleagues at BSL Management Consultants (Julia Ahrend, Caroline von Kretschmann, Mathias Lahrmann, Mirko Schnell, and, in particular, Jörn Meier-Berberich and Marc-Oliver Wille) and attorneys (in particular Sybille Barth and Lorenz Wachinger, BBG and Partner). I extend my thanks to all of my discussion partners for their useful remarks. Nevertheless, the usual disclaimer applies and sole responsibility for the proposed model is assumed by the author.[1]

12.2 A Proposal to Adjust Germany's Existing Institutional Framework

Based on the institutional framework presented in Chap. 4, the development of this framework over time presented in Chap. 5, international alternatives presented in Chap. 6 and the market developments for commercial and non-commercial services presented in Part III and Part IV, I conclude that:

- The German dichotomy between commercial and non-commercial services provides a greater variety of options for operators and PTAs (Public Transport Authorities) than in other parts of the world
- The German system is still characterized by a significant market share of direct awarding, making a fundamental change unrealistic in view of the intense debate about cases where competition has been introduced
- Still, there is ample room for improvements, as the existing framework prevents more dynamic market developments due to the many structural obstacles that increase uncertainty for market participants.

Regarding the numerous lawsuits and intense debate among legal professionals throughout the past decade (see Chap. 5 and Sect. 10.4.3), any proposed model must provide procedural clarity to market participants and ensure more smoothly functioning structures by avoiding the pitfalls identified in Part II and IV (such as uncertainty about whether to classify the service as commercial, activities to counter tendering procedures, lack of clarity about the role of the incumbent, legal uncertainty and lawsuits lasting for months or years).

Thus, I propose six objectives for a new model:

Six objectives of a proposed model for Germany

The new model should

1. Be flexible in the range of options to ensure efficient market organizations
2. Provide a variety of options for action to operators and PTAs

[1] Chapter 12 is based on Beck (2011b).

3. Offer possibilities for a high level of freedom to operators to design services
4. Provide a framework conducive to innovation
5. Contain well-defined regulations for awarding procedures and delegate defined roles and tasks to market participants
6. Avoid legal uncertainties due to unambiguous regulations on awarding procedures (transparency)

Below, I discuss how to adjust the existing German framework. The proposal aims to solve several of the problems identified during my research on the present regulations for awarding and contracting. At first glance, the process flow chart in Fig. 12.1 may appear complicated, since the system currently allows several processes for awarding. I preserve this diversity but clarify the decision paths to reduce uncertainty for market participants. The proposal assumes that licenses provide exclusivity during the license term.

The proposal consists of various decision nodes (explained in detail below). At a decision node there are usually several options and a single decision-making party. To facilitate my explanations in the following, the numbering in Fig. 12.1 corresponds to that of the subtitles, i.e. the main steps of the procedure.

12.2.1 Step 1: LA Determines Whether a Proposed Service is New

To promote innovations within the system, operators (or PTAs) can propose to provide a new (additional) service at any time. Upon request by the initiating stakeholder, and by involving the PTAs (Public Transport Authorities), the LA (Licensing Authority) determines whether a proposed service really is new.

If the service in question is classified as new, the LA checks whether the service is initiated by an operator and whether the operator claims exclusivity for its proposal. If the operator claims exclusivity, it will be the only player allowed to submit a bid to operate the service under a commercial license for the first license term. If the bid fulfills the usual minimum criteria of the LA,[2] the operator is directly awarded the license for one license term. Thus, this license shows similarities to a patent. By offering "patent"-like exclusivity to the operator initiating the process, the proposed model aims to promote innovations as is done in other industries, while recognizing that the number of such cases will be limited. Of course, a "patent" must be handled with care, for example by establishing some minimum criteria for a service to be classified as "new".

[2] The LA is responsible to check compliance with minimum criteria for: security, economic capability and reputation of the operator (e.g., adequate delivery of appropriate service according to previous PTPs [public transport plans]) and fulfillment of minimum quality standards for the service set by the PTP.

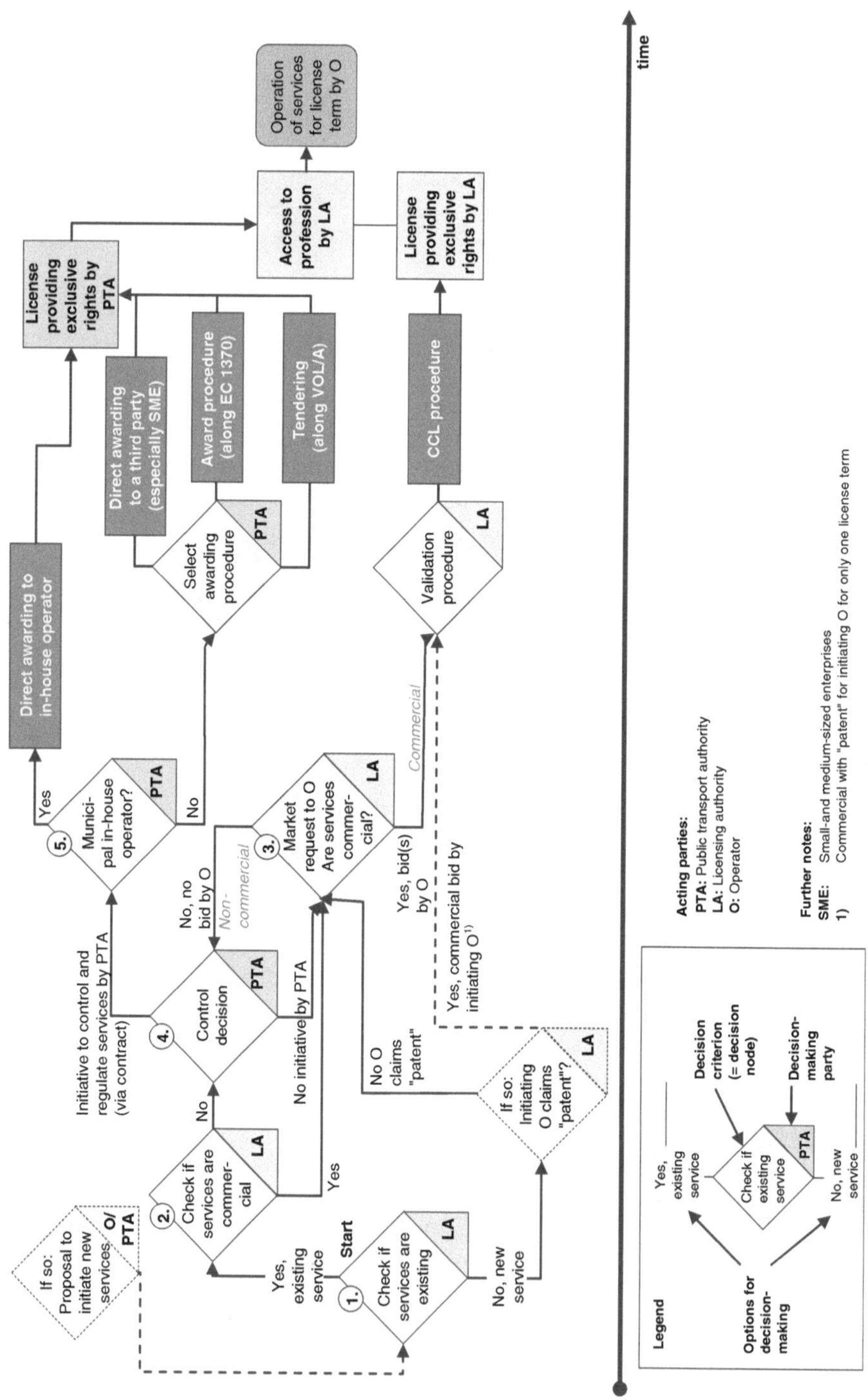

Fig. 12.1 Proposal for an adjusted award model for Germany (decision tree)

If the service in question is initiated by the PTA, or if the initiating operator does not claim exclusivity for its proposal, the LA proceeds by clarifying whether the service is commercial (i.e. Step 2).

12.2.2 *Step 2: LA Starts Clarification Whether Existing Service is Commercial for the Next License Term*

For existing services, the LA publishes the termination date of the license and the validation criteria for a possible CCL procedure (CCL: competition for commercial lines) to resolve the problem of unclear or non-existent validation criteria on the part of the LAs, and the confusion about termination dates that still exists in some regions (see Sects. 10.4.3 and 10.4.4).

The LA then verifies whether the service would be considered commercial for the upcoming license term by studying the expression of interest from either the incumbent operator and/or competing operators desiring to provide the service commercially for the next license term. Expressions of interest must be submitted within the time frame set by the LA in advance (limiting the problem of incorrect expectations as described in Sect. 4.6.3). Without a time limitation, a competitor could (and did in several cases; see Sects. 5.3.2 and 10.3.2) disrupt an ongoing awarding procedure by applying for a commercial service.[3]

The PTA always remains responsible for defining the minimum quality level (according to its definition of services of general interest) to be delivered via its PTP. In contrast to the situation today, the PTP is binding for the LA in the first instance, and the PTA is obliged to establish the PTP in a clear and non-discriminatory manner. Nevertheless, operators are still allowed to contribute to the PTP. The PTA can raise or lower the minimum quality level at the outset to reclassify the service in question from commercial to non-commercial and vice versa (see Sect. 4.6).

12.2.3 *Step 3: For Commercial Services, LA Submits Formal Market Request to Operators*

If the LA initially classifies the service as commercial based on the expressions of interest by operators as described above, the next step is a formal market request which is based on the binding bids submitted by the operators. In this case, the LA is obliged to avoid intolerable risks by ensuring transparency on relevant revenue data for newcomers (as already observed for several tendering procedures). This will reduce the problem of the winner's curse which arises when an operator's bid

[3] This may be due to strategic reasons; for other problems in this area see Sect. 4.6.3.

overestimates the revenue potential. Such a risk has been identified by numerous empirical studies as a clear market entry barrier for net-cost contracts tendered (see Sects. 7.4.2, 8.4.3, and 10.4.3). Nevertheless, with the aim of providing favorable incentives, operators should bear the full revenue risk. If the LA, upon its formal market request, receives no bids by operators to operate the service commercially, the LA hands the procedure to the PTA which awards supplementary direct subsidies (see Step 4).

If one bid is received, the LA checks whether it satisfies the minimum criteria and then validates it as part of a CCL procedure according to the validation criteria published prior to the formal market request. When more than one bid is received, the LA selects the best bid with respect to quality in a transparent validation procedure (quality competition).

In contrast to the current situation (described in Sect. 10.4.3), the procedure does not provide the incumbent with any special privilege. Moreover, the new CCL procedure contains a clear procedural framework similar to tendering procedures in order to avoid lawsuits lasting months (or years) and legal uncertainties for incumbents and newcomers (described for the current situation in Sect. 10.4.3).

Finally, the LA awards a license to operate the service under exclusivity for the license term to the winning bidder in the form of a contract pursuant to (EC) No 1370/2007 (for such a structure see Sect. 4.4.1).

12.2.4 Step 4: PTA Makes Control Decision

If no expression of interest or, finally, no binding bid for a commercial service is submitted, the LA hands the procedure to the PTA which then decides whether or not to control the service directly via a public service contract. If it opts for a public service contract, the PTA will then need to pay the supplementary direct subsidies necessary to satisfy the minimum quality level (see Step 5). For example, numerous experts expect that services currently operated by municipal operators will in reality be non-commercial.

On the other hand, if the PTA does not want to maintain direct control over the service for fiscal or political reasons,[4] it can hand the procedure back to the LA, thereby precluding a costly and time-consuming awarding procedure and the need for subsidy payments, contract controlling and settlement of accounts. The LA then (again) initiates the formal market request to operators as described above. This time, however, the LA permits bids that fail to meet the minimum quality level of the PTP. The LA then identifies the operator offering the best quality on a commercial basis, as described above in Step 3.

[4] E.g., due to the aim of limited public involvement in favor of more freedom for the operators to design the services as described in Sect. 4.4.2.

12.2.5 Step 5: PTA Decides on Direct Award or a Competitive Procedure

If the PTA decides to take direct control and wants to pay the supplementary direct subsidies necessary to provide the minimum quality level, the proposed model foresees a decision about whether or not the service will be provided in-house. (EC) No 1370/2007 Art. 5 (2) defines in-house as a provision by "a legally distinct entity over which the competent local authority ... exercises control similar to that exercised over its own departments", e.g., a municipal operator owned by the PTA. If the service in question will be provided by an in-house operator, competing operators are still free to submit expressions of interest to the PTA (already possible today). Nonetheless, the PTA is also free to mandate its in-house operator according to (EC) No 1370/2007 (EC 1370 in Fig. 12.1), e.g., for political reasons.

If no in-house operator is selected, the PTA can choose from the following options:

- A direct award of supplementary direct subsidies
  - To small- and medium-sized enterprises on the condition of Art. 5 (4) (EC) No 1370/2007
  - To other enterprises in small shares on the condition of Art. 5 (4) (EC) No 1370/2007
  - To any operator as an emergency measure on the condition of Art. 5 (5) (EC) No 1370/2007
- A competitive award of supplementary direct subsidies according to Art. 5 (3) (EC) No 1370/2007 (e.g., via negotiations with several operators)
- A formal tender of supplementary direct subsidies under VOL/A which represents a clear, formal and adjudicated framework (and, of course, also satisfies Art. 5 [3] [EC] No 1370/2007).

In any case, the LA checks the usual minimum criteria. Thereafter, the PTA concludes the contract with the preselected operator or the winning bidder, which includes a license that provides exclusivity for the license term.[5]

12.3 Model Assessment

This essay proposes a model to adjust the current awarding framework in Germany. Although there are many international models, a fundamental change seems unrealistic for Germany considering the intense debate about cases in which

[5] Again, access to the profession of being a bus operator is provided by the LA, here acting as a neutral authority between PTA and operator.

competition was already introduced. Thus, by using the decision tree illustrated in Fig. 12.1, the proposed model aims to clarify the existing framework by assigning more clearly the roles and tasks of PTAs, LAs and operators within a specified time frame.

The proposed model illustrates that the objectives for adjusting the existing German model are both administratively feasible and realistic. It preserves the dichotomy between commercial and non-commercial services and offers a variety of options for action to authorities and operators. Following the principle of subsidiarity promoted at the EU level, local market participants are free to select the procedure that fits their objectives, including the PTA's opportunity to select a municipal operator. The proposed model enables competition of different awarding modes within the market without any clear preference on the part of the legislative body. The number of options is nevertheless reduced in favor of a clear awarding structure, e.g., it does not allow CCL applications that would disrupt an ongoing tendering procedure.

At the same time, the general preferential treatment of market initiatives is one of the main pitfalls of the current system: if operators are licensed to provide commercial services under an excessively low minimum quality set by the PTA in its PTP, e.g., due to false expectations regarding commercial feasibility, the PTA cannot take full control of the service, even if it wants to do so. The dichotomy between two different authorities raises the issue of coordination. I suggest that it would be helpful to maintain a licensing authority on a state level as seen in Lower Saxony. As in New Zealand, the LA could also, upon request, support the PTAs with consultant services on awarding procedures, and assume full responsibility for the awarding if the PTA does not want to become involved.

Although the proposed model avoids any radical changes, the reduced level of overall uncertainty provided for new entrants has the potential to improve market development and reduce the entry barriers resulting from an unclear framework and non-transparent awarding procedures and revenue data. The potential of the incumbent to discriminate in a CCL procedure is mitigated by: (1) publication of the license's termination date (2) limiting the role of the incumbent in developing the PTP, (3) abolishing the incumbent's privilege in the CCL validation procedure, and (4) establishing minimum requirements for providing revenue data. Legal uncertainty can further be reduced by clearly-stated regulations about conducting awarding procedures over time.

If desired by the local authorities, the model allows a high level of freedom to operators and even promotes innovation by offering a "patent"-like exclusivity to innovators. In general, the model allows for competition among ideas between operators and for competition among models for market organizations.

Appendix

A.1 Annex for Chap. 8

A.1.1 General Remarks on Database I

Table A.1 Overview of criteria for collecting data for database I

Criteria	Description
Number of bidders	Level of competition with respect to the number of applicants for the specific services
Vkm p.a.	Volume of vehicle kilometers per annum for the specific lot
Number of lines	The quantity of lines in the specific lot
Start of operations (date)	Exact date for start of operations
Start of operations (year)	Year for start of operations
Incumbent type	Classification of the incumbent according to the majority of the shares as a municipal operator, private small- or medium-sized enterprise (SME), a subsidiary of the national railway operator Deutsche Bahn AG (DB, one of the largest bus operators in Germany) or a global player
Type of contract	Classification of the public service contract tendered out with respect to the revenue risk to be borne by the operator, either a gross-cost contract (revenue risk borne by the PTA) or a net-cost contract (revenue risk borne by the operator)
State	The name of the state in which the case is located
Source	Source of information for the specific case
Further information	Further information for the specific case

Table A.2 Pairwise Pearson correlation matrix of selected criteria for database I

	Number of bidders	Vkm p.a.	Number of lines	Start of operations (exact date)	Start of operations (year)
Number of bidders	1.0000				
Vkm p.a.	−0.1569	1.0000			
Number of lines	0.0455	0.4910	1.0000		
Start of operations (date)	−0.6778	0.1559	0.1759	1.0000	
Start of operations (year)	−0.5468	0.1436	0.1363	0.9907	1.0000

A. Beck, *Competition for Public Transport Services*, Contributions to Economics,
DOI 10.1007/978-3-7908-2802-3, © Springer-Verlag Berlin Heidelberg 2012

A.1.2 Results and Stata Program Code of Likelihood-Ratio-Test

Table A.3 Results of likelihood-ratio-test for number of bidders for database I

Model	(A)	(B)	(C)	(D)	(E)
Explanatory Variables	Number of bidders	Number of bidders	Number of bidders	Number of bidders	Number of bidders
Vehicle kilometers p.a.		-1.51×10^{-6}** (6.68×10^{-7})	-8.23×10^{-7} (5.78×10^{-7})	-8.62×10^{-7} (5.69×10^{-7})	2.17×10^{-7} (5.97×10^{-7})
Start of operations (year)			−1.0385*** (0.1655)	−0.9407*** (0.1697)	−0.6868*** (0.1612)
Gross-cost contract $\in \{0,1\}$				1.7120** (0.8320)	0.9148 (1.590)
Bavaria $\in \{0,1\}$					2.5776 (1.8690)
Hesse $\in \{0,1\}$					0.5972 (1.6477)
Rhineland-Palatine $\in \{0,1\}$					−0.4061 (1.6963)
Schleswig-Holstein $\in \{0,1\}$					−2.6256 (1.7335)
Constant	6.2647*** (0.3020)	7.0908*** (0.4703)	2089.587*** (331.9119)	1891.984*** (340.4453)	1382.009*** (323.6574)
Observations	102	102	102	102	102
F-value		5.11	23.22	17.40	15.14
Prob>F		0.0259	0.0000	0.0000	0.0000
R^2		0.0486	0.3193	0.3475	0.5300
Likelihood-Ratio Test for nested models		$LR_{(a)}$	$LR_{(a)}$	$LR_{(a)}$	$LR_{(a)}$
LR-$x^2_{(L)}$		5.09	39.23	43.55	77.02
Prob $> x^2_{(L)}$		0.0241	0.0000	0.0000	0.0000

Standard errors in parentheses; Significance ** 95%, *** 99%

Stata for Windows 9.1 program codes for selected models:

```
***Model (A):
Regress bidders
Estimates store A
***Model (B):
Regress bidders vkmp.a.
Estimates store B
***Model (C):
Regress bidders vkmp.a. startoyear
Estimates store C
***Model (D):
Regress bidders vkmp.a. startoyear grosscostcontract
Estimates store D
***Model (E):
Regress bidders vkmp.a. startoyear grosscostcontract
Bavaria Hesse Rhineland-Palatine Schleswig-Holstein
Estimates store E
***Likelihood-ratio test Model (B):
lrtest A B
***Likelihood-ratio test Model (C):
lrtest A C
***Likelihood-ratio test Model (D):
lrtest A D
***Likelihood-ratio test Model (E):
lrtest A E
```

A.1.3 Results and Stata Program Code for OLS-Regression

Table A.4 Results for single regression of dummy variables (selected models) for database I

Model	(a)	(b)	(c)
Dependent variables (x_i)	Number of bidders	Number of bidders	Number of bidders
Gross-cost contract $\in \{0,1\}$	3.0480*** (0.9299)		
Municipal $\in \{0,1\}$		−4.1319*** (1.1763)	
Private SME $\in \{0,1\}$		(dropped)	
Deutsche Bahn AG $\in \{0,1\}$		−1.0296 (0.8414)	
Global player $\in \{0,1\}$			(dropped)
Baden-Württemberg $\in \{0,1\}$			0.2500 (1.7885)
Bavaria $\in \{0,1\}$			5.6667*** (1.4121)
Hesse $\in \{0,1\}$			2.8846** (1.3904)
Rhineland-Palatine $\in \{0,1\}$			(dropped)
Schleswig-Holstein $\in \{0,1\}$			−0.5000 (1.5415)
Constant	3.5454*** (0.8784)	7.6875*** (0.7058)	3.0000** (1.3520)

(continued)

Table A.4 (continued)

Model	(a)	(b)	(c)
Dependent variables (x_i)	Number of bidders	Number of bidders	Number of bidders
Observations	102	63	102
F-value	10.74	6.37	18.60
Prob>F	0.0014	0.0031	0.0000
R^2	0.0970	0.1751	0.4341

Standard errors in parentheses; Significance ** 95%, *** 99%

(Code: regress Number of bidders x_i)

A.2 Annex for Chap. 9

A.2.1 List of Main Criteria

Table A.5 List of main criteria

Variable	Explanation	Scale of measurement	Measured by
p_i	Price per vehicle kilometer (vkm) to be paid by the PTA to the operator for lot *i* in the first contract year as a result of competitive tendering on a gross-cost basis. Note that net-cost contracts were made comparable to gross-cost contracts by using their net subsidy payment plus the fare revenues of that lot	Ratio	€ per vkm
P_i	p_i, adjusted by the effect of inflation (inflation measured by the real development of the operating costs) and other major impacts that affect the price over time (for example, adjustment of public co-funding for vehicle investments)	Ratio	€ per vkm
lot	Lot: the smallest part of a network tendered out for which a bidder is able to hand in an offer	Nominal	1
FP_i	Full price to be paid by the PTA per annum (p.a.) to the operator per lot *i*: $FP_i = P_i \times$ sum of vkm p.a. per lot *i*	Ratio	€ per lot p.a.
vkmpa	Vehicle kilometers (vkm) p.a. per *lot* within the first year of operations. Note that we count only those vkm p.a. provided on the specific lines according to the timetable of the *lot* usually set by the PTA; other tours, e.g., transfer between depot and start of a specific line, are excluded	Ratio	Kilometers per lot p.a.
linesno	Number of lines per *lot*	Interval	Number
novehcl	Number of vehicles per *lot*	Interval	Number
kmpervehcl	Vehicle kilometers per annum per vehicle in a specific *lot* on average	Ratio	Kilometers p.a. per vehicle

(continued)

Table A.5 (continued)

Variable	Explanation	Scale of measurement	Measured by
declwage	Minimum standard with respect to labour agreements as set by PTA with three occurrences: (1) no requirements, (2) closure of any labour agreement with employees required, (3) specific labour agreement set as a minimum standard	Ordinal	Number
lengthbus	Average length per vehicle in a specific *lot*	Ratio	Meters
term	Contract term in years per *lot*	Ratio	Years
deposit	Deposit which needs to be given to PTAs by operators as a security (security deposit) in percent of FP_i	Ratio	Percentage
submdays	The duration between the date of the public call for tenders and the date of submission as set by PTAs (days of submission)	Interval	Days
extopt	Option for PTA for term extension foreseen at the end of the contract term? Yes = 1, no = 0	Dummy	Yes/No
renewal	Do contract conditions exist that presuppose a renewal of vehicles during the contract period? Yes = 1, no = 0	Dummy	Yes/No
revrisk	Does the operator have to bear the revenue risk? Yes = 1 (classified as net-cost contract), no = 0 (classified as gross-cost contract)	Dummy	Yes/No
Expr	Experience of the PTA that has put out the *lot* to tender, measured by the specific number of the current lot tendered out by the PTA over time (e.g., 1: being the first tender ever of that PTA,; 10: being the 10th tender of that PTA over time)	Interval	Number
exprsum	Experience of the PTA that has put out the *lot* to tender, measured by the sum of all lots tendered out by the PTA	Interval	Number
startoyear	Year of start of operations	Interval	Year
bidders	Number of bidders per *lot*	Interval	Number
change	Has a change of the operator occurred due to the award of the specific tender? Yes = 1, no = 0.	Dummy	Yes/No
sme	Is the winning bidder a small or medium-sized enterprise (SME)? Yes = 1, no = 0.	Dummy	Yes/No
spatial	Spatial type to assess population density measured by five agglomeration types: (1) major city, (2) medium-sized town, (3) small town, (4) suburban area, (5) rural area	Ordinal	Number
fedstate	Abbreviation of the federal state where the lot is (primarily) located: BW: Baden-Württemberg, BY: Bavaria, HE: Hesse, NW: North Rhine-Westphalia, RP: Rhineland-Palatine and SH: Schleswig-Holstein.	Dummy per federal state	Yes/No

A.2.2 Results and Stata Program Code for Simple OLS-Regression

Table A.6 Simple OLS-Regression of the number of bidders on price for database II

Dependent variable (Code: `regress Pi bidders`)	P_i
Bidders	−0.0612*** (0.0137)
Constant	2.4167*** (0.0828)
Observations	157
F-value	19.79
Prob>F	0.0000
R^2	0.1132

Significant level: *** 99%, Standard errors in parentheses.

A.2.3 Stata Program Code for SUR-Analysis

```
rename vkmpamvv x11
rename kmpervehclmvv x12
rename lengthbusmvv x13
rename termmvv x14
rename extoptmvv x15
rename spatialmvv x16
rename startoyearmvv x17
rename vkmpahex x31
rename kmpervehclhex x32
rename lengthbushex x33
rename termhex x34
rename extopthex x35
rename spatialhex x36
rename startoyearhex x37
rename exprsumhex x38
rename vkmpaoth x51
rename kmpervehcloth x52
rename lengthbusoth x53
rename termoth x54
rename extoptoth x55
rename spatialoth x56
rename startoyearoth x57
rename exprsumoth x58
rename depositoth x60

regress P_imvv x11 x12 x13 x14 x15 x16 x17
foreach v of var P_imvv x11 x12 x13 x14 x15 x16 x17 {
replace `v'= `v' / e(rmse)
}
generate cons1 = 1/e(rmse)

regress P_ihex x31 x32 x33 x34 x35 x36 x37 x38
foreach v of var P_ihex x31 x32 x33 x34 x35 x36 x37 x38 {
replace `v'= `v' / e(rmse)
}
generate cons2 = 1/e(rmse)

regress P_ioth x51 x52 x53 x54 x55 x56 x57 x58 x60
foreach v of var P_ioth x51 x52 x53 x54 x55 x56 x57 x58
x60 {
replace `v'= `v' / e(rmse)
}
generate cons3 = 1/e(rmse)

save rescaled, replace
```

```
preserve
keep P_imvv x11 x12 x13 x14 x15 x16 x17 cons1 time
mark sample
markout sample P_imvv x11 x12 x13 x14 x15 x16 x17 cons1
rename P_imvv P_ix
gen id = 1
save data1, replace
restore

preserve
keep P_ihex x31 x32 x33 x34 x35 x36 x37 x38 cons2 time
mark sample
markout sample P_ihe x31 x32 x33 x34 x35 x36 x37 x38 cons2
rename P_ihex P_ix
gen id = 2
save data2, replace
restore

preserve
keep P_ioth x51 x52 x53 x54 x55 x56 x57 x58 x60 cons3 time
mark sample
markout sample P_ioth x51 x52 x53 x54 x55 x56 x57 x58 x60
cons3
rename P_ioth P_ix
gen id = 3
save data3, replace
restore

clear
use data1
append using data2
append using data3
mvencode x* cons* if sample, mv(0)

tsset time id

xtgee P_ix x* cons*, family(gaussian) link(identity)
corr(unstructured) noconstant
```

A.2.4 Stata Program Code for SFA-Analysis

```
generate lnFPi = ln(FPi)
generate lnvkmpamean = ln(vkmpamean)
generate lnkmpervehcl = ln(kmpervehcl)
*** declwage ordinal scale
generate lnlengthbus = ln(lengthbus)
*** renewal dummy scale
*** revrisk dummy scale
generate lnsubmdays = ln(submdays)
*** spatial ordinal scale

frontier   lnFPi   lnvkmpamean   lnkmpervehcl   declwage
lnlengthbus renewal revrisk lnsubmdays spatial
predict eff36, te

kwallis eff36, by(he)

kwallis eff36, by(expdummy)
```

A.3 Annex for Chap. 10

A.3.1 Tables Generated Using Database III

Note: The following tables are based on the CCL-database, defined as database III.

Table A.7 Overview of criteria where data was raised for CCL procedures

Criteria	Description
Vkm p.a.	Volume of vehicle kilometer p.a. for the specific services
Number of lines	The quantity of lines in the specific case
Federal state	The name of the federal state in which the case is located
Region	The name of the town or administrative district in which the CCL procedure is located
Description	Detailed description of the location and name of the services, e.g., location of main stops and/or denotation of the line or network
PTA	Competent public transport authority
Classification of services	Classification of the specific case (either: authority initiated, competitive application, prevention of tendering or new services with competition, see Sect. 10.2 for further explanations)
LA	Competent licensing authority

(continued)

Table A.7 (continued)

Criteria	Description
Number of bidders	Level of competition with respect to the number of applicants for the specific services
Start of operations	Exact date for start of operations
Year	Year for start of operations
Name of the incumbent	Exact name of that enterprise
Classification of the incumbent	Classification as a municipal operator, private small or medium sized enterprise (SME), a subsidiary of the national railway operator Deutsche Bahn AG (one of the biggest bus operators in Germany), or a global player
Name of the (first) competitor/ newcomer	Exact name of that enterprise
Classification of the (first) competitor/ newcomer	Classification as a municipal operator, a private SME, a subsidiary of the national railway operator Deutsche Bahn AG (one of the biggest bus operators in Germany) or a global player
Name of the winning bidder	Name of the applicant whose bid finally was approved by the LA (by the end of 2008 numerous CCL procedures were still under litigation, for which reason no information on this matter was available for numerous cases)
Further competitors	Name of further competitors (information was seldom available)
Litigation	Legal procedure as observed for the specific case (either: no litigation, contradiction, administrative court procedure, higher administrative court procedure or federal administrative court procedure)
Duration of litigations already finished	Length of legal procedure in months finished by the end of 2008
Duration of litigation not finished	Length of legal procedures in months not finished by the end of 2008 (compared to the planned date for start of operations)
Source	Source of information for the specific case
Further information	Further information for the specific case

Table A.8 Number of bidders for selected authority initiated CCL procedures (See Sect. 5.4.2 for a detailed description of the first Wittenberg case)

PTA	Quality of passenger revenue related data provided to operators by PTA	Number of applicants per CCL procedure	Expert interviewed
Verkehrsverbund Rhein-Neckar GmbH – VRN (Mannheim area)	Detailed information on passenger revenues per network provided to operators	3 cases with 8, 4 and 3 applicants	Peter Geisdorf
Rural district Wittenberg	Detailed information on passenger revenues per network provided to operators	3 procedures with 3 each	Holger Zubke
VerkehrsVerbund OstwestfalenLippe GmbH – VVOWL (Bielefeld area)	No information provided to operators	10 procedures with 1 each	Armin Hilger

(continued)

Table A.8 (continued)

PTA	Quality of passenger revenue related data provided to operators by PTA	Number of applicants per CCL procedure	Expert interviewed
Rural district Cuxhaven	No information provided to operators	3 cases with 1 bidder and 3 cases with 2 bidders	Gabi Kasten
Zweckverband Verkehrsverbund Süd-Niedersachsen – ZVSN (Göttingen area)	Basic information on passenger revenues per line or network was provided to operators	19 times 1 and 2 times 2 bidders	Carl-Michael Wieder

Please note that for Table A.8 only (experienced) PTAs with more than two procedure per PTA were selected. All other authority initiated procedures in the CCL database not mentioned here accounted for one to two applicants per procedure

Table A.9 Descriptive statistics of database III

	Obser-vations	Percent-age	Mean	Maximum	Minimum	Standard deviation
Number of bidders	117		1.82	8	1	1.01
Number of lines	117		6.7	50	1	8.90
Vehicle kilometers p.a.	46		600,728	3,400,000	20,000	625,229
Start of operations (date)	117			14/12/2008	01/01/2003	
Start of operations (year)	117			2008	2003	
Incumbent	117	100.00				
Municipal	36	30.77				
Private SME	43	36.75				
DB subsidiary	32	27.35				
Global player	6	5.13				
CCL classification	117	100,00				
Authority initiative	47	40.17				
Real market initiative	70	59.83				
Competitive application	43	36.75				
Prevention of tendering	22	18.80				
New services with compet.	5	4.27				
Federal state	117	100.00				
Baden-Wür-ttemberg	4	3.42				
Bavaria	7	5.98				
Brandenburg	7	5.98				
Hesse	17	14.53				
Mecklenburg-Western Pomerania	3	2.56				
Lower Saxony	46	39.32				
North Rhine-Westphalia	16	13.68				
Rhineland-Palatine	4	3.42				
Saxony	2	1.71				
Saxony-Anhalt	6	5.13				
Schleswig-Holstein	5	4.27				

Table A.10 Pairwise Pearson correlation matrix of selected criteria of database III

	Number of bidders	Vkm p.a.	Number of lines	Start of operations (date)	Start of operations (year)
Number of bidders	1.0000				
Vkm p.a.	0.2239	1.0000			
Number of lines	0.0364	0.7998	1.0000		
Start of operations (date)	−0.0252	0.1172	0.1748	1.0000	
Start of operations (year)	−0.0416	0.1174	0.1819	0.9582	1.0000

Table A.11 Results of empirical analysis of database III

Criteria	Hypothesis	Result	Note
Volume, measured by *number of lines*	The number of bidders decreases as the volume of a case increases	Hypothesis has to be rejected, no significant influence on the number of bidders	As data for vkm *p.a.* was available only for n = 46 cases, the analysis focused on the independent variable *number of lines*[a]
Federal state	The number of bidders depends on the federal state the case is located in, especially:	Some correlations were identified on a significant level, but have to be rejected because a significant bias must be assumed due to other factors	Every *federal state* represents an independent dummy variable
	Baden-Württemberg	Positive correlation, 99.99% significance level	Authority initiated procedures conducted by the VRN only, being altogether four cases, with one case in 2004 being the only authority initiated CCL procedure with more than four bidders (eight applicants), a bias has to be assumed
	Lower Saxony	Negative correlation, 90.00% significance level	A bias has to be assumed with respect to the high number of 19 authority initiatives conducted by the PTA ZVSN with only one bidder
	North Rhine-Westphalia	Negative correlation, 98.10% significance level	A bias has to be assumed with respect to the high number of 10 authority initiatives conducted by the PTA VVOWL with only one bidder

(continued)

Table A.11 (continued)

Criteria	Hypothesis	Result	Note
	Schleswig-Holstein	Positive correlation, 92.10% significance level	A low number of only five cases, three where the two applicants are always the same
Start of operations (time)	The level of competition increases over time	Hypothesis has to be rejected, no significant influence on the number of bidders	None
Classification of the incumbent	The number of bidders depends on the kind of the incumbent operator, especially:	Only one correlation identified (see below)	Every *classification of an incumbent* represents an independent dummy variable, being the classifications *municipal operator*, *SME*, *Deutsche Bahn AG* or *global player*
	Deutsche Bahn AG	Negative correlation, 99.40% significance level	A bias has to be assumed as 21 of all 32 CCL procedures with the incumbent operator *Deutsche Bahn AG* were the ones conducted by the ZVSN and the VVOWL with only one bidder
Classification of the (first) competitor/newcomer	The number of bidders depends on the kind of the (first) competitor/newcomer	Hypothesis has to be rejected, no significant influence on the number of bidders	None

[a]The data for this variable show a high correlation of 80% with the data from the independent variable *vkm p.a.*; see correlation matrix above

A.3.2 Tables Generated from Integrated Database IV

Note: The following tables are based on an integrated database IV, consisting of database I and database III.

Table A.12 Descriptive statistics of integrated database IV

	Observations	Percentage	Mean	Maximum	Minimum	Standard deviation
Number of bidders	230		3.99	8	10	3.14
CCL	117					
Vehicle kilometers	159		596,259	3,400,000	20,000	567,287
Number of lines	141		6.37	50	1	8.37
Start of operations (date)	198			14/12/ 2008	01/01/ 2003	
Start of operations (year)	230			2008	2003	
Incumbent	180	100.00				
Municipal	45	25.00				
Private SME	59	32.78				
DB subsidiary	70	38.89				
Global player	6	3.33				
Federal state	230	100.00				
Baden-Württemberg	8	3.48				
Bavaria	40	17.39				
Brandenburg	7	3.04				
Hesse	80	34.78				
Mecklenburg-Western Pomerania	3	1.30				
Lower Saxony	46	20.00				
North Rhine-Westphalia	16	6.96				
Rhineland-Palatine	7	3.04				
Saxony	2	0.87				
Saxony-Anhalt	6	2.61				
Schleswig-Holstein	15	6.52				

Table A.13 Pairwise Pearson correlation matrix of selected criteria of integrated database IV

	Number of bidders	CCL	Vkm p.a.	Number of lines	Start of operations (date)	Start of operations (year)
Number of bidders	1.0000					
CCL	−0.7034	1.0000				
Vkm p.a.	−0.0840	0.0050	1.0000			
Number of lines	−0.0448	0.1060	0.7565	1.0000		
Start of operations (date)	−0.5548	0.3642	0.1637	0.1540	1.0000	
Start of operations (year)	−0.5314	0.3762	0.1253	0.1714	0.9742	1.0000

Glossary

Application or application form (Genehmigungsantrag) Offer or request by an operator as an applicant to operate commercial or non-commercial services on a specific line or network bundle, filed with the licensing authority by using a specific application form (see Bezirksregierung Detmold 2008 for an example).

Authorization Other word used for license.

CCL – Competition for commercial lines or services (Genehmigungswettbewerb) Situation where at least two operators are filing an application for licenses for commercial services.

Commercial lines or services (Eigenwirtschaftliche Verkehre) Operating costs for these services are covered by fare and other operational revenues (see § 13 PBefG).

Common German Law for Railways (Allgemeines Eisenbahngesetz – AEG) Main legal basis for railway services.

Competition for non-commercial lines or services PTAs have the obligation to award subsidies for non-commercial services at lowest cost possible (see §§ 8 [4] and 13a PBefG). PTAs are obliged to award their supplementary direct subsidies through tendering procedures (Ausschreibungswettbewerb) similar to tendering procedures conducted in Denmark or Sweden.

Concession Another word used for *license*.

Exclusivity If a new application to operate a bus line competes with existing public transport services, and the operators of the existing lines claim convincingly that the profitability of these services is jeopardized; the licensing authority has to reject the new application. In reality this has resulted in a status of more or less exclusivity for holders of existing licenses (incumbent operators).

Gross-cost contract Contract where the PTA bears the revenue risk.

Incumbent The incumbent operator, possessing the existing (old) license to operate.

In-house Direct awarding to a municipal operator where the PTA is the owner.

Institutional or regulatory framework Legal framework for the public transport sector by bus as established at the national level (including the crucial laws AEG, PBefG and RegG).

A. Beck, *Competition for Public Transport Services*, Contributions to Economics,
DOI 10.1007/978-3-7908-2802-3, © Springer-Verlag Berlin Heidelberg 2012

LA – licensing authority (Genehmigungsbehörde) This authority grants the licenses to operators, who apply for them. This authority is entrusted with the obligation to safeguard security of operation for passengers and to ensure a continuous delivery of services.

Law on the Regionalization of Public Transport (Regionalisierungsgesetz – RegG) Legal framework to regionalize and re-finance public transport, established during market reform in the mid-1990s.

License or license for public transport services (Genehmigung) Authorization to operate public transport services as defined in the bid filed by the operator (application), and based on § 13 or § 13a PBefG. It is awarded by the licensing authority and provides exclusivity (see above) to operators.

License term (Laufzeit der Genehmigung) The period the operator is authorized to operate the services granted under the existing license.

Licensee (Genehmigungsinhaber) Operator holding a license to operate a specific line for the duration of the license term.

Local Authority Traffic Financing Act (Gemeindeverkehrsfinanzierungsgesetz – GVFG) Main legal basis for subsidies paid by national, state, and local authorities to support long-term investments in infrastructure and vehicles for public transport.

Market initiative Initiative to operate services by operators.

Market participants PTAs, LAs, and operators.

Net-cost contract Contract where the operator bears the revenue risk.

Non-commercial lines or services (Gemeinwirtschaftliche Verkehre) Operating costs for these services are not covered by fares and other revenues; supplementary direct subsidies by the PTA are necessary to ensure these services run at an adequate level (see § 13a PBefG).

Non-railway services All public transport services, including bus and light rail services, excluding heavy railway services.

Other operational revenues according to § 8 (4) PBefG (sonstige Unternehmenserträge im handelsrechtlichen Sinne) Direct or indirect subsidies granted by state authorities for a specific purpose, not accounted as "subsidies" for non-commercial services.

Passenger Transport Act (Personenbeförderungsgesetz – PBefG) Main legal basis for organizing the German public transport market for non-railway services.

Priority of commercial services In case the licensing authority has two applications to operate a specific service or line, one commercial and the other non-commercial, it is mandatory to grant the license to the operator applying for a commercial license, see § 8 (4) PBefG.

PTA – public transport authority (Aufgabenträger) Authority responsible for securing an adequate level of public transport services in its territory in accordance with the provision of services of general interest ("Sicherung der Daseinsvorsorge", see § 1 RegG).

PTP – (local) public transport plan (Nahverkehrsplan) Plan as set by PTAs on minimum quality standards (e.g., minimum frequency of service, junctions, vehicle standards such as air-conditioning and low-floor entry), and their goals for improving public transport in the near future within their territory.

Short distance services Regularly operated lines of up to 50 kilometers distance and/or one hour travelling time, as defined in both § 2 RegG and § 8 (1) PBefG.

Threshold Point where all operational costs for the minimum level of quality, as defined by the PTA in its PTP, are covered by fare and other operational revenues.

References

Literature and Documents

Achenbach H (2006) Der Wettbewerb im ÖPNV in Hessen am Beispiel des Rhein-Main-Verkehrsverbundes. In: Ifmo – Institut für Mobilitätsforschung (ed) Öffentlicher Personennahverkehr – Herausforderungen und Chancen. Springer, Berlin, pp 175–193

Agrell PJ, Bogetoft P, Cullmann A, Hirschhausen Cv, Neumann A, Walter M (2008a) Projekt GERNER IV Ergebnisdokumentation: Bestimmung der Effizienzwerte Verteilernetzbetreiber Gas. http://www.bundesnetzagentur.de/media/archive/14563.pdf. Retrieved 10 July 2009

Agrell PJ, Bogetoft P, Cullmann A, Hirschhausen CV, Neumann A, Walter M (2008b) Projekt GERNER IV Ergebnisdokumentation: Bestimmung der Effizienzwerte Verteilernetzbetreiber Strom. http://www.bundesnetzagentur.de/media/archive/14693.pdf. Retrieved 10 July 2009

Aigner D, Lovell CAK, Schmidt P (1977) Formulation and estimation of stochastic frontier production function models. J Econom 6(1):21–37

Alexandersson G, Hultén S, Fölster S (1998) The effects of competition in Swedish local bus services. J Transp Econ Policy 32(2):203–219

Alexandersson G, Hultén S (2009) The complexity of market structure – prospects for on-the-track competition in Sweden. In: van de Velde D, Beck A, Veeneman W (eds) Beyond competitive tendering – proceedings of the eleventh international conference on competition and ownership in land passenger transport. Next Generation Infrastructures Foundation, Delft, pp 187–209

Alexandersson G, Pyddoke R (2003) Bus deregulation in Sweden revisited: experiences from 15 years of competitive tendering. Paper presented at the eighth conference on competition and ownership in land passenger transport, Rio de Janeiro, 14–18 Sept 2003

Alexandersson G, Fearnley N, Hultén S, Longva F (2009) Impact of regulation on the performances of long-distance transport services: a comparison of the different approaches in Sweden and Norway. In: van de Velde D, Beck A, Veeneman W (eds) Beyond competitive tendering – proceedings of the eleventh international conference on competition and ownership in land passenger transport. Next Generation Infrastructures Foundation, Delft, pp 221–234

Amaral M, Saussier S, Yvrande-Billon A (2006) Does competition for the field improve cost efficiency? evidence from the london bus tendering model, Berlin University of Technology – Center for Network Industries & Infrastructure (ed) CNI-working paper, no. 2006-14, Berlin, 13 Sept 2006. http://www.cni.tu-berlin.de/index.php?id=15. Retrieved 10 Aug 2009

Amaral M, Saussier S, Yvrande-Billon A (2008) Auction procedures and competition in public services: the case of urban public transport in France and London. Utilities Policy 17(2):166–175

Arbeitsgruppe Verkehrsverträge und Qualitätsmanagement (2002) Abschlussbericht für die Europäische Kommission, DG Energie und Verkehr, report of the Citizens' Network Benchmarking Initiative, Brussels. Feb 2002. http://www.citizensnetwork.org/uk/download/WG2_Report_de.pdf. Retrieved 12 Sept 2008

A. Beck, *Competition for Public Transport Services*, Contributions to Economics, DOI 10.1007/978-3-7908-2802-3, © Springer-Verlag Berlin Heidelberg 2012

Ashmore DP, Mellor AD (2009) The 2008 New Zealand public transport management act: rationale, key provisions, and parallels with the United Kingdom. In: van de Velde D, Beck A, Veeneman W (eds) Beyond competitive tendering – proceedings of the eleventh international conference on competition and ownership in land passenger transport. Next Generation Infrastructures Foundation, Delft, pp 49–76

Atkins (2005) Monitoring local bus service tenders in England – bus tendering good practice guide, Department for Transport (DfT), London. http:/www.dft.gov.uk/pgr/regional/buses/tendering. Retrieved 12 Sept 2008

Augustin K, Walter M (2009) Operator changes through competitive tendering: empirical evidence from German local bus transport. In: Nash C, Wolanski M, Veeneman W, van de Velde D (eds) Benchmarking the competitive tendering outcome – proceedings of the eleventh international conference on competition and ownership in land passenger transport. Next Generation Infrastructures Foundation, Delft, pp 129–150

Bain JS (1956) Barriers to new competition. Harvard University Press, Cambridge

Banister D (1985) Deregulating the bus industry in Britain – (A) the proposals. Transp Rev 5(2):99–103

Barth S (2001) Die Regionalisierungsgesetze von Bund und Ländern. In: Barth S, Baumeister H, Berschin F, Werner J (eds) Recht des öffentlichen Personennahverkehrs, Section A 3, Hermann Luchterhand, Neuwied

Baumol W (1982) Contestable markets: an uprising in the theory of industry structure. Am Econ Rev 72(1):1–15

Beck A (2006) Der Fluch des Gewinners – Verlust- und Insolvenzgefahren beim Gewinn einer Ausschreibung von Verkehrsleistungen. Der Nahverkehr 24(4):29–33

Beck A (2007) Genehmigungswettbewerb: Das Problem der Auswahl des besten Genehmigungsantrages – Eine ökonomische Bewertung. Verkehr und Technik 60(11):425–430

Beck A (2009a) Der Ausschreibungswettbewerb im Schienenpersonennahverkehr – Markteintrittsbarrieren und Anreizmechanismen bei der Vergabe von Leistungen im SPNV. Erich Schmidt, Berlin

Beck A (2009b) The distinction between commercial and non-commercial bus services in Germany: given by nature? In: Technische Universität Berlin – Center for Network Industries & Infrastructure (ed) CNI-working paper, no. 2009-01, Berlin, 28 Mar 2009. http://www.wip.tu-berlin.de/typo3/index.php?id=2971. Retrieved 16 Mar 2010

Beck A (2009c) To tender or not to tender – the unanswered German question. In: Technische Universität Berlin – Center for Network Industries & Infrastructure (ed) CNI-working paper, no. 2009-02, Berlin. http://www.wip.tu-berlin.de/typo3/index.php? id=2971. Retrieved 16 Mar 2010

Beck A (2009d) Commercial public transport services by bus in Germany – how a market in motion struggles with its regulatory framework. In: van de Velde D, Beck A, Veeneman W (eds) Beyond competitive tendering – proceedings of the eleventh international conference on competition and ownership in land passenger transport. Next Generation Infrastructures Foundation, Delft, pp 87–116

Beck A (2009e) What are the effects of competitive tendering on bus services in Germany? In: Nash C, Wolanski M, Veeneman W, van de Velde D (eds) Benchmarking the competitive tendering outcome – proceedings of the eleventh international conference on competition and ownership in land passenger transport. Next Generation Infrastructures Foundation, Delft, pp 101–127

Beck A (2009f) The competitive market for commercial bus services in Germany: entry barriers for market initiatives? In: Technische Universität Berlin – Center for Network Industries & Infrastructure (ed) CNI-working paper, no. 2009-03, Berlin. http://www.wip.tu-berlin.de/typo3/index.php? id=2971. Retrieved 16 Mar 2010

Beck A (2009g) Experiences with competitive tendering of bus services in Germany. In: Technische Universität Berlin – Center for Network Industries & Infrastructure (ed) CNI-working paper, no. 2009-04, Berlin. http://www.wip.tu-berlin.de/typo3/index.php? id=2971. Retrieved 16 Mar 2010

Beck A (2010a) Barriers to entry in rail passenger services: empirical evidence for tendering procedures in Germany. In: Technische Universität Berlin – Center for Network Industries & Infrastructure (ed) CNI-working paper, no. 2010-02, Berlin, Spring 2009. http://www.wip.tu-berlin.de/typo3/index.php? id=2971. Retrieved 16 Mar 2010
Beck A (2010b) Commercial public bus transport services in Germany: how a market in motion struggles with its regulatory framework. Res Transp Econ (Special edition: Reforming public transport throughout the world) 29(1):183–194
Beck A (2011a) Barriers to entry in rail passenger services: empirical evidence for tendering procedures in Germany. Eur J Transp Infrastruct Res 11(1):20–41
Beck A (2011b) Public bus transport in Germany: a proposal to improve the current awarding system – discussion paper. In: Karlsruhe Institute of Technology – Faculty for Economics (ed) KIT Working Paper no. 19, Karlsruhe. http://econpapers.wiwi.kit.edu/. Retrieved 16 Apr 2010
Beck A (2011c) Experiences with competitive tendering of bus services in Germany. Transp Rev 31(3):313–339
Beck A (2012) The distinction between commercial and non-commercial bus services in Germany: given by nature? Transp Policy 19(1):26–35
Beck A, Wanner K, Zietz A, Christmann B, Schaaffkamp C (2006) Der Busverkehr im Wettbewerb – Zwischenfazit nach zehn Jahren Ausschreibungen im RMV, MVV und HVV. Study of the consultancy KCW for Rhein-Main-Verkehrsverbund GmbH (RMV), Münchener Verkehrs- und Tarifverbund GmbH (MVV) and Hamburger Verkehrsverbund GmbH (HVV), Berlin, Dec 2006 (unpublished)
Beck A, Kühl I, Schaaffkamp C (2007) Effekte des Ausschreibungswettbewerbs im regionalen Bahnverkehr in Deutschland. Die Volkswirtschaft 2007(3):18–20
Beck A, Schnell M (2008) Genehmigungswettbewerb in Deutschland – Ein häufig unterschätztes Risiko für Aufgabenträger, Genehmigungsbehörden und Unternehmen. Nahverkehrspraxis 56 (5):29–31
Beck A, Wanner K (2007) Was bewirken Ausschreibungen von Busverkehrsleistungen? Evaluation der Ausschreibungsergebnisse der vergangenen zehn Jahre im RMV, MVV und HVV. Der Nahverkehr 25(7–8):24–30
Beck A, Wanner K (2008) Entwicklung von Bestellerentgelten im Busverkehr – Analyse der Ausschreibungsergebnisse im RMV, MVV und HVV. Internationales Verkehrswesen 60 (9):322–327
Beck A, Walter M (2010) Tender prices in German local bus transport – an application of alternative regression techniques. In: Karlsruhe Institute of Technology – Faculty for Economics (ed) KIT Working Paper no. 13, Karlsruhe. Paper submitted to J Transport Econ Policy. http://econpapers.wiwi.kit.edu/. Retrieved 20 Mar 2011
Beck A, Wille M-O (2009) Genehmigungswettbewerb im deutschen ÖPNV – Aktuelle Entwicklungen im Markt für kommerzielle Busverkehre. Der Nahverkehr 27(4):8–11
Beck A, Wille M-O (2011) Zwischen Unternehmensverbund und Aufgabenträgerorganisation – Wohin geht die Entwicklung der Verkehrsverbünde in Deutschland? Der Nahverkehr 29(3):13–17
Beesley ME, Glaister S (1985) Deregulating the bus industry in Britain – (C) a response. Transp Rev 5(2):133–142
Berschin F (2003) Ausschreibungen im Busverkehr in Deutschland. In: Deutsche Verkehrswissenschaftliche Gesellschaft e.V. – DVWG (ed) 36. Verkehrswissenschaftliches Seminar Versteigerungen und Ausschreibungen in Verkehrs- und Versorgungsnetzen: Praxiserfahrungen und Zukunftsperspektiven, Schriftenreihe der Deutschen Verkehrswissenschaftlichen Gesellschaft e.V., Bd. B272, Berlin
Bester H (2003) Theorie der Industrieökonomik. Springer, Berlin
Beuven T, Dannenfeld D, Elsner R, Ubben E (2005) BUSfacts – Bestandsaufnahme und Perspektiven des Öffentlichen Straßenpersonenverkehrs in Deutschland und Europa, study of the Institut für Angewandte Wirtschaftsforschung und Regionalanalyse (ANWI), Omnibus-Wirtschaftsberatungsgesellschaft mbH (omnibera) (ed) Aug 2005. http://www.busfacts.de/index.php?option=com_content&task=blogsection&id=1&Itemid=9. Retrieved 20 Mar 2006

Bezirksregierung Arnsberg (2008) Linienverkehrsgenehmigungen. http://www.bezreg-arnsberg.nrw.de/dieBezirksregierung/aufbau/abteilungen/abteilung2/dezernat25/aufgaben/personenbefoerderung/linienverkehrsgenehmigungen/index.html. Retrieved 12 Dec 2008

Bezirksregierung Detmold (2008) Genehmigungen: StVO/StVZO/ÖPNV. http://www.brdt.nrw.de/400_WirUeberUns/030_Die_Behoerde/040_Organisation/020_Abteilung_2/050_Dezernat_25/060_Genehmigungen/index.php. Retrieved 12 Dec 2008

BLFA – Bund-Länder-Fachausschuss Straßenpersonenverkehr (2006) Vorschläge für die Gestaltung des Genehmigungsverfahrens im "Genehmigungswettbewerb". In: AG Genehmigungswettbewerb (Länder HE, NI, RP, ST) des BLFA, Niedersächsisches Wirtschaftsministerium (ed) writ with file number 44.1 – 10.02/01 – (30100/1023), Hannover, 26 July 2006 (unpublished document)

BMVBS – Bundesministerium für Verkehr, Bau und Stadtentwicklung (2005) Kontrollierter Wettbewerb im ÖPNV – Forschungsbericht FE-Nr 70.0663/2001, study within the research program FoPS – Forschungsprogramm Stadtverkehr of the German federal ministry of transport

Borrmann M (2003) Ausschreibungen im Schienenpersonennahverkehr – Eine ökonomische Analyse auf Basis der Vertrags- und Auktionstheorie. In: Hartwig K-H (ed) Beiträge aus dem Institut für Verkehrswissenschaften an der Universität Münster, vol 152. Vandenhoeck & Ruprecht, Göttingen

Branco F (1997) The design of multidimensional auctions. RAND J Econ 28(1):63–81

Bräuer C, Herr C, Pinz P, Wille M-O (2005) Erfolgsfaktoren für künftige Vergabeverfahren – Erfahrungen aus dem Planspiel "Virtuelle Ausschreibung" in den Ländern Niedersachsen und Bremen. Der Nahverkehr 23(6):10–16

Brenck A, Mitusch K, Winter M (2008) Die externen Kosten des Verkehrs. In: Schöller O, Canzler W, Knie A (eds) Handbuch Verkehrspolitik. VS Verlag für Sozialwissenschaften, Wiesbaden, pp 425–452

Brons M, Nijkamp EP, Rietveld P (2005) Efficiency of urban public transit: a meta analysis. Transportation 32(1):1–21

BSL – BSL Management Consultants GmbH & Co. KG (2008) Private Busunternehmen im Wettbewerb – Anforderungen, Chancen und Handlungsalternativen. In: Study for Landesverband Hessischer Omnibusunternehmer (LHO) (ed) Hamburg, Aug 2008

Burmeister J (2005) VLG verliert Verkehre an Hülsmann. stadtverkehr 50(10):16–18

Burmeister J (2006) Wettbewerb in Hessen – Erste Auswirkungen. Nahverkehrspraxis 54(10):8–10

Cantillon E, Pesendorfer M (2007) Combination bidding in multi-unit auctions. In: Centre for Economic Policy Research (ed) Discussion paper series, no. 6083, London, Feb 2007. http://www.cepr.org/pubs/dps/DP6083.asp.asp. Retrieved 10 Feb 2009

Capen EC, Clapp RV, Campbell WM (1971) Competitive bidding in high-risk situations. J Petrol Technol 23(6):641–653

CDU, CSU, FDP (2009) Wachstum. Bildung. Zusammenhalt – Koalitionsvertrag zwischen CDU, CSU und FDP – 17. Legislaturperiode, Berlin. http://www.cdu.de/portal2009/29145.htm. Retrieved 8 Dec 2009

Chadwick E (1859) On different principles of legislation and administration. J Royal Stat Soc 22:381–420

Che Y-K (1993) Design competition through multidimensional auctions. RAND J Econ 24(4):668–680

Coelli TJ, Rao DSP, O'Donnell CJ, Battese GE (2005) An introduction to efficiency and productivity analysis, 2nd edn. Springer, New York

Conpronet e.V. (2009) Ausschreibungspraxis im ÖPSV – Ergebnisse aus Hessen, study for bdo Bundesverband Deutscher Omnibusunternehmer e.V. and DB Stadtverkehr GmbH (ed) Emden, June 2009. http://www.bdo-online.de/fileadmin/Dateien/Pressemiteilungen_Anlagen/2009/AHA-02.Juni_2009.pdf. Retrieved 6 Aug 2009

Cowie J (2009) Contestability in the provision of bus services – evidence from the British deregulated market. In: van de Velde D, Beck A, Veeneman W (eds) Beyond competitive tendering – proceedings of the eleventh international conference on competition and ownership in land passenger transport. Next Generation Infrastructures Foundation, Delft, pp 1–15
Dalen DM, Gómez-Lobo A (2003) Yardsticks on the road: regulatory contracts and cost efficiency in the Norwegian bus industry. Transportation 30(4):371–386
Davis DD, Holt CA (1993) Experimental economics. Princeton University Press, Princeton
Demsetz H (1968) Why regulate utilities? J Law Econ 11(1):55–65
Eisenkopf A, Grotemeier C (2009) Ist der Fahrscheinvertrieb eine Essential Facility? – Diskussionsbeitrag zu Diskriminierungsproblemen beim Fahrscheinvertrieb im Schienenpersonennahverkehr. Der Nahverkehr 27(3):14–18
European Commission (2001) Communication from the commission – services of general interest in Europe, Official Journal of the European Communities, 44, C17/04, Brussels, 19 Jan 2001
European Commission (2006) Notification C (2006) 1847 endg. Brussels, 17 May 2006
European Court of Justice (2003) Judgment of the court of justice for the declaratory judgment proceeding C-280/00. Press note no. 64/03, 24 July 2003
Farsi M, Filippini M, Kuenzle M (2006) Cost efficiency in regional bus companies: an application of alternative stochastic frontier models. J Transp Econ Policy 40(1):95–118
Fees E (1997) Mikroökonomie – Eine spieltheoretisch- und anwendungsorientierte Einführung. Metropolis, Marburg
Fisher FM (1979) Diagnosing monopoly. Q Rev Econ Bus 19(2):7–33
Forsthoff E (1938) Die Verwaltung als Leistungsträger. W. Kohlhammer, Stuttgart
Freitag A (2009) The role and significance of Verkehrsverbünde within a market undergoing progressive liberalisation. In: Verband Deutscher Verkehrsunternehmen e.V. and VDV-Förderkreis e.V (eds) Transport alliances – promoting cooperation and integration to offer a more attractive and efficient public transport, DVV Media Group GmbH, pp 221–239
Gibson R (2009) Developing public transport procurement strategies in a new legislative environment – a New Zealand perspective. In: van de Velde D, Beck A, Veeneman W (eds) Beyond competitive tendering – proceedings of the eleventh international conference on competition and ownership in land passenger transport. Next Generation Infrastructures Foundation, Delft, pp 35–48
Gómez-Lobo A (2007) Why competition does not work in urban bus markets – some new wheels for some old ideas. J Transp Econ Policy 41(2):283–308
Gorter M (2009) Direct awards in Germany – design and effects. In: van de Velde D, Beck A, Veeneman W (eds) Beyond competitive tendering – proceedings of the eleventh international conference on competition and ownership in land passenger transport. Next Generation Infrastructures Foundation, Delft, pp 133–144
Graetz N, Gleixner H, Benzler G (2007) Die Rolle der ÖPNV-Aufgabenträger in der Bundesrepublik Deutschland – Eine Untersuchung in Zusammenarbeit mit der Bundesarbeitsgemeinschaft der ÖPNV-Aufgabenträger in der Bundesvereinigung der kommunalen Spitzenverbände Deutschlands (BAG ÖPNV). Deloitte (ed) Düsseldorf, Nov 2007
Griffiths T (2009) On rail competition: the impact of open access entry on the Great Britain rail market. In: van de Velde D, Beck A, Veeneman W (eds) Beyond competitive tendering – proceedings of the eleventh international conference on competition and ownership in land passenger transport. Next Generation Infrastructures Foundation, Delft, pp 161–171
Grzelec K, Wolanski M, Wyszomirski O (2009) Connecting competition and integration. A concept of new organizational framework for Polish local bus transport. In: van de Velde D, Beck A, Veeneman W (eds) Beyond competitive tendering – proceedings of the eleventh international conference on competition and ownership in land passenger transport. Next Generation Infrastructures Foundation, Delft, pp 77–86
Gwilliam KM (2007) Bus transport: is there a regulatory cycle? Paper presented at the tenth conference on competition and ownership in land passenger transport, Hamilton Island – Sydney, 12–17 Aug 2007

Gwilliam KM, Nash CA, Mackie PJ (1985) Deregulating the bus industry in Britain – (B) the case against. Transp Rev 5(2):105–132

Hensher DA, Wallis IP (2005) Competitive tendering as a contracting mechanism for subsidising transport: the bus experience. J Transp Econ Policy 39(3):295–321

Hermans G, Stoelinga A (2005) Competition in Dutch public transport. In: Hensher DA (ed) Competition and ownership in land passenger transport. Elsevier, Amsterdam, pp 291–301

Hickmann G (2004) Den Übergang in den Wettbewerb aktiv gestalten – Eckpunktepapier zur Gestaltung der zukünftigen Marktordnung im Öffentlichen Personennahverkehr (ÖPNV). In: Bündnis 90 Die Grünen Bundestagsfraktion (ed) Tübingen, 19 Oct 2004 (unpublished paper)

Hickmann G, Berschin F, Schaaffkamp C, Karwiese E, Schulze E (2008) Bundesland Brandenburg setzt die Reform der ÖPNV-Finanzierung fort – Anreizorientierte Bündelung der Fördermittel bei den kommunalen ÖPNV-Aufgabenträgern und Integration von §45a PBefG. Der Nahverkehr 26(3):36–41

HMWVL – Hessisches Ministerium für Wirtschaft, Verkehr und Landesentwicklung (2002) Eckpunkte für den Wettbewerb – Öffentlicher Personennahverkehr in Hessen. Position paper of the ministry of transport of the federal state of Hesse, Wiesbaden, Nov 2002. http://www.perspektive-wettbewerb.de/files/eckpunkte_wettbewerb.pdf. Retrieved 12 Mar 2007

HMWVL – Hessisches Ministerium für Wirtschaft, Verkehr und Landesentwicklung (2004) Konsequenzen aus dem EuGH-Urteil vom 24.07.2003 – Rs C-280/00 (Altmark Trans) – Auswirkungen auf die Genehmigungs- und Vergabepraxis in Hessen. Writ of the ministry of transport of the federal state of Hesse with file number AZ V9-66 I 28-59-02, Wiesbaden, 12 Mar 2004 (unpublished)

HMWVL – Hessisches Ministerium für Wirtschaft, Verkehr und Landesentwicklung (2005) Modernes Gesetz sichert Mobilität mit Bussen und Bahnen. Press release of the ministry of transport of the federal state of Hesse, Wiesbaden, 23 Nov 2005

HMWVL – Hessisches Ministerium für Wirtschaft, Verkehr und Landesentwicklung (2006a) Hessische Ausschreibungs- und Genehmigungspraxis im öffentlichen Personennahverkehr. Writ of the ministry of transport of the federal state of Hesse with file number AZ V8-66I28-59-02, Wiesbaden, 17 Feb 2006

HMWVL – Hessisches Ministerium für Wirtschaft, Verkehr und Landesentwicklung (2006b) Hessen setzt weiter vorrangig auf Ausschreibung, um Mobilität bei Bus- und Bahnverkehren zu erhalten. Press release of the ministry of transport of the federal state of Hesse, Wiesbaden, 9 Mar 2006

HMWVL – Hessisches Ministerium für Wirtschaft, Verkehr und Landesentwicklung (2006c) Hessen setzt weiter vorrangig auf Ausschreibung, um Mobilität bei Bus- und Bahnverkehren zu erhalten. Press release of the ministry of transport of the federal state of Hesse, Wiesbaden, 30 May 2006

HVV – Hamburger Verkehrsverbund GmbH (2003) Notification of the HVV. Within the Supplement to the Official Journal of the European Union: 2003/S 173-157309, 9 Jan 2003

HVV – Hamburger Verkehrsverbund GmbH (2004) Notification of the HVV. within the Supplement to the Official Journal of the European Union: 2004/S 108-089015. 4 June 2004

HVV – Hamburger Verkehrsverbund GmbH (2005) More than one way – A profile of the Hamburg public transport association. Hamburg. http://www.hvv.de/pdf/wissenwertes/unternehmensbroschuere.pdf Retrieved 16 Mar 2010

HVV – Hamburger Verkehrsverbund GmbH (2007) Bericht 2007, Hamburg, http://www.hvv.de/pdf/wissenwertes/verbundbericht_2007.pdf. Retrieved 16 Mar 2010

International Association of Public Transport (2005) A Market in Motion, UITP

Jamasb T, Pollitt MG, Triebs T (2008) Productivity and efficiency of US gas transmission companies: a European regulatory perspective. Energy Policy 36(9):3398–3412

Jondrow J, Lovell CAK, Materov IS, Schmidt P (1982) On the estimation of technical inefficiency in the stochastic frontier production model. J Econom 19(2–3):233–238

Kagel JH, Levin D (2002) Common value auctions and the winner's curse. Princeton University Press, Princeton

Klinger D (2006) Busverkehrsleistungen erfolgreich ausschreiben – Praxistipps unter Berücksichtigung der aktuellen vergaberechtlichen Rechtsprechung. Der Nahverkehr 24(4):48–51

Knieps M (2004) Aufgabenträger oder Verkehrsunternehmen als Gesellschafter von Verkehrsverbünden? – eine Analyse bestehender Verbundstrukturen und eine Bewertung unterschiedlicher Organisationsmodelle unter institutionenökonomischen Gesichtspunkten. Doctoral thesis, Gießen. http://geb.uni-giessen.de/geb/volltexte/2004/1644/. Retrieved 10 Feb 2009

Köberlein C (1997) Kompendium der Verkehrspolitik. Verlag Oldenbourg, Munich

Kohler U, Kreuter F (2008) Datenanalyse mit Stata – Allgemeine Konzepte der Datenanalyse und ihre praktische Anwendung. Oldenbourg, Munich

Kreis Dithmarschen (2003) Zweiter Regionaler Nahverkehrsplan für den Kreis Dithmarschen 2003–2007 – Fortschreibung des "Regionalen Nahverkehrplans" 2003–2007 des Kreises Dithmarschen. Nov 2003, Heide (Holst.) http://www.dithmarschen.de/index.phtml?La=1&sNavID=647.148&mNavID=164.804&object=tx|164.6338.1. Retrieved 6 Jun 2010

Krishna V (2002) Auction theory. Academic, San Diego

Kumarage AS, Jayaratne MDRP (2008) Lessons in ownership regulation and management from 100 years of bus transport in Sri Lanka. Res Transp Econ 22:109–117

Laffont J-J, Tirole J (1993) A theory of incentives in procurement and regulation. The MIT Press, Cambridge

Lalive R, Schmutzler A (2008a) Exploring the effects of competition for railway markets. Int J Ind Organ 26(2):443–458

Lalive R, Schmutzler A (2008b) Entry in liberalized railway markets: the German experience. Rev Netw Econ 7(1):37–52

Landesamt für Bauen und Verkehr Brandenburg (2008) Genehmigungen im Öffentlichen Straßenpersonenverkehr. http://www.lbv.brandenburg.de/Oeff_spv_pverkehr.htm. Retrieved 12 Dec 2008

Landesdirektion Dresden (2008) Personenverkehr. http://www.ld-dresden.de/index.asp? ID=1491&art_param=168, Retrieved 16 Dec 2008

Landkreis Wittenberg (2005a) Nahverkehrsplan Landkreis Wittenberg 2007–2014. Wittenberg, 30 June 2005. http://www.landkreis-wittenberg.de/pics/download/1_1206695307/Nahverkehrsplan.pdf. Retrieved 12 Sept 2008

Landkreis Wittenberg (2005b) Satzung für die Schülerbeförderung im Landkreis Wittenberg. Amtsblatt für den Landkreis Wittenberg 9 July 2005

Landkreis Wittenberg (2005c) Satzung zur Unterstützung eigenwirtschaftlicher Verkehrsleistungen im Landkreis Wittenberg, DS-Nr. 112/06 Amtsblatt 06 2006, Wittenberg, 18 Mar 2006. http://www.landkreis-wittenberg.de/pics/download/1_1266580845/Satzung_Unterst.eigenwirtsch.Verkehrsleistungen.pdf&sa=X&ei=V84tTOPQNp6cOJ-K9PgB&ved=0CBoQzgQoATAA&usg=AFQjCNF1zYp88CNvR8qAvhGpi7RrwTJItg. Retrieved 12 Sept 2008

Landkreis Wittenberg (2006) Notification of the suburban district Wittenberg. Supplement to the Official Journal of the European Union, 2006/S 8-0090005. 13 Jan 2006

Landkreise im MVV (1999) Positionspapier im MVV zum Wettbewerb im straßengebundenen ÖPNV. Munich, 20 July 1999. http://www.mvv-muenchen.de/web4archiv/objects/download/positionspapierlandkreisewettbewerb.pdf. Retrieved12 Sept 2008

Landsberg G (2003) Genehmigungswettbewerb im ÖPNV. Verkehr und Technik 54(10):411–413

Leopairojna SK, Hanoaka S (2007) Market analysis of passenger vans in Bangkok, In: Macário R, Viegas JM, Hensher DA (eds) Competition and ownership in land passenger transport. Selected papers from the 9th international conference (Thredbo 9), Lisbon, Sept 2005, Elsevier, Amsterdam, pp 303–329

LNVG – Landesnahverkehrsgesellschaft Niedersachsen mbH (2008) ÖPNV genehmigen. http://www.lnvg.de/. Retrieved 10 Dec 2008

Lundin U, Biörklund UC, Nilsson A-C, Pettersson S (2009) En ny kollektivtrafiklag – Delbetänkande av Utredningen om en ny kollektivtrafiklag. In: Statens Offentliga Utredningar (ed), Stockholm, Apr 2009. http://www.sou.gov.se/koll/PDF/SOU2009_39_bilaga1-5.pdf. Retrieved 10 Aug 2009

Macário R (2005) Institutional frameworks, regulatory agencies and the land passenger transport industry – Reflections on recent evolutions. In: Hensher DA (ed.) Competition and ownership in land passenger transport. Selected refereed papers from the 8th international conference (Thredbo 8), Rio de Janeiro, Sept 2003, Elsevier, Amsterdam, pp 541–558

Mathisen TA, Solvoll G (2008) Competitive tendering and structural changes – an example from the bus industry. Transp Policy 15(1):1–11

MBV ST – Ministerium für Bau und Verkehr des Landes Sachsen-Anhalt (2005) Plan des öffentlichen Personennahverkehrs des Landes Sachsen-Anhalt – ÖPNV-Plan – Zeitraum 2005 bis 2008/2015. Magdeburg. http://www3.nasa.de/fileadmin/media/oepnv/pdf/OEPNV-Plan_2005.pdf Retrieved 6 Mar 2007

MBV ST – Ministerium für Bau und Verkehr des Landes Sachsen-Anhalt (2006) "Wittenberger Modell" sichert öffentlichen Nahverkehr in hoher Qualität. Press release from the ministry of transport of Saxony-Anhalt, Magdeburg, 23 May 2006

MBV NW – Ministerium für Bauen und Verkehr des Landes Nordrhein-Westfalen (2008) Hinweise zur Durchführung des Genehmigungswettbewerbs. 1 Nov 2008 (unpublished)

McAfee R, Mialon M, Williams MA (2004) What is a barrier to entry? Am Econ Rev 94 (2):461–465

McAfee R, McMillan J (1987) Auctions and bidding. J Econ Lit 25(6):699–738

McDowell A (2004) From the help desk: seemingly unrelated regression with unbalanced equations. Stata J 4(4):442–448

Meeusen W, van den Broeck J (1977) Efficiency estimation from Cobb-Douglas production functions with composed error. Int Econ Rev 18(2):435–444

Miller D (1970) Differences among cities, differences among firms, and costs of urban bus transport. J Ind Econ 1:22–32

MIR – Ministerium für Infrastruktur und Raumordnung des Landes Brandenburg (2007) Hinweise zur Erteilung von Liniengenehmigungen mit Kraftfahrzeugen nach dem Personenbeförderungsgesetz. In: Referat 40 (ed), Summer 2007. http://www.lbv.brandenburg.de/dateien/MIRHinweisezurErteilungvonLiniengenehmigungen1.pdf. Retrieved 12 Sept 2008

MVV – Münchner Verkehrs- und Tarifverbund GmbH (1996) Call for offers for the route 838. Publication notice for the Supplement of the Official Journal of the European Community, 19 Sept 1996

MVV – Münchner Verkehrs- und Tarifverbund GmbH (2005a) Wettbewerbsbericht 2005 – MVV-Regionalbusverkehr. Munich. http://www.mvv-muenchen.de/web4archiv/cobjects/download/mvv-wettbewerbsbericht2005.pdf. Retrieved 12 Sep 2008

MVV – Münchner Verkehrs- und Tarifverbund GmbH (2005b) Verbundbericht 2005 – Münchner Verkehrs- und Tarifverbund. Munich. http://www.mvv-muenchen.de/web4archiv/objects/download/1/verbundbericht_2005.pdf Retrieved 12 Sept 2008

MVV – Münchner Verkehrs- und Tarifverbund GmbH (2009) Ausschreibungsunterlagen MVV-Regionalbuslinie 466. Munich, 9 Jun 2009 (unpublished)

MVV – Münchner Verkehrs- und Tarifverbund GmbH (2010) MVV in Zahlen. http://www.mvv-muenchen.de/de/home/dermvv/unternehmen/mvv_in_zahlen/index.html. Retrieved 21 May 2010

Nareike A, Walter J (2006) Berufsfreiheit und Genehmigungspraxis im Personenverkehrsgewerbe. Verkehr und Technik 59(8):315–320

Nash C (2009) European rail reform – the next steps. In: van de Velde D, Beck A, Veeneman W (eds) Beyond competitive tendering – proceedings of the eleventh international conference on competition and ownership in land passenger transport. Next Generation Infrastructures Foundation, Delft, pp 145–159

Nash C, Nilsson J-E (2009) Competitive tendering of rail services – a comparison of Britain and Sweden. In: Nash C, Wolanski M, Veeneman W, van de Velde D (eds) Benchmarking the competitive tendering outcome – proceedings of the eleventh international conference on competition and ownership in land passenger transport. Next Generation Infrastructures Foundation, Delft, pp 1–22

Nash C, Smith A (2006) Passenger rail franchising – British experience. Paper presented at the ECMT workshop on competitive tendering for passenger rail services, Paris, 12 Jan 2006

OFT – Office of Fair Trading (2009) Local bus services – Report on the market study and proposed decision to make a market investigation reference, London, Aug 2009. http://www.oft.gov.uk/shared_oft/consultations/oft1112con.pdf. Retrieved 21 May 2010

OVN and ver.di – Omnibus Verband Nord (OVN) e.v. and ver.di – Vereinte Dienstleistungsgewerkschaft (ver.di) Landesbezirk Nord (2007) Lohntarifvertrag für die gewerblichen Arbeitnehmer/innen des privaten Omnibusgewerbes in Schleswig-Holstein. Kiel/Lübeck, valid from 1.Sept 2007 (unpublished document)

Peter B (2008) Railway reform in Germany: Restructuring, service contracts, and infrastructure charges. Doctoral thesis, Berlin University of Technology, Berlin. http://opus.kobv.de/tuberlin/volltexte/2008/1870/. Retrieved 21 May 2010

Preston J, Whelan G, Nash C, Wardman M (2000) The franchising of passenger rail services in Britain. Int Rev Appl Econ 14(1):99–112

Pucher J, Kurth S (1996) Verkehrsverbund: the success of regional public transport in Germany, Austria and Switzerland. Transp Policy 2(4):279–291

Raad voor Verkeer en Waterstaat (2009) Ondernemend regionaal openbaar vervoer voor meer reizigers – Een advies over reizigersgroei door modernisering van de toepassing van het concessiestelsel, Den Haag, Mar 2009. http://www.verkeerenwaterstaat.nl/kennisplein/3/8/386106/RVW_ondernemend_regionaal_openbaar_vervoer.pdf. Retrieved 10 Aug 2009

Rausch W (2004) Die offensive hessische Strategie zum Wettbewerb im ÖPNV – Die Aufregung um den Erlass vom 12.03.2004. Verkehr und Technik 55(8):319–322

Recker E (2007) Genehmigungswettbewerb im Personenbeförderungsgesetz – Novellierungsvorschlag der Länder. Verkehr und Technik 60(2):69–70

Region Hannover (2008) Nahverkehrsplan 2008, Hannover, Nov 2008. http://www.hannover.de/de/wirtschaft/mobilitaet/RH_Nahverkehr/RH_Wer_macht_was/nvp2008_text.html. Retrieved 6 Jun 2010

Rehn W, Valussi R (2005) Wettbewerb im kommunalen ÖPNV – Erste Erfahrungen in Frankfurt am Main. Der Nahverkehr 23(1–2):59–63

Reim U, Reichel B (2010) Öffentlicher Personennahverkehr mit Bussen und Bahnen 2008. In: Federal statistical office of germany (DESTATIS) (ed) Wirtschaft und Statistik, 2010 (2):129–137

Rhiel A (2005) Das Besteller-Ersteller-Prinzip – Ein Kernstück des neuen Hessischen ÖPNV-Gesetzes. Nahverkehrspraxis 53(9):1

Richter R, Furobotn EG (1999) Institutions and economic theory – the contribution of the new institutional economics. The University of Michigan Press, Michigan

RMV – Rhein-Main-Verkehrsverbund GmbH (2005) Mustervergabeunterlagen für BPNV-Leistungen, Hofheim (Taunus) (unpublished)

Roberts C (2005) Is the current ownership structure of the British bus industry capable of meeting public policy objectives? In: Hensher DA (ed) Competition and ownership in land passenger transport. Selected refereed papers from the 8th international conference (Thredbo 8), Rio de Janeiro, Sept 2003, Elsevier, Amsterdam, pp 681–695

Romilly P (2001) Subsidy and local bus service deregulation in Britain – a re-evaluation. J Transp Econ Policy 35(2):161–194

Ronellenfitsch M (2004) Das Altmark-Urteil des Europäischen Gerichtshofs. Verwaltungsarchiv 95(3):425–442

Saito T (2009) Conflict between commercialism and public transport policy purpose: unique feature of policy dispute in Japan. In: van de Velde D, Beck A, Veeneman W (eds) Beyond competitive tendering – proceedings of the eleventh international conference on competition and ownership in land passenger transport. Next Generation Infrastructures Foundation, Delft, pp 235–246

Schenck M, Metzner D, von Hoerschelmann O (2003) Wettbewerb im Regionalbusverkehr: Liberalisierung zum Nutzen aller Beteiligten gestalten – Ein Erfahrungsbericht des Münchner Verkehrs- und Tarifverbundes. Der Nahverkehr 21(6):14–18

Schmidt R, Schäfer R, Seyb W (2004) Jeder Fahrschein zählt: Einnahmeaufteilung im SH-Tarif – Entwicklung und Einführung eines vertriebsdatengestützten Abrechungsverfahrens in Schleswig-Holstein. Der Nahverkehr 22(12):32–34

Schnell M (2009) Wettbewerb im ÖPNV – Aktuelle Beobachtungen und Erwartungen. Nahverkehrspraxis 57(6):24–25

SCI – SCI Verkehr GmbH (2006) Verwendung der Regionalisierungsmittel durch die Bundesländer – Eine Analyse für das Haushaltsjahr 2004 im Auftrag der Allianz pro Schiene. In: Allianz pro Schiene (ed) Berlin, 12 Apr 2006. http://www.allianz-pro-schiene.de/presse/pressemitteilungen/2006/2006-16/studie-verwendung-regionalisierungsmittel.pdf Retrieved 6 Mar 2007

Séguret S (2009) Is competition on track a real alternative to competitive tendering in the railway industry? Evidence from Germany. In: van de Velde D, Beck A, Veeneman W (eds) Beyond competitive tendering – proceedings of the eleventh international conference on competition and ownership in land passenger transport. Next Generation Infrastructures Foundation, Delft, pp 173–186

Sharaby N, Shiftan Y (2008) The economic benefits from competition in bus public transport – the Israeli case. Int J Transp Econ 35:391–413

Stammler H, Pulkkinen K (2008) Brutto oder Netto? – Verkehrsverträge im SPNV: Das Problem der Erlöskalkulation in SPNV-Ausschreibungen aus Sicht eines Eisenbahnunternehmens. Der Nahverkehr 26(3):8–13

Stanley J, van de Velde D (2008) Risk and reward in public transport contracting. ResTransp Econ 22:20–25

Sterzenbach R (2006) (2006) 'Lohnkutscher in Hessen – Von wegen Vorbild: Mit seinem allzu eingeschränkten Wettbewerb im öffentlichen Nahverkehr ist das Land auf dem Irrweg'. Frankfurter Allgemeine Zeitung 66:13

Sterzenbach T (2008) Reformaufgaben im Rahmen einer Neuordnung der Finanzierung des öffentlichen Personennahverkehrs (ÖPNV). Kovač, Hamburg

VDV – Verband Deutscher Verkehrsunternehmen (2004) VDV schlägt "marktorientierte Direktvergabe" als Alternative in der künftigen Marktordnung für den ÖPNV vor. Press release of the Association of German Transport Undertakings, Cologne, 23 Jan 2004

VDV – Verband Deutscher Verkehrsunternehmen (2007) Ausgestaltung öffentlicher Ausschreibungen von Busverkehrsleistungen nach VOL/A – Gemeinsames Diskussionspapier der Sparten "Bus" und "Verbund- und Aufgabenträgerorganisationen", Cologne. http://www.vdv.de/medienservice/stellungnahmen_entry.html?secure_type=download&secure_filename=2534bb957ae11c8d3a8c9b872e3ae27b&secure_targetname=ausgestaltung_oeffentlicher_ausschreibungen_von_busverkehrsleistungen_nach_vol.pdf. Retrieved 12 Sept 2008

VDV – Verband Deutscher Verkehrsunternehmen (2008) Stellungnahme zum Referentenentwurf eines Gesetzes zur Änderung personenbeförderungsrechtlicher Vorschriften (27 Aug 2008), Berlin, 23 Sept 2008 (unpublished)

Veeneman W, de Groot F (2009) A trip to the new world: public transport governance change in the main Dutch cities. In: van de Velde D, Beck A, Veeneman W (eds) Beyond competitive tendering – proceedings of the eleventh international conference on competition and ownership in land passenger transport. Next Generation Infrastructures Foundation, Delft, pp 117–132

van de Velde D (1999) Organisational forms and entrepreneurship in public transport – Part 1: classifying organisational forms. Transp Policy 6(3):147–157

van de Velde D (2005) The evolution of organizational forms in European public transport during the last 15 years. In: Hensher DA (ed) Competition and ownership in land passenger transport. Selected refereed papers from the 8th international conference (Thredbo 8), Rio de Janeiro, Sept 2003, Elsevier, Amsterdam, pp 481–513 van de Velde D (2009) Long-distance coach services in Europe: concessions or free market? 18th international symposium on transport economics and policy: the future for interurban passenger transport, Madrid (Spain), 16–18 Nov 2009, Joint OECD ITF transport research centre, international transport forum, OECD (Paris)

van de Velde D, Beck A (2010) Workshop report – beyond competitive tendering. Res Trans Econ (Special Edition: Reforming Public Transport throughout the World), 29(1):145–151

van de Velde D, Beck A, van Elburg J, Terschüren K-H (2008a) Contracting in urban public transport. In: Study by NEA, inno-V, KCW, RebelGroup, TØI, SDG and TIS.PT for the European Commission – DG TREN (ed) Amsterdam, 14 Jan 2008. http://ec.europa.eu/transport/urban/studies/doc/2008_contracting_urban_public_transport.pdf. Retrieved 12 Sept 2008

van de Velde, D, Beck A, van Elburg J, Terschüren K-H (2008b) Contracting in urban public transport – Appendix: contracting tables. In: Study by NEA, inno-V, KCW, RebelGroup, TØI, SDG and TIS.PT for the European Commission – DG TREN (ed) Amsterdam, 14 Jan 2008. http://ec.europa.eu/transport/urban/studies/doc/2008_contracting_urban_public_transport_annex.pdf. Retrieved 12 Sept 2008

van de Velde D, Jacobs J, Stefanski M (2009a) Development of railway contracting for the national passenger rail services in the Netherlands. In: van de Velde D, Beck A, Veeneman W (eds) Beyond competitive tendering – proceedings of the eleventh international conference on competition and ownership in land passenger transport. Next Generation Infrastructures Foundation, Delft, pp 211–220

ver.di hessen – Vereinte Dienstleistungsgewerkschaft Landesbezirk Hessen (2007) Tarifverträge: Entgelte und Ausbildungsvergütungen für die Arbeitnehmerinnen und Arbeitnehmer des privaten Personenverkehrs mit Omnibussen in Hessen (LHO). Frankfurt on the Main, valid from 1Oct 2007 (unpublished document)

Vickrey W (1961a) Counterspeculation, auctions, and competitive sealed tenders. J Finance 16(1):8–37

von Berlepsch HJ (2005) Wettbewerb im ÖPNV – "Einsparpotenzial ist erheblich" – In Frankfurt werden seit 2003 Buslinien ausgeschrieben. Zeitung für kommunale Wirtschaft 10 Sept 2005

Walter M (2011a) Some determinants of cost efficiency in German local public transport. J Transp Econ Policy 45(1):1–20

Walter M, Haunerland F, Moll R (2009) Heavily regulated but promising prospects: entry in the German express coach market. Dresden University of Technology – Chair of Energy Economics and Public Sector Management (ed) Working Paper Transport Economics 16. http://www.tu-dresden.de/wwbwleeg/projekte/tr.html?7 #mark3. Retrieved 20 Dec 2009

Wanner K, Zietz A (2008a) Busverkehrsdienstleistungen im Ausschreibungswettbewerb. Internationales Verkehrswesen 60(3):77–82

Werner J (1998a) Nach der Regionalisierung – der Nahverkehr im Wettbewerb: Rechtlicher Rahmen, Verantwortlichkeiten, Gestaltungsoptionen. Dortmunder Vertrieb für Bau- und Planungsliteratur, Dortmund

Werner J (2001) Verkehrsgewerberecht. In: Barth S, Baumeister H, Berschin F, Werner J (eds) Recht des öffentlichen Personennahverkehrs, Section A 4, Hermann Luchterhand, Neuwied

Werner J (2004a) Der Zugang zum Personenbeförderungsgewerbe im Lichte aktueller Entwicklungen in der Rechtssprechung. Gewerbearchiv 50(3):89–128

Werner J, Wolf M, Landsberg G, Schaaffkamp C (2004) Zur Anwendbarkeit der VO (EWG) 1191/69 in Deutschland. Study of KCW GmbH for the ministry of transport of the state of Hesse, Berlin, 24 Feb 2004. http://www.kpv-ibb.de/55001/Uploaded/admin%7CGutachten_KCW_VO-1191.pdf. Retrieved 6 Mar 2007

Westin P (2009) Review of public transport in Sweden: Implementation on the passenger rail market and plans for the local public transport market. Paper presented at the eleventh conference on competition and ownership in land passenger transport, Delft, 20–25 Sept 2009. http://ses.library.usyd.edu.au/bitstream/2123/5918/1/P4-02-z03-Westin-Review-of-public-transport-in-Sweden-doc.pdf. Retrieved 21 May 2010

Wewers B (2004a) Vom Interregio zum Schleswig-Holstein-Express – Erfahrungen und Lehren aus Sicht eines Aufgabenträgers. Der Nahverkehr 22(9):48–51

White P (2009a) Future opportunities for local bus services in Britain following the local transport act 2008. In: van de Velde D, Beck A, Veeneman W (eds) Beyond competitive tendering – proceedings of the eleventh international conference on competition and ownership in land passenger transport. Next Generation Infrastructures Foundation, Delft, pp 17–33

White P, Tough S (1995a) Alternative tendering systems and deregulation in Britain. J Transp Econ Policy 29(3):275–289

Williamson OE (1976a) Franchise bidding for natural monopolies – in general and with respect to CATV. Bell J Econ 7:73–104

Wilson R (1977a) A bidding model of perfect competition. Rev Econ Stud 44(3):511–518

Winnes M (2007a) Das Wettbewerbskonzept des Verkehrsverbund Rhein-Neckar. Verkehr und Technik 61(7):263–268

Wissenschaftlicher Beirat beim BMVBS – Bundesminister für Verkehr, Bau und Stadtentwicklung (2008a) Die Zukunft des ÖPNV – Reformbedarf bei Finanzierung und Leistungserstellung. Zeitschrift für Verkehrswissenschaft 79(2):75–101

Wolanski M (2009a) How much do we save on competitive tendering? Quantitative study of Polish cities' experience. In: Nash C, Wolanski M, Veeneman W, van de Velde D (eds) Benchmarking the competitive tendering outcome – proceedings of the eleventh international conference on competition and ownership in land passenger transport. Next Generation Infrastructures Foundation, Delft, pp 233–248

Wolfstetter E (1999a) Topics in microeconomic theory – industrial organization, auctions and incentives. Cambridge University Press, Cambridge

Wooldridge JM (2002a) Econometric analysis of cross section and panel data. MIT Press, Cambridge, MA

Zellner A (1962a) An efficient method of estimating seemingly unrelated regressions and tests for aggregation bias. J Am Stat Assoc LVII(June, 1962):348–368

Acts of law

(EC) No 1370/2007 Regulation (EC) No 1370/2007 of the European Parliament and of the Council of 23 Oct 2007 on public passenger transport services by rail and by road and repealing Council Regulations (EEC) Nos 1191/69 and 1107/70, published in the Official Journal L 315/1, 3 Dec 2007

(EEC) No 1191/69 Council Regulation (EEC) No 1191/69 of 26 June 1969, on action by member states concerning the obligations inherent in the concept of a public service in transport by rail, road and inland waterway, published in the Official Journal L 156/1, 28 June 1969

(EEC) No 1893/91 Council Regulation (EEC) No 1893/91 of 20 June 1991 amending Regulation (EEC) No 1191/69 on action by member states concerning the obligations inherent in the concept of a public service in transport by rail, road and inland waterway, published in the Official Journal L 169/1, 29 June 1991

Common German Law for Railways (Allgemeines Eisenbahngesetz – AEG) Railway act as amended and promulgated on 27 Dec 1993 (see BGBl. I, 2378 (2396) (1994, 2439)), last amended by article 8 of the law from 26 Feb 2008 (see BGBl. I, 215)

Demerger Act (Gesetz zur Entflechtung von Gemeinschaftsaufgaben und Finanzhilfen, or Entflechtungsgesetz – EntflechtG) Law as of 5 Sept 2006 (see BGBl. I, 2098, 2102)

Law for Public Transport in Hesse (Gesetz über den öffentlichen Personennahverkehr in Hesse – ÖPNVG) Law as amended and promulgated on 7 Dec 2005 (see GVBl. for the Federal State Hesse II, 60)

Law for Public Transport in Saxony-Anhalt (Gesetz über den öffentlichen Personennahverkehr im Land Sachsen-Anhalt – ÖPNVG LSA) Law as amended and promulgated on 20 Jan 2005 (see GVBl. for the Federal State Saxony-Anhalt I, 16)

Law for the Advancement of Public Transport Services in Hesse (Gesetz zur Weiterentwicklung des öffentlichen Personennahverkehrs in Hesse) Law as amended and promulgated on 19 Jan 1996 (see GVBl. for the Federal State Hesse I, 50)
Law on the Regionalisation of Public Transport (Regionalisierungsgesetz – RegG) Law as amended and promulgated on 27 Dec 1993 (see BGBl. I, 2378, 2395), last amended by article 1 of the law from 12 Dec 2007 (see BGBl. I, 2871)
Local Authority Traffic Financing Act (Gemeindeverkehrsfinanzierungsgesetz – GVFG) Law as amended and promulgated on 28 Jan 1988 (see BGBl. I, 101), last amended by article 4 of the law from 22 Dec 2008 (see BGBl. I, 2986)
Ninth Code of Social Law (Neuntes Buch Sozialgesetzbuch – Rehabilitation und Teilhabe behinderter Menschen – SGB IX) Article 1 of the law as of 19 June 2001 (see BGBl. I, 1046), last amended by article 5 of the law from 22 Dec 2008 (see BGBl. I, 2959)
Official German Contracting Terms for Award of Service Performance Contracts, Part A (Verdingungsordnung für Leistungen, Teil A – VOL/A) (2006) Revised version, published in the Bundesanzeiger 58 (100a), dated 30 May 2006
Passenger Transport Act (Personenbeförderungsgesetz – PBefG) Law as amended and promulgated on 8 Aug 1990 (see BGBl. I, 1690), last amended by article 27 of the law from 7 Sept 2007 (see BGBl. I, 2246)

FSC
www.fsc.org
MIX
Papier | Fördert
gute Waldnutzung
FSC® C083411

Kolibri 360 GmbH
Ferdinand-Jühlke-Straße 7
99095 Erfurt, Deutschland
produktsicherheit@kolibri360.de